BRIDGE

25 WAYS TO COMPETE
IN THE BIDDING

BARBARA SEAGRAM & MARC SMITH

MASTER POINT PRESS • TORONTO

Master Point Press
331 Douglas Ave.
Toronto, Ontario Canada
M5M 1H2
(416) 781-0351
Internet www.masterpointpress.com

Canadian Cataloguing in Publication Data
Seagram, Barbara
Bridge: 25 ways to compete in the bidding

ISBN 1-894154-22-3

1. Contract bridge — Bidding. I. Smith, Marc, 1960-   II. Title: Bridge: 25 ways to compete in the bidding

GV1282.4.S418 2000   795.41'52   C00-931331-1

Editor	Ray Lee
Cover and Interior design	Olena S. Sullivan
Interior format and copyediting	Deanna Bourassa

Printed and bound in Canada

 5 6 7 812 11 10 09

To my children, Heather and Chris, and my wonderful husband, Alex Kornel. Bridge is my passion but you are my life.

Barbara

To my wife, Charlotte, and my dogs, Benito and Giorgio.

Marc

ACKNOWLEDGEMENTS

Our sincere thanks to Eddie Kantar, everyone's favorite author and teacher, who has helped us so much over the past year. His humor and wisdom kept us afloat throughout all crises. Many thanks also to Alan LeBendig, who was always a willing sounding board for hands and auctions. His support and patient advice have been invaluable.

The loyal students, members and staff of the Kate Buckman Bridge Studio are a constant source of encouragement and inspiration — grateful thanks to all of them.

Finally, thanks to Ray Lee, a wonderful editor who does much more than just edit. It is such a pleasure to work with him.

Barbara Seagram
Marc Smith

C O N T E N T S

Suit Overcalls

Takeout Doubles

Notrump Overcalls

Bidding Over Opponents' 1NT Opening

Bidding Over Preempts

General Competitive Issues

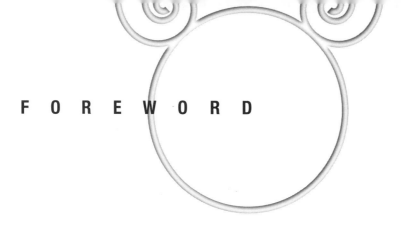

F O R E W O R D

If this were Las Vegas, Barbara and Marc would have hit the jackpot — twice. Their first book, *25 Bridge Conventions You Should Know,* was a clear-cut winner and lo and behold, they've done it again. This time they have selected a topic that screams for exposure: explaining those bread and butter competitive bidding sequences; your side doing the competing, their side doing the sweating and vice versa. They show you how to make life miserable for your opponents. No longer are you going to sit there like a bump on a log and let the opponents bid merrily to their best contract. With an eye on the vulnerability you *will* (army talk) put maximum pressure on your opponents by overcalling, jump overcalling, doubling, balancing, and preempting, including preemptive jump raises in many sequences. In short, you are about to become a feared opponent.

Included are some wonderful chapters about deciding whether to double an opening bid or overcall, how to handle an opponent's 1NT opening bid, when to balance, and how to deal with those miserable preempts that they are always throwing at you. My two favorite chapters were the ones entitled 'The Law of Total Tricks' and 'Hand Evaluation', the two absolute keys to improving your competitive bidding judgement, what it's all about. Each topic is explained clearly with neat example hands. The kicker is the quiz at the end of each chapter which nails down the whole chapter and gives you a final chance to see what you have absorbed. Another plus is the length of each chapter, not too long, not too short, just right. What was impressed upon me, even though I know it well, is how difficult high-level preempts are to deal with, even for world-class players. True, you are given some tools to help reduce your trauma, but the authors level with you and tell you that you simply are not going to land on your feet every time they stick it to you. How true, how true, how true.

This book can and should be used as a reference book. Think back. How often do doubles, overcalls, balancing bids, preempts, and bidding over an opponent's 1NT opening bid, come up? Did you say, "On almost every hand?" Right on. But now you have a place to go to see if you handled the sequence properly, how you should have handled the situation, or more likely, what your partner should have bid. You are holding a winner in your hands; just make sure you get one in your partner's hands as well!

Eddie Kantar

I N T R O D U C T I O N

 It is possible to sit an entire evening at the bridge table and never play a hand. *Florence Irwin,* **Auction Highlights,** *1913.*

To bid or not to bid? When you started to play bridge, you were undoubtedly taught some rules that would help you decide whether or not to open the bidding. With a good hand, say thirteen points or more, you were allowed to open at the one-level, while with a weaker hand but a very good suit you were encouraged to open with a preemptive bid — a bid at the three- or four-level designed to make life difficult for your opponents. At that time nobody talked very much about why or how you get into the bidding once one of the opponents has made an opening bid.

Once an opponent has opened the bidding, you are immediately on the defensive. You have two choices: pass and let the enemy bid unimpeded to their optimum contract, or get in amongst them. There are numerous reasons why you might choose action rather than inaction. In the first place, it's more fun than passing all the time! Moreover, just because they opened the bidding, it doesn't necessarily mean the hand belongs to them. You may be able to outbid the opponents and make a contract of your own; perhaps only a partscore, but game or even slam may not be out of the question. Maybe you can just push them up enough that they cannot make what they bid, or maybe you can use up so much of their bidding space that they find it hard to get to the best contract. And even if they do get to the right spot, your side may be able to find a profitable sacrifice, a contract which goes down only a trick or two, costing you much less than letting them play their game.

If you are happy to pass once the enemy has opened the bidding, you don't need this book — you should buy one on opening leads and signaling, since you are going to be doing plenty of defending. If you would prefer to be in the bidding, however, then this is the book for you. We are going to show you how to get into the auction effectively and safely after the opposition has opened the bidding.

One thing that it is important to understand is that there are relatively few absolute rights and wrongs in the area of competitive bidding. Often, the way you decide to do things will be a matter of personal preference for you and your partner. As in most aspects of bridge, the critical thing is that you and your partner are on same wavelength. Many of the ideas that are presented in this book are almost universally accepted, while others are popular in some form or another with many players around the world. Where there is more than one way to approach a particular situation, we shall give you our recommendation, while pointing out that it may not be the only playable method.

You should understand, too, that a subject as complex as this one cannot be covered comprehensively in a book such as this. As you gain experience, you will realize that we have left many questions unanswered, and indeed that we have failed to mention a good number of the ideas and agreements that the modern tournament player will encounter. But it is not our goal to be all-encompassing. Our objective is to describe a set of sound general principles for defensive bidding so that you have a firm foundation to build from with your favorite partner; at the same time, if you happen to sit down one day with a strange partner, you will be more confident that you know basically what they are going to expect of you in these situations.

Barbara Seagram
Marc Smith

BRIDGE

25 WAYS TO COMPETE
IN THE BIDDING

AUTHORS' NOTE

In the course of this book we frequently refer to 'points'. If you are bidding notrump, then this means 'high card points' (HCP) since you cannot count distribution for notrump purposes. However, when bidding suits, 'points' means total points (HCP + distributional points) unless we specifically say 'HCP'.

Your opponents are referred to as LHO (Left-hand Opponent) and RHO (Right-hand Opponent) respectively. If LHO opens the bidding, partner bids next, then RHO, then you. A diagram of the table seen from above would look like this:

If you have played organized duplicate bridge, then you will probably have come across the Alert Procedure. Some of the methods contained in this book, although fairly standard, must be alerted — you must warn your opponents when you use them so that they have the chance to ask for an explanation if they wish. Exactly which bids require an alert varies from country to country and even from area to area or from club to club. You can check with your local club organizer, but if in doubt, err on the side of alerting too much rather than too little.

Within this book we always use the terms 'he', 'his' and 'him' when referring to partner or an opponent. We appreciate that these persons may be male or female, of course; the use of the male pronoun exclusively avoids such awkward constructions as 'his or her' and 'he or she', and should not be construed as implying any gender bias on our part.

Final note: The quotations that begin each chapter are taken from *Auction Highlights* by Florence Irwin, published by Putnam in 1913. Some of them are quaint and amusing from the lofty perspective of ninety years experience; others still ring strangely true. We hope you enjoy them.

C H A P T E R

SIMPLE
SUIT OVERCALLS

♥ There are many players who practically always hold poor hands, and their only defense, up to now, has been to reduce their losses by not bidding and by letting the other side win.
Florence Irwin, **Auction Highlights,** *1913.*

Once the opponents have opened the bidding, there are only two ways in which you can get into the auction — by doubling for takeout or by bidding something yourself, which is termed overcalling. We shall deal with takeout doubles at some length later in this book; for now, we'll just assume that you know what they are (if you don't, we suggest you take a quick skim through Chapter 6 before continuing). First, let's talk about the kinds of hand on which you might want to get into the bidding with an overcall, and why.

When would you want to make an overcall?

The answer to this question is very similar to the answer to, "When should you open the bidding?" — when you have either a good hand or a good suit. If you have a good five-card suit or better, you probably want to make an overcall (we'll worry about hand strength a little later). However, to judge whether a hand is worth an overcall, it is important to understand what you are trying to achieve by bidding. There are three main reasons for making an overcall (often, a hand will justify overcalling for more than one of these reasons).

1. *You have a good hand or a good suit so you wish to compete for the partscore or perhaps even look for game if partner has some values and a fit.*
2. *You want to harass the opponents, either by using up their bidding space or by pushing them to bid too high.*
3. *You want to suggest a good lead to partner in case your LHO becomes declarer.*

These reasons for overcalling are listed in order of importance. You may be surprised to hear that the most important reason to make an overcall is constructive — you want to try to play the hand. For years, overcalls were viewed as merely obstructive maneuvers. That is no longer the majority view, but it is still a widely-held belief in some circles that an overcall shows a bad hand, and that if you have an opening bid or better you must start with a takeout double. However, as we shall see, it is now common practice to overcall on quite strong hands, with the intention of bidding again later to show extra values.

What does an overcall look like?

First, let's define our terms. We are going to start with one of the basic building blocks of competitive bidding — the simple overcall, which means an overcall that is made at the lowest possible level of the suit you bid (you can also overcall in notrump, too, but we'll be talking about that later on). These auctions are both examples of simple overcalls:

LHO	Partner	RHO	You		LHO	Partner	RHO	You
1♣	1♥				1♥	2♦		

In both cases, partner has bid his suit at the lowest level that he could. By comparison, look at these auctions:

LHO	Partner	RHO	You		LHO	Partner	RHO	You
1♣	2♥				1♥	3♦		

In both cases here partner has made what is called a **jump overcall** (he has not bid his suit at the lowest possible level) and as you might suspect, this kind of overcall shows a somewhat different type of hand. We're going to ignore jump overcalls for now, and come back to them in Chapter 5.

When an opponent opens the bidding, he is announcing that the hand belongs to his side. What's more, he is probably right. The enemy probably does have more points than your side. It is also now less risky for them to double you if you bid too much, since they already know that they probably have the balance of strength. In fact, if they are looking at trump tricks as well as a good hand, they will find it very easy to double. However, when you have a strong suit for your overcall, it will be more difficult for your opponents to double you, since they will not have good trumps. Your first requirements for overcalling are therefore:

1. *A good suit, at least five cards in length* **or**
2. *A good hand (an opening bid or better)* **and preferably**
3. *Both.*

So when deciding whether or not to overcall, it is not just a matter of counting your high-card points. Indeed, there are many 14-point hands on which you should pass, while there are plenty of 8-point hands on which an overcall is clearly correct. The key is to have a suit that is good enough to take some tricks if it is the trump suit, or to have enough high cards instead. For example:

♠ A Q J 10 7　♥ 10 9 6 4　♦ 4　♣ 8 6 3

♠ J 10 6 3 2　♥ A K 4　♦ A K 4　♣ 6 3

Both these hands are very reasonable 1♠ overcalls if your RHO opens, say, 1♣. You would not dream of opening one spade with the first hand — you have only 7 HCP! However, it is a perfectly respectable overcall. Now look at this example:

♠ K J 7　♥ A J 10　♦ K 8 6 4　♣ Q 6 3

You have 14 HCP and would not consider passing if you were the dealer. However, you cannot make an overcall (or any other positive bid) once RHO opens, say, 1♣. You have no five-card suit, and (as you will see when we get to Chapter 6) you cannot make a takeout double with three cards in the enemy's suit. If you were a little stronger, you might consider a notrump overcall (again, we'll get to that in a later chapter), but you don't have enough points for that bid. So like it or not, you must pass.

The point is that when you are thinking about overcalling, playing strength is more important than high-card points. 'Playing strength' is a way of talking about the capacity of your hand to take tricks, which comes from a combination of your high-cards and your long-suit tricks. Compare the three hands above; the first, with only 7 HCP, has much more playing strength than the third, despite its 14 HCP. On the first hand, you can expect to make four spade tricks (if they are trumps). On the third example hand, though, what tricks are you going to make? The ace of hearts and maybe a couple more in the wash, but that's about it.

'Suit quality' is another important factor, which relates not just to the high cards in your suit, but also the intermediate spot cards. A suit like ♠QJ1098 is clearly much better in terms of trick-taking potential than ♠QJ432 and yet both count as 3 HCP. Look at your spot cards in the suit you plan to overcall, and ask yourself, "How many tricks can I count on in this suit if it ends up as trumps and partner has only two or three small ones?" If the answer is, "Not many," you should be reluctant to overcall without aces and kings elsewhere to compensate.

What if you have a really good hand?

As we shall see in a later chapter, one special meaning of the takeout double is that you have too good a hand for a simple overcall. How good is 'too good'? Modern style is to start with an overcall on quite strong hands, especially if your good suit is one of the main features that you want to tell partner about. Remember that you will often get the chance to show your extra values by taking a second bid later in the auction. As a very rough guideline, we shall say that you can overcall on a hand with up to about 18 points.

Here is an example of a pretty good hand on which you should nevertheless start by overcalling:

♠ A Q 8 7　♥ 9　♦ K Q J 9 6 4　♣ K 3

RHO opens 1♣. You have three features you want to show: really good diamonds, a secondary spade suit, and a good hand. In a competitive auction, there is some risk that the bidding will be uncomfortably high when you next get a chance to speak. You therefore need to get the main features of your hand described as fast as possible. Although you have a very good hand here, it is still best to start with a 1♦ overcall. You will probably get a chance to bid your spades later, and at the same time to show your extra values just by taking a second bid.

How does my overcall make life difficult for the opponents?

You'll remember that we gave three important reasons why you might decide to overcall. We also mentioned that often, more than one of them will apply. Suppose your RHO deals and opens 1♣, and you have:

♠ A J 10 8 7　♥ A 4　♦ 9 8 7 5　♣ 8 6

There are two advantages to making a 1♠ overcall. First, you may be able to buy the contract — maybe both sides can make nine tricks in their best suit. Since you hold the boss suit, you can outbid your opponents whatever their best suit happens to be. You have the spades and it is up to you to bid them — after all, you cannot expect your partner to bid the suit with only ♠Qxx, for example. However, a second reason for overcalling is that you are taking away the opponents' bidding space. Without your overcall they might have a happy, undisturbed auction such as:

LHO	Partner	RHO	You
		1♣	pass
1♥	pass	1NT	pass
2♣	all pass		

By sticking in a 1♠ bid, you can take the whole one-level away from them. If LHO has the right kind of hand, he may be able to use a negative double to help describe it (see our previous book, *25 Bridge Conventions You Should Know* if you are not familiar with Negative Doubles), but even then it will be hard for them to stop in 2♣, and that may be their best contract. Things get even worse for them if your partner happens to be able to raise spades (we'll talk about what kind of hand he would have for this in the next chapter). Now the auction might go:

LHO	Partner	RHO	You
		1♣	1♠
dbl	2♠	?	

Do you see what has happened? You and your partner have just taken the two-level away from the opponents as well as the one-level, and you may even steal the hand in 2♠ if opener feels the three-level is too high for him. Even if they can make three of a suit, it may be hard for them to figure that out.

Making life difficult for the opponents by using up their bidding space is a major reason for choosing to overcall. Bidding 1♠ over a 1♣ opening can be very disruptive. However, notice that the reverse is also true. If you bid 1♦ over their 1♣, or 1♠ over their 1♥, you're not taking up any of their room, so you had better be overcalling for one of our other two reasons — either you think it may be your hand, or you want to suggest a lead.

When should you overcall for the lead?

We have dealt so far with hands on which you overcall with at least some expectation of competing for and making a contract, or are trying to take up some of the opposition bidding space. But what if you hold:

♠ A Q J 10 6 ♥ 4 3 ♦ 8 7 5 ♣ 10 7 6

You can be fairly frisky at the one-level, since you won't often get doubled there, and it's certainly worth bidding 1♠ over 1♣ or even over 1♦ since it takes up a good chunk of their space. What about over a 1♥ opening, though? You have few enough high cards that it seems likely that the opponents will play the hand, probably in hearts or in notrump. You are only going to get one chance to suggest that partner lead a spade and, if LHO declares 3NT, you are not likely to have much chance of beating it except on a spade lead. So you should overcall 1♠ on this hand even if they open 1♥, for the third of the three main reasons — you want to make a strong suggestion to partner about what he should lead.

Obviously, the main requirement for this kind of overcall is to have a really good suit — probably not worse than the one in this example.

What about overcalls at the two-level?

LHO	Partner	RHO	You
		1♠	2♥

We pointed out at the start of the chapter that this 2♥ bid is still a simple overcall, since this is the lowest level at which you could bid hearts. However, in contrast to the situation when you bid, say, 1♥ over 1♣, you are now committing your partnership to the two-level, and you won't be surprised to learn that the requirements to do this are a touch more stringent.

You should realize that the two-level is much more dangerous than the one-level — you are more likely to be doubled and you are a trick higher. It is therefore wise to resist the temptation to overcall at the two-level on a poor suit, particularly when vulnerable, although avoiding large penalties is only one reason for this. You should have at least a good five-card suit and a hand on which you would open the bidding. Many players insist on a six-card suit for a minor-suit overcall, and there is good reason for this. When you overcall in a major, the most likely game contract, if the hand belongs to your side, is in your suit. However, when you overcall in a minor, the best game contract is very likely to be 3NT. Having a strong six-card suit that will provide tricks is therefore a major asset. These hands would be good examples of sound two-level overcalls over an opponent's 1♠ opening:

| ♠ 8 3 ♥ K Q 10 9 8 ♦ A 4 3 ♣ A J 7 | Bid 2♥ |
| ♠ A 3 ♥ 9 8 3 ♦ 7 4 ♣ A K J 9 7 3 | Bid 2♣ |

If you're feeling aggressive, here is a hand where you might think seriously about overcalling 2♣ over a 1♦ opening, even though it has relatively few high card points:

♠ J 9 8 3 ♥ 8 ♦ 7 4 ♣ A K J 9 7 3

You'd hate to pass and have LHO get to 3NT without suggesting to your partner that a club is the best lead. In addition, 2♣ takes up a great deal of bidding space. With five tricks or so in your own hand, you are unlikely to get damaged too badly in 2♣, and you may even get a chance to show your second suit if partner shows signs of life. Especially not vulnerable, most good players would overcall with this hand.

That is not the case, however, with our final example:

♠ K Q 5 ♥ A 5 ♦ A 7 3 ♣ J 8 6 4 3

If RHO opened 1♦, overcalling 2♣ on this hand would be an atrocity. Yes, you have 14 HCP and yes, your overcall uses up lots of the opponent's bidding room, but because your suit is so bad, it won't be worth many extra tricks as a trump suit. You will take just about as many tricks on defense as you would if you played the hand. So it doesn't seem likely the opponents can make much (although from time to time they'll enjoy defending 2♣ doubled!). The most likely consequence of your overcall is that the opponents will stay out of a contract that would fail or, if they don't, that partner will lead a club and let them make it. Remember, that when you overcall, partner will almost certainly lead your suit; now look at the hand and ask yourself which suit you least want led!

Are the rules any different if both opponents have bid?

You should be more careful about getting into the auction when the bidding is opened on your left and RHO responds. The primary reason for this is that the danger is greater (because both opponents have shown values) and the bidding may even be at an uncomfortably high level. We will deal later with overcalling when LHO opens and the next two players pass — this is called **balancing**, and is covered later on. For now, let us assume that RHO does respond to his partner's opening bid.

LHO	Partner	RHO	You
1♣	pass	1♥	?

When responder bids a new suit at the one-level, you must be more careful than when the opening bid is on your right. If you come in now, you are entering a live auction in which both opponents have already shown some strength. It is now unlikely that it is your hand, since LHO has at least 13 points or so and RHO at least 6.

You can still overcall with the same kind of hand on which you would make the bid in second seat. However, when deciding whether to come into this type of auction, remember that the preemptive value of your bid is greatly reduced — you're not really taking up much bidding space if any, and they have already exchanged some information. So you should usually have some expectation of outbidding the opponents to offset the risk of entering the auction when both opponents have shown values. Remember also that when LHO has opened the bidding and RHO has bid a new suit, both hands are unlimited in strength. Responder could have as few as 6 HCP but he also could have much more, so you should be very cautious. In these auctions, the opponents can double you for penalties much more easily than they can when only one of them has bid.

This situation is slightly different, but many of the same warnings apply:

LHO	Partner	RHO	You
1♥	pass	1NT	?

Even in this auction, where RHO has shown a fairly weak hand (6 to 9 or 10 points), entering the bidding is still dangerous. RHO is certain to have length in at least one of the minors and, quite probably, in both. Remember, he could not bid 1♠, so he has at most three of those, and he could not raise hearts, so he is short there too. To come in with a 2♣ or 2♦ overcall, you need at least a strong six-card suit and a decent hand. Even then, there is no guarantee of safety.

Finally, what about this kind of auction?

LHO	*Partner*	*RHO*	*You*
1♥	pass	2♣	?

When responder bids a new suit at the two-level, it is a guarantee that your side is outgunned. Opener has shown 12+ points, and responder has suggested at least 10 (or a full opening bid himself if they are playing the modern Two-over-One style). Even if you have a good hand, say 15 points or so, how many do you think partner will have? Right — not many.

To enter the fray now, you must have a decent hand with plenty of distribution — in other words, what we earlier called 'playing strength', which in this case is going to mean the ability to take tricks without necessarily having many high cards. A strong six-card suit or five cards in each of the unbid suits would be a minimum. Remember that partner will produce little in terms of high cards. If you do not find a good fit, even a two-level overcall could lead to a substantial penalty.

Summary

✓ Overcalls at the one-level show at least a good five-card suit, but may be made on fewer high-card points than would be required to open the bidding.

✓ An overcall does not imply a poor hand. You can overcall with quite a good hand (up to about 18 HCP), intending to bid again later to show your extra values, if that is the most descriptive bid available to you.

✓ Because overcalls tend to show good suits, partner will strain to lead your suit if your LHO becomes declarer. Holding a good suit and little else, you may therefore consider overcalling at the one-level solely to direct the lead.

✓ Overcalls at the two-level show opening bid values and at least a good five-card suit. If the overcall is in a minor suit, it should be a six-card suit.

✓ Overcalling after RHO responds to the opening bid is much more dangerous. You must therefore have both a good hand and a strong suit in this situation.

Simple Suit Overcalls

NOW TRY THESE...

1. On each of these hands, your RHO opens 1♣. Neither side is vulnerable. What is your next bid?

a
- ♠ A J 10 4 2
- ♥ 7 6
- ♦ K 6 5 2
- ♣ 3 2

b
- ♠ A J 10 4 2
- ♥ 7 6
- ♦ A K 5 2
- ♣ 3 2

c
- ♠ A J 10 4 2
- ♥ K Q 8 4
- ♦ 3
- ♣ 8 5 4

d
- ♠ A J 10 4 2
- ♥ K Q 4
- ♦ 3
- ♣ A 8 5 4

e
- ♠ K J 4 2
- ♥ 4
- ♦ K Q J 8 6
- ♣ 8 5 4

f
- ♠ A K 4 2
- ♥ 7 4
- ♦ J 8 7 6 3
- ♣ Q 4

2. On each of these hands, your RHO opens 1♥. Neither side is vulnerable. What is your next bid?

a
- ♠ K Q J 4
- ♥ 9 7
- ♦ A Q 8 6
- ♣ K J 4

b
- ♠ A Q J 4 2
- ♥ 4
- ♦ Q J 8 6
- ♣ A 9 3

c
- ♠ 4 2
- ♥ 4
- ♦ A K J 8 6 3
- ♣ K 8 6 5

d
- ♠ Q J 4 2
- ♥ 4
- ♦ A K J 8 6 3
- ♣ 6 4

e
- ♠ K Q 2
- ♥ K 4
- ♦ J 8 6 3 2
- ♣ A 8 5

f
- ♠ A K Q 9 7 5
- ♥ 8
- ♦ A K 7 5
- ♣ A 4

3. Neither side is vulnerable. What is your next bid on each of these hands?

a
- ♠ K Q 4
- ♥ 4
- ♦ K Q 10 6 3 2
- ♣ K 7 5

LHO	Partner	RHO	You
1♥	pass	1NT	?

b
- ♠ Q 5 4 2
- ♥ 4
- ♦ K J 8 6
- ♣ A J 6 5

LHO	Partner	RHO	You
1♥	pass	1♠	?

ANSWERS

1 **a** 1♠ It may be your hand if partner has some values and a fit, but this is essentially an obstructive (and lead-directing) overcall.

    b 1♠ This time you have more expectation of buying the hand. Anything else would be wrong at this point.

    c 1♠ Were you tempted to make a takeout double because you have both majors? Wrong for two reasons: your double promises support for *all* the unbid suits, and your best fit is likely to be spades.

    d 1♠ For similar reasons to those given for 1(c) above, 1♠ is again correct. If the opponents compete you may be able to do something on the next round that will show your extra values.

    e 1♦ An overcall shows a good five-card suit, and your spades don't qualify. You may get the chance to bid spades later.

    f pass Bidding 1♦ over a 1♣ opening shows a decent hand and/or a really good suit, as it takes up no room. This hand has neither. You have marginal values and a poor suit — best to keep quiet.

2 **a** dbl You have support for all three unbid suits. Overcalling 1♠ would show five spades, and there's no reason to suggest that this will be your best trump suit anyway. If partner has three spades and four diamonds, you obviously prefer to play in the minor.

    b 1♠ Although you have support for all unbid suits, doubling is wrong. You probably belong in spades, and partner will not bid spades in response to your double with only three of them. You should be able to show your extra strength on the next round.

    c 2♦ You have a good suit, and you should be pleased if partner advances towards game, whether it be 5♦ or 3NT.

    d 2♦ It would be a mistake to double in the hope that partner will bid spades. More likely, he will bid clubs (they always do!). You may get a chance to bid spades on the next round anyway.

    e pass Although you have an opening bid, your hand is the wrong shape for a takeout double and your moth-eaten diamonds are not even close to being good enough for an overcall.

    f dbl This time you are too strong for a simple overcall. Double first and then bid your spades on the next round. This shows a very good hand with at least six good spades (see Chapter 6).

3 **a** 2♦ You have a strong suit but, without aces, you still have a minimum. Even 2♦ could get doubled and suffer a large penalty.

    b pass You are risking much to gain little if you double; you are more likely to find the minors with LHO than with partner. What do you think your partner's longest suit is? Right — hearts!

RAISING PARTNER'S SUIT

 To pass when you can raise is to shirk your responsibilities; but raising your partner's bid properly requires a perfect knowledge of the raising rules.
Florence Irwin, **Auction Highlights***, 1913.*

In our opening chapter, we looked at the various reasons for making an overcall. Now let's move around the table — LHO opens the bidding and partner makes an overcall. What do you do now?

In an uncontested auction, where only your side is in the bidding, you can often adopt a strategy designed to describe your hand accurately in two or even three bids. You cannot afford such luxuries in a contested auction — by the time you get a second turn, the bidding may already have reached an uncomfortably high level. Your objective is therefore to describe the nature of your hand immediately. It is vital that you make sure your partner knows what is happening as quickly as possible. In particular, if you have support for your partner's suit, tell him right away. In other words,

Support with support!

Your objective when you have found a fit is twofold — to reach your best contract, and to do so as quickly as possible, denying the enemy the time and space to explore for a contract of their own. What follows is a general guide to the meaning of various bids that show support for partner. The point counts given are only approximate since, as before, playing strength is more important than high cards in deciding how good your hand is.

When do you just raise partner's suit?

You should rarely pass when you have a fit for partner's overcalled suit. As we saw in the first chapter, he could have quite a good hand (up to18 HCP or so) and still only have made a simple overcall. Remember too, that partner shows at least a good five-card suit with his overcall, so you should not be shy about supporting with only three trumps. However, it's also important to be able tell partner how good a hand you have so he can make an intelligent decision about bidding on. We're going to divide the possible hands into two groups: those where you have limit raise values or better (in other words, you at least want to invite partner to bid game) and those where you have less than a limit raise. To qualify for a limit raise, you should have 10+ points and at least three-card trump support.

Let's look at the weaker hands first.

LHO	Partner	RHO	You
1♦	1♠	pass	?

♠ Q 9 7 ♥ K 8 7 6 ♦ 8 7 ♣ 9 7 6 4

Just as you would if partner opened 1♠, you should raise to 2♠. Admittedly, this rather unappealing collection is a minimum, but you should always try to find an excuse to bid if you have support. As we saw in the first chapter, owning the spade suit means never having to say you're sorry — every time you bid it, you take a whole level of the auction away from the opponents.

Extra length in partner's suit is a liability defensively. It is easy to see why... Let's say your partner overcalls on a suit such as ♠AKQ74. If the opponents end up playing hearts and you have a singleton spade, then the odds favor partner's being able to cash two or three spade tricks. Now let's say that you have four spades. How many spade winners is partner likely to make? He may get two on a very good day, but one is more likely and perhaps even none. If you have five spades, at most your side will take one trick in the suit on defense. The more cards you have in your partner's suit, the more likely it is that his winners will be ruffed if your side ends up on defense. **So the more cards you have in support of partner, the less suitable your hand is for defending.** Reread that. Again.

All direct raises of partner's suit show hands that are weaker than a limit raise — hands in the 6-9 point range. How do you decide how high to raise partner? Easy — you just count trumps! The more you have, the higher you raise. We've seen that, with three-card support, you can give a single raise. Even though you may have relatively few high cards, you can afford to be very aggressive when you hold four-card (or longer) support for partner's five-card suit. So with four-card trump support, jump raise partner's suit.

LHO	Partner	RHO	You
1♦	1♠	pass	?

♠ K 9 7 3　♥ K 8 7　♦ 8 7　♣ 9 7 6 4

♠ J 9 7 3　♥ K 8　♦ 8　♣ 10 9 7 6 4 2

Bid 3♠ with either of these hands. It is important to remember that your jump to 3♠ is not invitational and does not show a good hand. This is a pre-emptive raise — you are simply trying to make life difficult for the opponents by using up bidding space. (Although this method is now very commonly played, it is still something that you must agree on with your partner and it must be alerted when it comes up.)

It is easy enough to see why preemptive jumps in response to overcalls have grown in popularity. If taking the two-level away from the opponents made life tough for them, imagine how disruptive it is if you can also steal the three-level. You have no idea who can make what, but the chances are that the hand belongs to the enemy. *Make the opponents take the last guess!*

With even more trumps, you can take extreme liberties...

♠ K 7 6 4 2　♥ 7　♦ 8 2　♣ 9 7 6 5 4

LHO	Partner	RHO	You
1♦	1♠	dbl	?

You do not want to defend a high-level contract with hearts or diamonds as trumps, so you must make life as difficult as you dare for the opponents. You have at least a ten-card spade fit, so you should contract for ten tricks. Bid 4♠.

What if you have a good hand with support?

Very simple. Since we have said that all direct raises (single and jump raises of partner's overcall) are used on relatively weak hands, largely for preemptive purposes, you start with a cuebid (a bid of the opponents' suit) on any good hand with support.

♠ K 7 4　♥ A 8 7 3　♦ 8 7　♣ K 6 4 2

LHO	Partner	RHO	You
1♦	1♠	pass	2♦

As a rough guide, a cuebid shows 10+ points (including distribution) with at least a three-card fit for partner. Note that the cuebid is unlimited — it shows a sound limit raise or better. If partner has a good opening bid or better for his overcall, game is quite possible. However, it is also possible that eight tricks are the limit of the hand.

This, however, is where things get a little trickier than they are in an uncontested auction. Partner can have quite a wide range for his overcall (anything from 7 to about 18 HCP), while your cuebid has, so far, merely promised at least about 10. We're going to have to do some fancy footwork to get to the right spot from here.

LHO	Partner	RHO	You
1♦	1♠	2♦	3♦

You are still showing a limit raise or better in spades by bidding 3♦.

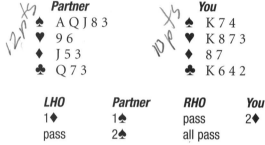

BY THE WAY

If you are a passed hand, your cuebid shows exactly a limit raise, since you cannot have more than that or you would have opened the bidding.

How does the auction continue after a cuebid?

Partner assumes that you have 10-12 for your cuebid, until further notice. With a minimum hand, partner will simply rebid his spades. (Remember, your cuebid shows at least three-card support, so partner can happily rebid his five-card suit.) If either of you has more than advertised, then taking one more bid is usually the way to get the message across. The best way to see how this works is by looking at some examples. Here are some typical auctions, with hands to match:

Partner		**You**	
♠ A Q J 8 3		♠ K 7 4	
♥ 9 6		♥ K 8 7 3	
♦ J 5 3		♦ 8 7	
♣ Q 7 3		♣ K 6 4 2	

LHO	Partner	RHO	You
1♦	1♠	pass	2♦
pass	2♠	all pass	

Partner has little to spare for his overcall, so he simply repeats his suit at the lowest available level. You have a bare 10 points for your cuebid, so you pass.

Partner		**You**	
♠ A Q J 8 3		♠ K 7 4	
♥ 9 6		♥ K 8 7 3	
♦ A 5 3		♦ 8 7	
♣ Q 7 3		♣ K 6 4 2	

LHO	Partner	RHO	You
1♦	1♠	pass	2♦
pass	3♠	all pass	

This time partner has extra values, so he bids more than just 2♠. He is not quite strong enough to commit to game facing a balanced 10-count though, so he invites game by jumping to 3♠. Again however, you have a minimum, and you pass.

	Partner		You
♠	A Q J 8 3	♠	K 7 4
♥	9 6	♥	K 8 7 3
♦	K 5 3	♦	8 7
♣	A Q 3	♣	K 6 4 2

LHO	Partner	RHO	You
1♦	1♠	pass	2♦
pass	4♠	all pass	

With this hand (17 points) partner is happy to play game even if you have a minimum limit raise. As he also knows that you have at least three-card spade support, there is no need to investigate alternative contracts, and he jumps directly to 4♠.

Now let's make your hand a little stronger...

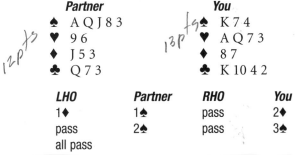

	Partner		You
♠	A Q J 8 3	♠	K 7 4
♥	9 6	♥	A Q 7 3
♦	J 5 3	♦	8 7
♣	Q 7 3	♣	K 10 4 2

LHO	Partner	RHO	You
1♦	1♠	pass	2♦
pass	2♠	pass	3♠
all pass			

Partner again has a minimum overcall, and so he rebids 2♠. You are worth one more effort though, and invite him to bid on by raising to 3♠. This sequence, a cuebid followed by an invitational raise, typically shows around 13-14 points. On this hand, partner is still not quite strong enough to bid game, so he passes.

Here's one last sequence:

	Partner		You
♠	A Q J 8 3	♠	K 7 4
♥	Q 6	♥	A K J 3
♦	J 5 3	♦	8 7
♣	Q 7 3	♣	K 6 4 2

LHO	Partner	RHO	You
1♦	1♠	pass	2♦
pass	2♠	pass	3♠
pass	4♠	all pass	

Partner's values are scattered, and also somewhat soft — he doesn't know whether those queens and jacks will be really useful. He does not want to venture beyond 2♠ facing a balanced 10-count — hence the 2♠ rebid. However, once you show extra by inviting with 3♠, partner is happy to accept the game try.

Summary

✓ If you have support for partner's suit, tell him so immediately. Since partner's overcall promises a good five-card suit, you have a fit any time you have at least three of his suit.

✓ Direct raises, both single raises and jumps, show about 6-9 points. They are primarily defensive bids intended to get in the opponents' way. Make a single raise with three trumps and jump raise with four.

✓ Even with relatively few high-card points, you can afford to raise to the level of the number of known combined trumps.

✓ With good hands containing support for partner's suit (10+ points), start with a cuebid.

✓ In response to a cuebid, overcaller makes a minimum rebid to deny extra values. Repeating his suit does not show extra length in it.

✓ If RHO bids over partner's overcall, make your normal bid, including cuebidding opener's suit if you need to show a limit raise or better.

RAISING PARTNER'S SUIT

NOW TRY THESE...

What is your next bid on each of these hands (neither side is vulnerable)?

1
- ♠ J 4 2
- ♥ 9 8 7 6 3
- ♦ K 6 5 2
- ♣ 3

LHO	Partner	RHO	You
1♣	1♠	pass	?

2
- ♠ J 10 4 2
- ♥ 7 6
- ♦ K 8 6 5 2
- ♣ 3 2

LHO	Partner	RHO	You
1♣	1♠	pass	?

3
- ♠ J 9 7 4 2
- ♥ 4
- ♦ J 8 7 6 5 2
- ♣ 4

LHO	Partner	RHO	You
1♣	1♠	pass	?

4
- ♠ A J 4
- ♥ K Q 4 3
- ♦ 3 2
- ♣ 9 8 5 4

LHO	Partner	RHO	You
1♣	1♠	pass	?

5
- ♠ K J 4
- ♥ 4
- ♦ K J 8 6 4
- ♣ A 8 5 4

LHO	Partner	RHO	You
1♣	1♠	pass	?

6
- ♠ A K 4 2
- ♥ A 4
- ♦ K J 7 6 3
- ♣ Q 4

LHO	Partner	RHO	You
1♣	1♠	pass	?

7
- ♠ K Q J 4 2
- ♥ 8 4
- ♦ 8 5
- ♣ K 8 6 3

LHO	Partner	RHO	You
		1♦	1♠
pass	2♦	pass	?

8
- ♠ K Q 8 4 3
- ♥ K 7
- ♦ 8 6
- ♣ K J 4 3

LHO	Partner	RHO	You
		1♦	1♠
pass	2♦	pass	?

9
- ♠ A Q J 4 2
- ♥ 4 3
- ♦ A 8
- ♣ K Q 9 3

LHO	Partner	RHO	You
		1♦	1♠
pass	2♦	pass	?

10
- ♠ A Q J 8 4
- ♥ K Q 7
- ♦ J 6 3
- ♣ 6 5

LHO	Partner	RHO	You
		1♦	1♠
pass	2♦	pass	?

ANSWERS

1 2♠ You have a weakish hand with three-card support for partner's overcall. Make a defensive raise to make life difficult for opener to re-enter the auction.

2 3♠ You still have a weak hand, but this time you have four-card support for partner. Preempt the auction as high as you dare.

3 4♠ You have a terrible hand unless spades are trumps, and the opponents can surely make at least game if you give them room to find their best fit. You know your side has at least ten spades, so preempt to the four-level. You probably won't make 4♠, but the Law of Total Tricks (see Chapter 24) assures us that if they double you, the penalty will be less than the value of their game. Trust us, it works!

4 2♣ Cuebid the opener's suit to show a limit raise. This is a minimum hand for a cuebid, so if partner rebids 2♠, showing no extras, you will pass. If partner encourages by bidding 3♠, you will have a decision to make.

5 2♣ This time, you have enough to invite game. You should start with a cuebid, and then make one more effort — if partner rebids 2♠, you can raise to 3♠.

6 2♣ You plan to bid game, even if partner has no extra values. By starting with a cuebid, you can investigate slam prospects at a safe level.

7 2♠ You are minimum for your initial overcall. If partner is also minimum for his cuebid (a 10-count with three-card spade support), then there is no reason to expect that you can make more than eight tricks. Show your minimum hand by making the weakest rebid available.

8 3♠ You have extras this time. Game will be on if partner has anything more than a totally minimum cuebid. Invite partner to bid game by jumping to 3♠. More experienced players may consider bidding 3♣ here instead of 3♠. This descriptive game try allows partner to go on if he likes clubs.

9 4♠ Even opposite a minimum cuebid (10 points and three-card spade support) you want to play in game.

10 3♠ *or* 4♠. So do you feel lucky? This 14-point hand is right on the cusp; aggressive players will just bid game, while others will feel more comfortable just inviting. Who's right? Vulnerable, we would just bid 4♠ (remember that game bonus!), but we've gone down before, and probably will this time too!

CHAPTER 3

RESPONDING TO OVERCALLS WITHOUT SUPPORT

 But think, oh think, of those awful and numerous times when the hand does not fit! *Florence Irwin,* **Auction Highlights,** *1913.*

In the last chapter, we looked at the various options you have available if you want to raise the suit partner has overcalled. But what if you don't have support for partner's suit?

First of all, you should not bid at all on a poor hand (less than about 8 points) if you have no support for partner. You must not introduce a new suit just because you want to rescue your partner.

	Partner		*You*
♠	Q 10 3	♠	K 7 4
♥	K Q J 10 7 3	♥	—
♦	3	♦	Q 9 8 7 6 4
♣	A Q 8	♣	9 7 4 2

LHO	*Partner*	*RHO*	*You*
1♣	1♥	pass	?

Here you hate hearts and you have a six-card suit of your own. However, bidding 2♦ would be like jumping from the frying pan into the fire. Looking at both hands, it is clear that 1♥ is a much better contract than 2♦; to begin with, partner is going to make 1♥, while 2♦ is a very sick puppy indeed. Not only that but, as we shall see shortly, partner is not even allowed to pass 2♦ — it is forcing! Whatever partner bids over 2♦ will just get you into worse trouble.

When you do not like partner's suit and you have a poor hand, keep the bidding low by passing. If the hand is a misfit for your side, then it probably will be for the opponents too. Often they will bid again, with the result that they get into trouble, rather than you.

What if you have a decent hand, though?

If you have at least 8 points or so, you should try to bid something even without support for partner. After all, if partner can have as much as 18, you're now in a range where game is not out of the question, depending on how good his hand actually is. Since, as we saw in the last chapter, a cuebid promises support for partner's suit, you have only two options: bid your own suit or bid notrump.

You won't always have a convenient bid available but, if you have at least 10 points counting distribution and a reasonable five-card suit, you can bid it now. Let's take a look at some hands on which you should bid your own suit:

♠ K J 9 7 6 4   ♥ 8   ♦ A 8 7   ♣ Q 9 2

LHO	Partner	RHO	You
1♦	1♥	pass	?

In this example, you have a decent suit of your own (decent means at least a good five-card suit), and sufficient values to expect that it will be your hand if a fit can be found. If partner has enough high cards, you may be able to bid and make 3NT even if you don't have a good trump fit somewhere. However, before we look at how the auction might continue, there is very important point to make: your new suit bid is forcing — partner is not allowed to pass. There is good reason for this — since a cuebid shows a good raise of partner's suit, you cannot also use it just to tell him you have a good hand if you do not have support. So there are going to be hands where you don't have support for partner, but have enough high cards that you don't want him to pass just yet. Perhaps these are the two hands:

	Partner		You
♠	10 8 3	♠	A K J 9 7 6
♥	K Q J 10 7	♥	8
♦	K 3	♦	A 8 7
♣	J 8 3	♣	Q 9 2

LHO	Partner	RHO	You
1♦	1♥	pass	1♠
pass	?		

Partner has a fairly minimum hand to overcall 1♥ over 1♦, yet it is enough to give you quite a good play for 4♠. You're not going to get there if he is allowed to pass your 1♠ response!

How does the auction continue after you bid a new suit?

The answer is pretty straightforward: partner does what comes naturally to describe his hand. His weakest bids are a rebid of his own suit, or a single raise of yours:

	Partner		*You*
♠	10 8	♠	K J 9 7 6
♥	K Q J 10 7 2	♥	8
♦	J 3	♦	A 8 7 4
♣	K 8 3	♣	Q 9 2

LHO	**Partner**	**RHO**	**You**
1♦	1♥	pass	1♠
pass	2♥	all pass	

With a minimum hand, and no support for you, partner simply rebids his suit. Notice that this doesn't promise extra length, or indeed anything much at all — he has to bid something, after all.

Here's a hand on which partner would raise your new suit:

	Partner		*You*
♠	10 8 3	♠	K J 9 7 6
♥	K Q J 10 7	♥	8
♦	K 3	♦	A 8 7 4
♣	J 8 3	♣	Q 9 2

LHO	*Partner*	*RHO*	*You*
1♦	1♥	pass	1♠
pass	2♠	all pass	

Note again that your partner does not show any extra values when he raises spades. Since 1♠ is forcing, he has to bid something, even with this minimum overcall. When he holds a stronger hand in support of your suit, he must therefore do more than make a simple raise. Look at these two hands:

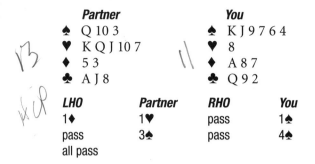

	Partner		You
♠	Q 10 3	♠	K J 9 7 6 4
♥	K Q J 10 7	♥	8
♦	5 3	♦	A 8 7
♣	A J 8	♣	Q 9 2

LHO	Partner	RHO	You
1♦	1♥	pass	1♠
pass	3♠	pass	4♠
all pass			

This time, partner has a better than minimum hand and good support for your spade suit. Your singleton heart is not an asset, but you do have an extra spade so you decide to push on to game. You're probably going to need the club finesse to work but, since LHO opened the bidding, he figures to have most of the high cards too, and it probably will.

With a solid overcall, partner may be able to suggest playing in notrump:

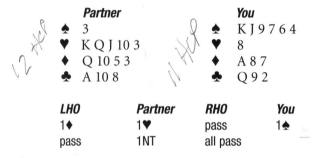

	Partner		You
♠	3	♠	K J 9 7 6 4
♥	K Q J 10 3	♥	8
♦	Q 10 5 3	♦	A 8 7
♣	A 10 8	♣	Q 9 2

LHO	Partner	RHO	You
1♦	1♥	pass	1♠
pass	1NT	all pass	

This time, you reach a safe haven even though neither of you has a fit for the other's major. Having shown some values with 1♠, there is no need for you to bid again. Of course, with a better hand you are allowed to raise:

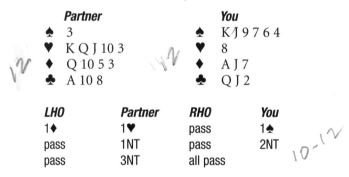

	Partner		You
♠	3	♠	K J 9 7 6 4
♥	K Q J 10 3	♥	8
♦	Q 10 5 3	♦	A J 7
♣	A 10 8	♣	Q J 2

LHO	Partner	RHO	You
1♦	1♥	pass	1♠
pass	1NT	pass	2NT
pass	3NT	all pass	

Notice that you reached an excellent game contract with only 24 HCP between you. This also brings us conveniently to the topic of bidding notrump after an overcall.

What kind of hand do you need to bid notrump after partner overcalls?

When partner's suit is a major, you deny three-card support by bidding notrump. You also need at least one (and preferably two) stoppers in the opponents' suit, and you have a fairly balanced hand, probably without a good suit of your own:

♠ 8 4   ♥ K Q 7 5   ♦ Q J 8 6   ♣ K 10 3

LHO	Partner	RHO	You
1♦	1♠	pass	?

I over part overcall

Bid 1NT, showing about 8-11 HCP. The range for a 1NT bid as responder to an overcall is higher than it would be if partner has opened, because partner may have a lower point-count for his overcall than he would for an opening bid.

♠ J 4   ♥ K Q 7 5   ♦ Q J 8 6   ♣ A J 10

LHO	Partner	RHO	You
1♦	1♠	pass	?

Bid 2NT on this hand. You cannot commit to game when partner might have only 7-8 points. 2NT here shows around 12-14 HCP and is highly invitational. With extra values, partner will be happy to raise you.

Things are slightly different if partner has overcalled at the two-level, promising at least opening bid values:

LHO	Partner	RHO	You
1♠	2♥	pass	?

Now 2NT by you would show about 8-11 HCP (the minimum range), as well as a balanced hand, fewer than three hearts, and a spade stopper or two. With a better hand, just bid 3NT right away.

Does any of this change if you are a passed hand?

If you had a chance to open the bidding and did not do so, there is the implication that you have neither a particularly strong hand nor a very good suit. Most players, therefore, treat a new suit bid by a passed hand as showing moderate values; however, it is no longer forcing.

BY THE WAY

Often in competitive auctions, you can bid aggressive games on slightly less than the normal amount of high card points. This is because you may be able to judge that your high cards will be well-placed relative to the opening bidder, who will have most of the ones you are missing. This is very different from the normal 26-point game contract where the opposing high cards could be anywhere – they could be split 7-7, 10-4, 4-10, and so forth. If you know during the auction that all the kings are lying under your ace-queens, it's a whole new ball game.

Partner	You
♠ 3 2	♠ A J 10 7 6
♥ K Q J 10 3	♥ 8
♦ 10 5 3	♦ 9 8 7
♣ A 10 8	♣ K 9 3 2

LHO	Partner	RHO	You
		pass	pass
1♦	1♥	pass	1♠
all pass			

BY THE WAY

If you want to bid a new suit at the three-level as a passed hand, you have to pay some attention to safety, so you must have at least some tolerance for his suit.

LHO	Partner	RHO	You
			pass
1♠	2♥	2♠	3♣

Partner's two-level overcall has promised at least an opening bid, and you may be just shy of one. Clearly, too, you have a good club suit. But what if partner doesn't like clubs and can't bid notrump? You must be able to stand it if he rebids 3♥ — so you need a doubleton heart (with more you would just raise).

Partner has a minimum hand for his 1♥ overcall, and while he's not thrilled about spades, at least he has a couple of them. Since you are a passed hand, he's allowed to pass, and would probably do so happily.

What happens if RHO bids?

In the auctions we have so far discussed, opener's partner has passed over your partner's overcall. That will not always be the case.

Just as was the case when you had support for partner, the simplest way to proceed is to ignore RHO.

♠ Q 9 2   ♥ 8   ♦ A 8 7   ♣ K J 9 7 6 4

LHO	Partner	RHO	You
1♦	1♥	1♠	?

With this hand, you can bid 2♣ just as you would have done if RHO had passed. There is, however, one common situation that we need to mention, which is when RHO raises opener's suit, and your hand is not really good enough to bid your own suit.

Using a Responsive Double

Throughout this book, we will be looking at numerous ways in which you can employ a double to help your competitive bidding. Many of you will be used to playing a double for penalties in most situations. As we shall see, that is often not the best use for the call.

♠ Q 2　♥ K J 8 4　♦ 9 4　♣ K 10 7 6 4

LHO	Partner	RHO	You
1♦	1♠	2♦	?

On this hand, you would have bid 2♣ if RHO had passed, but 3♣ is something of a stretch. The answer, as those who have read our previous book will know, is to use a conventional double. This is called a **responsive double**, and it tells partner that you have support for both of the unbid suits, tolerance for his suit (usually), and sufficient values to compete — perfect! Think of it as a type of takeout double. Let's look at another example:

♠ K 7　♥ A Q 6 3　♦ K 6 3　♣ Q 8 5 2

LHO	Partner	RHO	You
1♦	1♠	2♦	?

Without the intervention, you would have chanced 2NT, but the 2♦ call has given you the opportunity to tell partner a lot more about your hand. Perhaps he has four hearts and a minimum hand, in which case you can now get to play 2♥ instead of 2NT. So, make a responsive double and partner will know you have values and no clear-cut bid.

Now, what about this auction?

LHO	Partner	RHO	You
1♦	1♠	1NT	dbl

Is this double still responsive? No, because RHO didn't raise opener's suit. This is a penalty double.

Summary

✓ If you have support for partner's suit, tell him immediately.

✓ Do not attempt to rescue partner just because you have a bad hand with shortness in his suit.

✓ A new suit bid in response to an overcall by an unpassed hand is forcing. It shows 10+ points (including distribution) and a good five-card suit, and is a constructive move forwards.

✓ Overcaller does not show extra values when he makes a simple raise of your new suit. As your bid was forcing, he has to bid something, even with a minimum hand.

✓ Overcaller can show extra values with support for your suit by cuebidding or making a jump raise.

✓ Notrump bids in response to an overcall show more points than they would if partner had opened the bidding. Typically, bidding notrump at the minimum level shows 8-11 HCP.

✓ A new suit bid by a passed hand in response to an overcall is not forcing, but is still forward-going. If the new suit bid forces the auction to the three-level, it also shows a tolerance for over-caller's suit.

✓ If RHO bids over partner's overcall, make your normal bid if possible. If he raises opener's suit, you have the opportunity to make a responsive (takeout) double if you have the right kind of hand.

RESPONDING TO OVERCALLS WITHOUT SUPPORT

NOW TRY THESE...

What is your next bid on each of the following hands?

1
- ♠ Q 8 4
- ♥ —
- ♦ J 8 7 6 5 2
- ♣ J 9 3 2

LHO	Partner	RHO	You
1♣	1♥	pass	?

2
- ♠ A J 10 4 2
- ♥ 7 6
- ♦ K J 5 2
- ♣ 3 2

LHO	Partner	RHO	You
1♣	1♥	pass	?

3
- ♠ A J 10 4 2
- ♥ 4
- ♦ A Q 8 7 3
- ♣ 8 5

LHO	Partner	RHO	You
1♣	1♥	pass	?

4
- ♠ A Q J 10 4 2
- ♥ Q 4
- ♦ K 3
- ♣ A 5 4

LHO	Partner	RHO	You
1♣	1♥	pass	?

5
- ♠ K J 4 2
- ♥ 4
- ♦ J 10 8 6
- ♣ K 9 8 4

LHO	Partner	RHO	You
1♣	1♥	pass	?

6
- ♠ Q J 9
- ♥ 8 7
- ♦ A J 9 6 3
- ♣ A Q 4

LHO	Partner	RHO	You
1♣	1♥	pass	?

7
- ♠ Q J 9 2
- ♥ 9 7
- ♦ A 9 6 3
- ♣ 10 7 4

LHO	Partner	RHO	You
1♣	1♥	pass	?

8
- ♠ K J 9 2
- ♥ 4
- ♦ K 10 9 7 3
- ♣ A Q 4

LHO	Partner	RHO	You
1♠	2♥	pass	?

9
- ♠ K Q J 4 2
- ♥ 4
- ♦ 8 7 4
- ♣ K 8 6 4

LHO	Partner	RHO	You
		1♦	1♠
pass	2♥	pass	?

10
- ♠ K Q J 4 2
- ♥ 4 3 2
- ♦ 8
- ♣ K 8 6 4

LHO	Partner	RHO	You
		1♦	1♠
pass	2♥	pass	?

11
- ♠ K Q J 4 2
- ♥ A 4 2
- ♦ 8
- ♣ K 8 6 4

LHO	Partner	RHO	You
		1♦	1♠
pass	2♥	pass	?

12
- ♠ K Q J 4 2
- ♥ 4
- ♦ K 10 7 4
- ♣ A 8 7

LHO	Partner	RHO	You
		1♦	1♠
pass	2♥	pass	?

ANSWERS

1 pass There is no reason to suppose that your side can make any contract, so keep the bidding as low as possible. With luck, the opponents will bid again, and then they will be the ones to get into trouble on this misfit.

2 1♠ You are just about worth a bid, although opposite a minimum overcall you may be turning a plus score into a minus by moving. Partner might have quite a good hand though and, if he also has a spade fit, then making game is not out of the question.

3 1♠ Although you have a good hand, there is no guarantee that you have a fit. Bid 1♠ and hope to get a chance to introduce your second suit cheaply too.

4 1♠ As this is forcing, there is no need to do more at this stage.

5 1NT This shows 8-11 HCP and denies a fit for partner's hearts. Do not be surprised if you cannot make anything, though.

6 2NT This time you have to make an effort to get to game opposite anything but a completely minimum overcall. However, you should still not be surprised if you find yourself too high sometimes.

7 pass Much though you'd like to take a bid in case partner has a really good hand, you have only 7 HCP, no heart support, no club stopper, and no five-card suit of your own.

8 3NT Partner has overcalled at the two-level, and should have an opening bid, so just bid game.

9 2♠ You don't promise extra spades since 2♥ was forcing. Don't even think about bidding 3♣ — that shows better clubs and serious extra values.

10 3♥ Again, you're not promising a rose garden, just admitting to three-card heart support.

11 4♥ This time you really like hearts; you have a ruffing value and your spades will produce some tricks even opposite a singleton.

12 2NT You have a good enough hand to make a move towards game, even if it isn't going to be in a major suit. This is just a natural, descriptive bid, and partner can do what he wants from here, including pass.

OVERCALLS THAT SHOW TWO SUITS

 It is obvious from the outset that such bids are of necessity, false bids. No sane person would bid this and mean what he said.
Florence Irwin, **Auction Highlights, 1913.**

There are two conventions (Michaels Cuebids and the Unusual Notrump) that allow you to make an overcall showing two suits at the same time. Not a bad idea, is it? Let's begin by seeing how a Michaels Cuebid works:

LHO	Partner	RHO	You
		1♦	2♦

This immediate cuebid of the suit RHO has opened used to mean you could make game with no help from partner — the kind of hand you would have opened with a strong 2♣ if RHO had passed. However, you don't often get to use such a bid, so you are not giving up much by assigning a different meaning to it. In any case, as we'll see later, you can deal with those hands by starting with a takeout double. Mike Michaels, a Florida bridge teacher, had the idea of using a direct cuebid of opener's suit to show various two-suited hands. If you play this convention, then when the opening bid is a minor, as in the example above, your cuebid shows both majors.

LHO	Partner	RHO	You
		1♠	2♠

When the opening bid is a major, a Michaels Cuebid shows the unbid major and one of the minors. In the example above, you would have hearts and either clubs or diamonds.

Here is a summary of the different possibilities.

Michaels Cuebids

RHO opens

1♣	2♣	*shows spades and hearts*
1♦	2♦	*shows spades and hearts*
1♥	2♥	*shows spades and a minor*
1♠	2♠	*shows hearts and a minor*

This makes hands that are otherwise difficult to describe much easier to bid. Bidding is a language that includes very few words, so any time you can tell partner a great deal about your hand with one bid, it must be a good thing. Suppose you have the following hand:

♠ A J 10 5 3   ♥ A K J 7 2   ♦ 4 2   ♣ 5

Your RHO opens 1♦. If you have no way to show both suits at once, you will presumably bid 1♠, hoping to get the chance to bid hearts later. That's a fond hope, but what if the auction continues 1NT from LHO and RHO raises to 3NT? Obviously, this isn't your hand, and bidding 4♥ is simply laying your head on the block and asking the opponents to chop it off. Trust us, they will. There's another problem, too — partner's going to lead a spade against 3NT and, for all you know, the only lead to beat it is a heart. Unfortunately, partner doesn't know about your heart suit...

What do you need to use Michaels?

Let's start with the shape requirements for a Michaels Cuebid: you must be at least 5-5 in your two suits. There is an old bridge expression 'Five-five, come alive,' which refers to the enormous playing strength of a hand with 5-5 distribution. Never use Michaels with a 5-4 hand; partner will bid expecting two five-card suits and will not be happy to find that he has made the wrong choice because you are a card short somewhere. By the same token, don't talk yourself into a Michaels bid when you are 6-4, just because you have ten cards in your two suits. It's not OK. You must have at least five cards in each of your two suits.

The most common method to play is that the Michaels bidder has either a weak hand (less than 10 points) or a very strong hand (16+ points). This is called 'Mini-Maxi Michaels'. If you have a hand in the middle range (10-15), then just make an overcall in the higher-ranking of your two suits, and hope you get a chance to bid the other one later. How weak can you be? Well, at favorable vulnerability, you might bid 2♣ over 1♣ with as little as

♠ K 10 6 4 3   ♥ Q J 7 5 2   ♦ 4 2   ♣ 7

There's no guarantee you won't get damaged, but the odds are in your favor.

How do you respond to Michaels?

With a fit for one of partner's known suits, simply raise to the appropriate level. Bid assuming partner has the weak hand — if he has the Maxi, he'll bid again. After a major suit cuebid, you don't know which minor partner has, of course. Here's a typical situation:

♠ Q 10 6 ♥ 7 2 ♦ J 5 4 3 ♣ J 10 6 4

LHO	Partner	RHO	You
1♠	2♠	pass	?

Obviously, you want to settle in partner's minor, but which minor does he have? To find out, bid 2NT; this is not natural — it tells partner you are not enthusiastic about hearts, but would prefer to play in his minor, which he will now bid. You will, of course, pass — quickly!

What is the Unusual Notrump?

What if you have the wrong two suits for a Michaels bid? Suppose RHO opens 1♠ and you have:

♠ 6 ♥ A 2 ♦ A J 10 4 3 ♣ K Q J 3 2

A Michaels Cuebid would show hearts and a minor, so that's out. However the Unusual Notrump (or UNT for short) comes to the rescue — a jump over-call of 2NT. There's no real need to preserve any natural meaning for this bid. As we'll see later, in Chapter 6, if you have a really strong balanced hand (with 19+ HCP) you can double first and then bid notrump, so you do not need a natural 2NT overcall. UNT is very similar to Michaels — it shows at least 5-5 in two suits and either a strong or a weak hand, but this time it promises the two lowest suits above 2NT that have not yet been bid. If RHO has opened a major suit, UNT shows both minors. If RHO opens a minor, then UNT promises hearts and the other minor.

Here's another summary table:

Unusual Notrump

RHO opens

1♣	2NT *shows hearts and diamonds*
1♦	2NT *shows hearts and clubs*
1♥	2NT *shows diamonds and clubs*
1♠	2NT *shows diamonds and clubs*

The requirements for making a UNT overcall are the same as Michaels: you must be at least 5-5, and the Mini-Maxi agreement is again useful. This time, however, both your suits are known, and partner gives preference at the appropriate level for his fit and hand strength, assuming you have the weak hand until further notice.

Note: using Unusual Notrump is more dangerous than using a Michaels Cuebid because you are always forcing your partner to at least the three-level.

When RHO opens a minor suit and you make a Michaels Cuebid, partner is only forced to give preference between the majors at the two-level. When vulnerable, you should refrain from using the Unusual Notrump on marginal hands as the opponents will find it very easy to double you

Summary

✓ When an opponent opens the bidding, a direct cuebid of the opponent's suit or a jump overcall of 2NT both show different two-suited hands.

✓ You must have at least five cards in each of your two suits.

✓ Cuebidding a minor shows both majors.

✓ Cuebidding a major shows the other major and an unknown minor.

✓ Overcalling 2NT over a major shows both minors.

✓ Overcalling 2NT over a minor shows hearts and the other minor.

✓ It is useful to agree that both Michaels and UNT show either a weak hand (how weak will depend on vulnerability) or a very strong hand.

✓ If the Michaels bidder has an unknown suit, his partner can bid 2NT to ask him to show it.

OVERCALLS THAT SHOW TWO SUITS

NOW TRY THESE...

What is you next bid on each of these hands?

1
- ♠ A Q 8 4 3
- ♥ A K J 4 3
- ♦ 5
- ♣ K 9

LHO	Partner	RHO	You
		1♣	?

2
- ♠ A K J 4 3
- ♥ 4 3
- ♦ A
- ♣ K Q 10 9 5

LHO	Partner	RHO	You
		1♥	?

3
- ♠ 5
- ♥ 2
- ♦ K 10 8 6 4
- ♣ Q J 9 5 3 2

LHO	Partner	RHO	You
		1♠	?

4
- ♠ A Q 8 4 3
- ♥ A 3
- ♦ K Q J 7 3
- ♣ 9

LHO	Partner	RHO	You
		1♣	?

5
- ♠ A Q 8 4
- ♥ J 3
- ♦ A 5 3
- ♣ 9 7 5 2

LHO	Partner	RHO	You
1♣	2♣	pass	?

6
- ♠ Q J 3
- ♥ K 8 6 4 3
- ♦ 9
- ♣ 5 4 3 2

LHO	Partner	RHO	You
1♣	2♣	pass	?

7
- ♠ 3
- ♥ Q 7 4 3
- ♦ K 7 2
- ♣ 7 6 4 3 2

LHO	Partner	RHO	You
1♥	2♥	pass	?

8
- ♠ A Q 3
- ♥ K J 3
- ♦ 8 6 4 3 2
- ♣ A 9

LHO	Partner	RHO	You
1♣	2♣	3♣	?

9
- ♠ 3
- ♥ 4 3
- ♦ Q 6 4 3
- ♣ K 10 7 6 4 2

LHO	Partner	RHO	You
1♣	2♣	pass	?

10
- ♠ 8 4 3
- ♥ K J 5 3 2
- ♦ 5
- ♣ A 10 9 4

LHO	Partner	RHO	You
1♦	2NT	pass	?

ANSWERS

1 2♣ This shows both majors. You have a very strong hand, and you intend to bid again even if partner only gives you a simple preference to his better major.

2 2♥ Ideal. A very good hand with five spades and a five-card minor. Here, too, you will bid again whatever partner does.

3 2NT Whether you bid on this hand will depend on the vulnerability. If partner fits either or both of your suits, your excellent shape gives you a lot of playing strength even though you have very few high cards. Vulnerable against not, you should probably pass, but bid 2NT at other vulnerabilities.

4 1♠ You don't have the right suits for either Michaels or UNT, so just overcall 1♠ for now. Maybe you will get to show diamonds later.

5 4♠ If partner has the strong hand, you expect to make game; if he is weak, then maybe the opponents have a game. Either way, you tell partner you have a good fit and some values.

6 4♥ Because you have a fit for both partner's suits, you expect to make this if he is strong. If he is weak, the opponents can make game and you will not come to much harm in 4♥ doubled. If you bid confidently, sometimes you will steal the hand in 4♥ even when partner is weak!

7 2NT You don't like spades, and suspect strongly that partner's second suit is diamonds. It cannot hurt to bid 2NT and find out, though. On a good day, partner will bid clubs now!

8 4♣ Bidding 4♥ or 4♠ would not be wrong here, but this is a better alternative. Obviously you are not bidding clubs naturally here, any more than partner was! The cuebid, however, shows enough values for game and asks to partner to choose the major he prefers — he might be 6-5, for example. Also, slam is not impossible if partner has the right hand.

9 2♥ A typical Michaels auction, unfortunately. You don't like either of partner's suits, but you have to bid something. Did you consider passing with all those clubs? You shouldn't have — partner could easily be void, and opener could have six of them too! You are required to bid one of partner's suits in this situation, so bid a confident 2♥ and maybe they'll bid on instead of doubling. Whichever side plays this hand is likely to be in deep trouble.

10 4♥ Where are the spades? Partner has hearts and clubs, and so do you — time to make it as hard as possible for the opponents to find the right spot. With at least ten trumps, you are safe at the four-level.

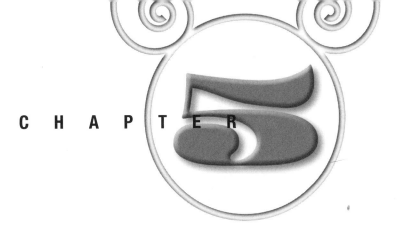

JUMP OVERCALLS

> Give me a partner who knows how to stop bidding his own suit
> and leave me in my better one.
> *Florence Irwin,* **Auction Highlights, 1913.**

So far, we have only considered simple (non-jump) suit overcalls. Jump over-calls are used to show single-suited hands with few high-card points but reasonable playing strength. When you are the dealer (or after RHO passes), you think of such hands as preemptive opening bids. You can still bid on these hands after RHO has opened the bidding, by using jump overcalls.

What do you need to make a weak jump overcall at the two-level?

Let's say you pick up a hand on which, as the dealer, you would have opened with a Weak Two-bid — 6-10 points and a good six-card suit with two of the top three honors. RHO stifles your intentions by opening the bidding, though. Fortunately, opener's suit is lower-ranking than the one you were going to bid. No problem — you can still make the same two-level bid that you had in mind.

Think of a jump overcall at the two-level as being the same as an opening Weak Two-bid. Thus:

♠ A Q J 9 6 5   ♥ 8 6   ♦ 8 3   ♣ 9 5 4

If RHO had passed as dealer, you would have opened with a weak 2♠ bid. When instead RHO opens with a bid of 1♣, 1♦ or 1♥, you can still show this hand by making a jump overcall of 2♠.

By contrast, look at this example hand:

♠ Q 7 6 5 4 3   ♥ A 6   ♦ K 5   ♣ 9 5 4

You have a hand with a six-card suit and you are within the normal 6-10 HCP range for a Weak Two opening. However, if you had been first to speak, you would not have started with a 2♠ opening because that would show a better suit than this. So, what do you do with this hand after RHO opens the bidding 1♣, 1♦ or 1♥?

We said earlier that you should think of a jump overcall as being like a Weak Two, and the requirements for a decent suit still apply. However you have a six-card suit and adequate values to make a simple overcall. Do not allow the sixth spade to lure you into a jump overcall when that would not describe your hand accurately. Overcall 1♠.

What if your jump overcall would be at the three-level?

Sometimes opener's suit will be higher-ranking than yours. What this means is that a two-level overcall would not now be a jump, and to make a jump overcall you have to come in at the three-level. That's okay though, and the same criteria we have just discussed can be applied to these bids. If you would have opened with a three-level preemptive bid as dealer, you can make a jump overcall to that same level.

♠ 8   ♥ 9 3   ♦ A Q J 8 6 4 3   ♣ 8 6 3

If you were first to speak, you would open with a preemptive bid of 3♦. Little changes when RHO opens the bidding — if he opens 1♥ or 1♠, you can still jump to 3♦. The same requirements in terms of suit quality can be applied to overcalls as you would use for deciding whether to preempt as dealer. For example:

♠ 9   ♥ A   ♦ Q 8 6 5 4 3 2   ♣ K 9 6 3

You would not open 3♦ with this hand. Preempts show hands suitable for play in only one suit with little defensive strength outside of the long suit. Clearly, this hand does not therefore qualify for a 3♦ opening bid. For exactly the same reasons, it also does not qualify for a jump overcall. If you decide to bid, make a simple 2♦ overcall on this hand.

What about jumping more than one level?

A 'jump overcall' usually only jumps the bidding one level — i.e.

LHO	Partner	RHO	You
		1♦	2♠

LHO	Partner	RHO	You
		1♥	3♣

Higher-level preemptive overcalls can also be judged by exactly the same criteria. Let's look at a hand we have already seen once:

♠ 8   ♥ 9 3   ♦ A Q J 8 6 4 3   ♣ 8 6 3

We have already established that you would open 3♦ with this. We have also agreed that you can make a jump overcall of 3♦ with it over a 1♥ or 1♠ opening bid. Now, let's say that RHO opens 1♣. You could make a jump overcall to 2♦, but you would do that with one fewer diamond. Since this hand would have been worth an opening 3♦ bid, that is the bid you should still make, even though it is a double jump.

The same applies to this hand:

♠ 7   ♥ K Q J 8 7 5 2   ♦ Q 7 3   ♣ 8 2

As dealer, you would open 3♥. If RHO opens 1♠, you should therefore make a jump overcall to 3♥. If RHO opens 1♣ or 1♦, you are still worth a preemptive jump to 3♥. Easy, isn't it?

One more example should suffice:

♠ —   ♥ A Q J 10 8 7 6 2   ♦ 7 5 3   ♣ 8 3

As dealer, few people would disagree with a 4♥ opening bid. Thus, if RHO opens with 1♣, 1♦ or 1♠, you should overcall 4♥ with this hand.

Summary:

Good 6-card suit	*Jump overcall at the 2-level*
Good 7-card suit	*Jump overcall at the 3-level*
Good 8-card suit	*Jump overcall at the 4-level*

Does the vulnerability affect the decision to make a jump overcall?

The summary above offers only a rough guideline. You must always bear in mind the vulnerability when deciding how high to overcall, just as you would when making a preemptive opening bid. The best time to preempt is when you are not vulnerable against vulnerable opponents — this is known as 'favorable' vulnerability. The opponents will have to beat you four tricks doubled to show a profit if they can make a vulnerable game.

When learning about opening preemptive bids, you were taught to be more cautious when your side is vulnerable. With a not quite perfect preempt, the risk of bidding is probably worthwhile if you are not vulnerable. When vulnerable, though, discretion is the better part of valor, and you should err on the side of caution by passing instead. Exactly the same criteria should be applied to jump overcalls.

Remember that it is easier for the opponents to double you once one of them has shown strength by opening the bidding. When you preempt as dealer, you may be allowed to steal the contract if each opponent holds around 12-14 points. That cannot happen once RHO has opened. If opener's partner has 12+ points, he knows already that the hand belongs to his side. Your potential gain from a jump overcall is therefore slightly less than when you preempt as the dealer, while your risk is substantially greater. If your hand isn't quite a textbook preempt, you should usually refrain from acting when vulnerable (particularly if your opponents are not vulnerable).

How do you respond to a jump overcall?

The easy answer is to bid over a jump overcall as you would in response to a preemptive opening bid. Most of the time, you will pass, but if you do have a good enough hand to bid, a new suit is natural and forcing. A direct raise is not invitational, and usually designed to take up bidding space. There are one or two differences that apply though. For example, after a two-level jump overcall:

LHO	Partner	RHO	You
1♥	2♠	pass	?

With an invitational hand including spade support, you cuebid the opponents' suit. For example:

♠ Q 7 6 ♥ 6 5 ♦ A K J 7 5 ♣ K Q 4

LHO	Partner	RHO	You
1♥	2♠	pass	3♥

Partner's continuations after the cuebid are similar to the ones we discussed in Chapter 2 (when you made a cuebid in response to a simple overcall to show a limit raise or better with support for his suit). Partner will rebid his suit with a minimum or jump to game with a decent hand for his jump overcall.

Other bids are natural. As over any preempt, direct raises do not invite partner to bid again:

♠ Q76 ♥ 65 ♦ KJ754 ♣ K54

LHO	Partner	RHO	You
1♥	2♠	pass	3♠

With nine trumps between you, you can safely raise to 3♠ and make them bid at the four-level if they dare. But this is only safe if partner is not allowed to take you seriously and bid 4♠!

Notrump bids are also natural:

♠ Q7 ♥ AJ105 ♦ QJ75 ♣ AK5

LHO	Partner	RHO	You
1♥	2♠	pass	2NT

With a maximum hand for his preempt, partner can bid 3NT. Nine tricks in notrump may be easier than ten in spades since he won't be able to ruff anything in your hand.

How do you respond to higher jump overcalls?

As you might expect, responding to a three-level overcall is similar to bidding over partner's opening preemptive bid.

LHO	Partner	RHO	You
1♥	3♣	pass	?

If your partner had opened 3♣, then a bid of a new suit would be natural and forcing. Bids of 3♦ and 3♠ are exactly that here too. Again, a cuebid is available to show most other good hands you might hold. As in all other situations we have discussed, this cuebid asks partner to describe his hand further. For example, he might be able to bid 3NT with a heart stopper. Failing that, he can repeat his suit (bid 4♣) with a minimum or jump to game (bid 5♣) with better than a minimum.

Summary

✓ Jump overcalls at the two-level show a hand that would have opened a Weak Two-bid if given the chance.

✓ Higher jump overcalls show a hand suitable for the same bid as dealer. Thus, a jump to the three-level tends to show a seven-card suit with few defensive values, and a jump to the four-level suggests an eight-card suit.

✓ As with any preempt, look at the vulnerability before deciding to make a jump overcall. Be careful when vulnerable, and be more aggressive at favorable vulnerability.

✓ In response to jump overcalls, bids of new suits are natural and forcing. A cuebid of the opponent's suit is a strong move asking the overcaller to describe his hand further. A cuebid promises a fit for overcaller's suit and at least invitational values.

JUMP OVERCALLS

NOW TRY THESE...

What is you next bid on each of the following hands?

1
- ♠ A K J 4 3
- ♥ 4 3
- ♦ 8 7 6 5
- ♣ 9 5

LHO	Partner	RHO	You
		1♥	?

2
- ♠ A Q J 9 4 2
- ♥ 6
- ♦ 8 5 2
- ♣ J 3 2

LHO	Partner	RHO	You
		1♥	?

3
- ♠ 8 2
- ♥ K 4
- ♦ A K J 7 6 3
- ♣ Q 8 5

LHO	Partner	RHO	You
		1♥	?

4
- ♠ 2
- ♥ 4 3
- ♦ A K 10 9 8 5 3
- ♣ 5 4 2

LHO	Partner	RHO	You
		1♥	?

5
- ♠ K 9 8 5 4 2
- ♥ A 4
- ♦ J 10 8 6
- ♣ 4

LHO	Partner	RHO	You
		1♥	?

6
- ♠ A Q 10 9 7 6 4 2
- ♥ 4
- ♦ J 6 3
- ♣ 9

LHO	Partner	RHO	You
		1♥	?

7
- ♠ A K J 10 3
- ♥ 4
- ♦ K J 7 5
- ♣ A 9 5

LHO	Partner	RHO	You
1♥	3♣	pass	?

8
- ♠ A 9 5 4 2
- ♥ 6
- ♦ K 5 2
- ♣ J 8 3 2

LHO	Partner	RHO	You
1♥	3♣	pass	?

9
- ♠ A K Q 3
- ♥ 8 4
- ♦ A K 6 3
- ♣ Q 8 7

LHO	Partner	RHO	You
1♥	3♣	pass	?

10
- ♠ A 5 4 3
- ♥ K 4
- ♦ A 6 3 2
- ♣ K Q 7

LHO	Partner	RHO	You
1♥	3♣	pass	?

ANSWERS

1   **1♠**   Partner will expect a six-card suit if you make a jump overcall. He may therefore misjudge your playing strength and bid too much on a good hand or sacrifice wrongly. A simple overcall is enough on this hand.

2   **2♠**   You would have opened a Weak 2♠, and that bid still describes your hand perfectly now.

3   **2♦**   You have a good six-card suit and an opening bid. You are far too strong to preempt, but a simple overcall gets the message across.

4   **3♦**   You would have opened 3♦, so that is what you should bid over RHO's opening bid.

5   **1♠**   You are within the range for a Weak Two and you have six spades, but jumping to 2♠ would not tell partner that your suit is weak and that you have some defensive values outside spades — quite the opposite, in fact. A simple 1♠ overcall is a better description of this hand.

6   **4♠**   You would have opened 4♠ if RHO had passed, so make the same bid now.

7   **3♠**   You could raise to 5♣, but it's easier to take ten tricks than eleven. If partner has three spades, you will probably be safer in 4♠. If partner can bid 3NT over 3♠, that should be a safe spot. Perhaps he has ♥Kx and seven clubs headed by the king.

8   **5♣**   This is clearly not your hand. You have no idea what the opponents can make, so get the auction as high as possible as quickly as you can to prevent them from fully investigating the hand. This is the same principle that we talked about in Chapter 2 — partner has seven clubs, you have four, so you can raise to an eleven-trick contract.

9   **3♥**   If partner has a minimum 3♣ overcall, then ten tricks might be the limit of the hand. However, with very good trumps, partner will jump to 5♣. Alternatively, with a heart stopper partner can try 3NT.

10   **3NT**   Partner is supposed to have a 'good' seven-card suit, and you have the king and queen! He must have the ace, and likely the jack too, so you can count seven club tricks and two aces in notrump. If they lead a heart, that will be an overtrick!

TAKEOUT DOUBLES AT THE ONE-LEVEL

 It is, according to my opinion, the only conventional call for which there is the slightest excuse.
Florence Irwin, **Auction Highlights,** *1913.*

Strictly speaking, when you make the call of 'double' it says that you believe the opponents have bid too much and have arrived at a contract you think will fail. It signifies confidence that you will collect a penalty and that you wish to double the stakes for which the hand is played. This 'penalty double' (or 'business double') comes in handy if you think the opponents have bid too much. If declarer's contract is defeated, he will lose more points because he was doubled.

LHO	*Partner*	*RHO*	*You*
		1♣	dbl

However, in situations like this one, there are other (much more useful) meanings for the call 'double', the one most commonly encountered being the takeout double. To see why, consider the following hand:

♠ A J 7 4   ♥ K Q 8 3   ♦ K J 9 5   ♣ 6

Your RHO opens 1♣. You cannot make an overcall because you do not have a five-card suit, but you do not want to pass and let the opponents buy the contract cheaply when you have a nice opening bid yourself. So, what can you do?

You would like to have a magic word that will force partner to bid his longest suit. In fact you do have such a word, and that word is 'double'. Since you will very rarely have a hand where you want to double an opening bid of one of a suit for penalties, you give up very little by using the double for takeout.

How do you know when a double is for takeout?

Now there's a question. What's your final answer? These are the four rules that define a *basic* takeout double:

1. *The bidding is below the game level.*
2. *The doubler has not made a call other than pass.*
3. *The doubler's partner has not made a bid other than pass.*
4. *The opponents' last bid was a suit, not notrump.*

If a double meets all these requirements, it is a takeout double. The double in each of these auctions is for takeout; notice how in each case, all four of the conditions are satisfied.

Auction 1

LHO	Partner	RHO	You
		1♠	dbl

Auction 2

LHO	Partner	RHO	You
1♠	pass	2♠	dbl

Auction 3

LHO	Partner	RHO	You
1♠	pass	pass	dbl

Auction 4

LHO	Partner	RHO	You
3♣	dbl		

On the other hand, the final double in each of these auctions is not for takeout:

Auction 5

LHO	Partner	RHO	You
	1NT	2♥	dbl

Partner has bid, so this is not for takeout.

Auction 6

LHO	Partner	RHO	You
1NT	dbl		

Doubles of notrump bids are not for takeout, except by special agreement.

Auction 7

LHO	Partner	RHO	You
1♠	pass	3♠	pass
4♠	dbl		

Since 4♠ is a game bid, this double is for penalties.

Auction 8

LHO	Partner	RHO	You
			1♦
pass	1NT	2♣	dbl

This double is not a takeout double for two reasons: partner has made a bid other than pass, and so have you.

What do you need to make a takeout double?

There are three types of hand on which you can make a takeout double. What can be regarded as a 'normal takeout double' is by far the most common of these three hand types and has the following requirements:

1. *At least opening bid values (including distribution)*
2. *Adequate trump support (at least three) for all of the unbid suits*
3. *Shortness in the opponent's suit (at most a doubleton)*

The purpose of the normal takeout double is to show a hand with sufficient strength to wish to compete in the bidding and to ask partner to choose his best from the three unbid suits. As we shall see later, there is no upper limit for your strength when you make a takeout double. However, to qualify as a 'normal takeout double' your hand must fit all three requirements. Let us therefore start with the kind of hand on which you cannot double.

♠ A K 7 4 ♥ 8 4 ♦ A 9 2 ♣ Q 9 6 3

LHO	Partner	RHO	You
		1♣	?

You should not say 'double'; partner is too likely to bid hearts. You are not strong enough to bid twice, and your partner will not approve if you put this hand down in dummy having promised support for all of the unbid suits.

Here is an example of a typical takeout double after RHO has opened 1♦:

♠ K Q 7 4 ♥ Q J 6 4 ♦ 5 ♣ A 10 7 4

You have opening bid strength, shortness in the opener's suit, and support for all unbid suits. Whichever suit partner chooses, he will be happy with dummy's support.

You should not be afraid to double with few high cards, if your shape makes up for it. Look at this collection:

♠ K J 10 4 ♥ A 10 9 4 ♦ — ♣ Q 9 8 7 5

Again, RHO opens 1♦. Although you have only 10 HCP, the fantastic shape more than compensates for that. This is a clear takeout double of a 1♦ opening. The better your shape, the fewer high cards you need for a double, and vice versa.

We mentioned earlier that there are two other hand types on which you can also start with a double. Basically, these are the two types of hand that are too strong for any other action:

1. *A very strong one-suited hand — double then bid your suit next round (16+ points and a six-card suit, or 18+ points and a five-card suit)*

2. *A hand too strong to overcall 1NT — double then bid notrump next round (19+ points and a balanced hand)*

Summary

✔ A normal takeout double shows all of the following:

— strength at least equivalent to an opening bid

— support (at least three cards) for all unbid suits

— shortness in the opponents' suit.

✔ You may also start with a takeout double on very strong hands (either balanced or single-suited) that are too strong for any other initial action.

TAKEOUT DOUBLES AT THE ONE-LEVEL

NOW TRY THESE...

What do you bid with each of these hands?

1
♠ A Q 4 2
♥ 6
♦ Q J 5 2
♣ K J 3 2

LHO	Partner	RHO	You
		1♥	?

2
♠ K Q 8 2
♥ K 4
♦ A 10 6 3
♣ Q 8 5

LHO	Partner	RHO	You
		1♥	?

3
♠ K 9 8 5
♥ A 8 3
♦ K 10 9 8
♣ K 2

LHO	Partner	RHO	You
		1♥	?

4
♠ A K J 4 3
♥ 3
♦ J 7 6 5
♣ A 9 5

LHO	Partner	RHO	You
		1♥	?

5
♠ A Q 5
♥ 7 2
♦ K J 6
♣ K 8 7 5 4

LHO	Partner	RHO	You
		1♥	?

6
♠ A K Q 6 4 2
♥ A 7 4
♦ A J 3
♣ 9

LHO	Partner	RHO	You
		1♥	?

7
♠ A 7 4 2
♥ A 6
♦ J 9 7 5 2
♣ K 2

LHO	Partner	RHO	You
		1♥	?

8
♠ K 10 9 2
♥ —
♦ J 9 7 5 2
♣ A Q 9 8

LHO	Partner	RHO	You
		1♥	?

ANSWERS

1   dbl   This is a classic takeout double of 1♥.

2   dbl   Your shape is not as good this time, but the extra high cards compensate for that.

3   pass   Although you hold a solid opening bid, you have both too many hearts and not enough clubs for a takeout double.

4   1♠   Although your hand is suitable for a takeout double, the chances are that you belong in a spade contract. Partner will not bid spades on ♠Qxx, and if he responds to your double by bidding 2♣, you are not strong enough to bid spades later. If you are to reach your 5-3 spade fit, you must overcall now.

5   dbl   Your suit is not strong enough for a 2♣ overcall. You have adequate support for the other two suits and short hearts, so make a takeout double.

6   dbl   You are too strong for an overcall. If you overcall 1♠, you will miss game when partner has a few scattered values but short spades. If you overcall 4♠, you will miss slam when partner has just the right cards. (A 4♠ overcall would be preemptive and show more spades but fewer aces — usually less than 10 HCP and at least seven and often eight spades). There is no rush with hands this strong. Start slowly with a double, conserving bidding space, so that you can investigate fully. As we have seen, when you double and later bid your own suit, you are showing a very good hand.

7   pass   You have the wrong shape for a double, and a 2♦ overcall on that suit would be asking for trouble. Sometimes you just have to bite the bullet and hope the opponents bid to a contract that you might beat.

8   dbl   Despite having only 10 HCP, you should make a takeout double and not be ashamed of it. Compare this to Hand 2, which has 4 HCP more. This is a much better takeout double than that was. A void is a powerful feature as it provides ruffing power in the dummy and reduces the value of the enemy high cards.

RESPONDING TO A TAKEOUT DOUBLE

 There is no part of bridge that has made more strides in the last year than team-work. The combining of the two hands, by means of bidding and overcalling, has reached the height of perfection.
Florence Irwin, **Auction Highlights, *1913.***

If there is no intervening bid, you must respond to partner's takeout double. You must bid your longest of the three unbid suits even if you have no points. Always remember this saying: 'Takeout doubles are to be taken out'. However weak you are, you must still respond — even if the opener has already bid your best suit.

♠ J 8 6 3 ♥ K Q 7 4 ♦ 4 3 ♣ 9 6 2

LHO	*Partner*	*RHO*	*You*
1♥	dbl	pass	?

Hearts is your favorite suit, but that does not mean that you can pass partner's double. To understand why, think about what passing really means — it would be converting partner's takeout double into a penalty double.

Responding to a Takeout Double **59**

If you really do want to defend 1♥ doubled (which will happen about once
every five years if you play a lot of
bridge) you can pass partner's takeout
double, of course. Your hand would
have to be something like:

♠ A5 ♥ QJ10972 ♦ 76 ♣ 843

Your side would then have to take seven or more tricks with hearts as trumps. You therefore should have at least three sure trump tricks and an outside ace or so. With the kind of hand in our example, you should just choose the longest of the three unbid suits as partner has asked you to — on this hand, bid 1♠.

When partner makes a takeout double of an opening bid of one of a suit, he has promised to like whichever of the unbid suits that you choose, particularly unbid majors. Imagine that his double said, "I have an opening bid, probably with four cards in your best suit (excluding opener's suit)", and bid your hand accordingly.

How does partner know how good a hand you have?

Responding to the double is not quite as simple as choosing your longest suit. You also need to tell partner if you have some goodies. To start with, let's assume that RHO passes partner's takeout double. The following is a good guide to your responses (these point ranges are high-card points plus distributional points):

0-8 points: *bid your best suit at the cheapest level*
9-11 points: *bid your best suit one level higher than necessary or bid notrump (see below)*
12+ points: *force to game*

Notice that you can immediately add distributional points to your HCP as you know you have a fit. Partner has promised to have support for your longest suit. To understand why you need to jump with as few as 9 points, look at this hand:

♠ 8643 ♥ 864 ♦ 8653 ♣ 93

You pick up one of our normal rubber bridge hands, and hear partner make a takeout double of LHO's 1♦ opening bid. Since you cannot defeat the opponents in 1♦, you cannot pass. You therefore respond 1♠, which you would do on any hand with 0-8 points.

Now ask yourself how you feel about this hand after partner doubles a 1♦ opening:

♠ KJ85 ♥ 7 ♦ 9643 ♣ KJ32

If partner had opened the bidding (with 1♥, for example), you would have responded 1♠. There would be no need to jump. Why, then, must you jump in response to a takeout double? To see why, go back to the previous hand. With that rotten collection, you would simply pass if your partner opened the bidding. This is not an option when responding to a takeout double — you have to

Bidding notrump instead of a 'bad'
suit just because you don't like your
hand is not an option either. When
you bid notrump in response to a
takeout double it almost always
denies holding a four-card or longer
major suit. Notrump responses also
show specific point ranges, as you'll
see shortly.

bid 1♠ even with no points at all. This second hand is infinitely better, so you cannot make the same bid with this relative monster.

This hand comfortably falls within the 9-11 point range (including distribution). In fact, it is really a pretty good hand when you consider what you might have held. Jump to 2♠ with this hand, and do not feel that you have overbid.

How do you force to game holding an opening bid?

With 12+ points opposite partner's takeout double, you know that you both have opening bids, which means that you want to reach game. If you have a five-card major, you can simply jump to game in that suit (partner has guaranteed support for it). If you do not, then you can cuebid the opponents' suit — this simply tells partner that you have a good hand and that your side has to keep bidding until game is reached.

After making a cuebid, you both bid your best suits until either you find one you both like (and then someone can bid game in it) or you find you have no suit that you both like (in which case you'll probably bid 3NT). To understand how this works, look at the following auction:

	Partner		You
♠	K Q 9 6	♠	A J 8 3
♥	A Q 8 4	♥	K 7 3
♦	5	♦	Q 8 4 2
♣	Q 9 7 6	♣	K 5

LHO	Partner	RHO	You
1♦	dbl	pass	2♦
pass	2♥	pass	2♠
pass	4♠	all pass	

Your 2♦ cuebid just says that you have enough points to force to game, but that you have no five-card major. Partner made his cheapest available bid in a four-card suit, hearts, and you then bid your four-card major. Having found a 4-4 major-suit fit, partner is happy to jump to game.

When should you bid notrump in response to a takeout double?

With 8+ points you can choose to respond in notrump, particularly if you do not have a four-card major to show. You must also have a stopper in the opponents' suit to bid notrump, of course. Here is a summary of the meanings of notrump bids in response to a takeout double:

Notrump responses to a takeout double

8-10 HCP, stopper in opponents' suit:	*bid cheapest level of NT*
11-12 HCP, 1+ stoppers in opponents' suit:	*jump to 2NT*
13+ HCP, 1+ stoppers in opponents' suit:	*bid 3 NT*

Once again, it's important to emphasize that you cannot bid 1NT just because you do not like any of the unbid suits — 1NT is a positive response to a takeout double, and shows 8-10 HCP. Here's a good example:

♠ 9 3   ♥ 9 7 6 5 4   ♦ 7 5 3   ♣ J 8 5

LHO	Partner	RHO	You
1♥	dbl	pass	?

Many players make the mistake of bidding 1NT on this type of hand. You must not do this. If partner has around 15-16 HCP for his double, he will raise you to 3NT and someone will double. The ensuing penalty will be large enough to dial internationally. When he doubled originally, partner asked you to pick your longest unbid suit, so grit your teeth and bid 2♣. If your only long suit is the one that the opponents have already bid, then you simply have to respond in your cheapest three-card suit.

What if you have more than one suit to bid?

Say you hold this hand:

♠ K J 7 5   ♥ 8 7 4   ♦ Q 8 7 6 3   ♣ 4

LHO	Partner	RHO	You
1♣	dbl	1♥	?

With good support for both of the unbid suits, you are worth a free bid. So, should you bid 1♠ or 2♦?

As a general principle, you should tend to look for a **major-suit fit** before worrying about the minors. Following this principle here will lead you to correct answer — bid 1♠.

Bidding 1♠ may also allow you to bid both of your suits economically. Compare these two auctions:

LHO	Partner	RHO	You
1♣	dbl	1♥	1♠
2♣	pass	pass	2♦

LHO	Partner	RHO	You
1♣	dbl	1♥	2♦
all pass			

In the first auction, you have been able to bid both suits. Holding four spades, partner will correct to the higher-scoring spot.

If your suits are reversed, the choice is easy.

♠ K J 8 6 5   ♥ 8 6   ♦ Q 9 7 5   ♣ 8 4

LHO	Partner	RHO	You
1♣	dbl	1♥	1♠
2♣	pass	pass	2♠

You know that partner has at least three spades, so this time do not bother telling the opponents that you also have diamonds. That can only help them when it comes to defending the hand. Just compete in your strongest suit.

What difference does it make if opener's partner bids?

Until now, we have assumed that opener's partner passed over partner's double. If he makes a bid, things change dramatically as you can now pass whenever you have a poor hand. You should have 8+ points (including distribution) to respond if you are not forced to do so. This is called making a 'free bid.'

♠ K J 8 5   ♥ 7   ♦ 9 6 4 3   ♣ K J 3 2

LHO	Partner	RHO	You
1♦	dbl	pass	?

If RHO passes, jump to 2♠ with this hand — think of this hand as being the dummy for partner's assumed four-card spade suit... You will remember that this was the example we gave earlier illustrating a hand that is far too good for a minimum response to the double. Now let's change the auction slightly:

♠ K J 8 5   ♥ 7   ♦ 9 6 4 3   ♣ K J 3 2

LHO	Partner	RHO	You
1♦	dbl	1♥	?

With a very weak hand, you would simply pass, so you can now bid a simple 1♠ — a free bid — and show your values (8+ points).

Let's stick with this second auction and look at various other hands you might hold:

♠ K J 7 5   ♥ 8 6   ♦ Q J 9 6   ♣ A Q 3

LHO	Partner	RHO	You
1♦	dbl	1♥	?

If RHO had passed partner's takeout double, you would have bid 2♦ — an artificial, game-forcing cuebid. How does RHO's 1♥ bid affect that? It doesn't; you can still cuebid opener's suit (i.e. bid 2♦) to show a strong hand that wants to go to game. After all, 4♠, 3NT or even 5♣ might be the best spot, but you need to consult partner to discover which.

Here's a slightly different problem that RHO can create for you:

♠ K7 ♥ AJ96 ♦ 8642 ♣ Q5

LHO	Partner	RHO	You
1♦	dbl	1♥	?

Once again, RHO bids 1♥ over partner's double of the 1♦ opening bid. This time hearts is your best suit, and you have a decent hand. Any thoughts?

To spot the answer, think back to what partner's double really means. He said he had an opening bid with good support (at least three cards and usually four cards) in all three other suits — clubs, spades and hearts! If you like, imagine that partner has already bid hearts too (although it is not as if he has opened 1♥, promising five of them). Now that your opponent has bid one of partner's suits, a **double** is for penalties — it shows hearts and some positive values. Perfect!

The opponents will rarely play in hearts, but your bid shows values as well as hearts, and partner may be able to double them somewhere else. Also, just because RHO has four small hearts does not mean that you should necessarily avoid playing in the suit — hearts may still be *your* best trump suit!

What if RHO raises opener's suit?

♠ AJ42 ♥ Q865 ♦ 963 ♣ 97

LHO	Partner	RHO	You
1♦	dbl	2♦	?

Here you want to compete in a major, but you don't know whether to bid 2♥ or 2♠. Partner should have at least one four-card major, but why try to guess which one it is? This is another place to use a **responsive double**, which we first encountered in Chapter 3. When the opponents have bid and raised a minor, a responsive double asks partner to bid his longer major.

In all cases, you need sufficient values to compete at the level to which you are making partner bid, but since partner has at least an opening bid, you don't have to have that much. We suggest a minimum of 6 points (including distribution) at the two-level, and at least 9 points at the three-level.

If they have bid and raised a major, a responsive double tends to imply interest in the minors:

♠ 42 ♥ 865 ♦ QJ96 ♣ AQ97

LHO	Partner	RHO	You
1♥	dbl	2♥	?

A double by you here asks partner to bid his longer minor. Notice that you can't have four spades, since with a hand like:

♠ A J 4 2   ♥ 8 6 5   ♦ 9 6   ♣ Q 9 7 3

LHO	Partner	RHO	You
1♥	dbl	2♥	?

you would simply bid 2♠ and not mess around. With a slightly better hand you will jump to 3♠, inviting partner to bid game.

When the opponents are bidding spades, and you have hearts, there is no room left to jump with invitational values:

♠ 5 4 2   ♥ A J 6 5   ♦ 9 6   ♣ K Q 7 3

LHO	Partner	RHO	You
1♠	dbl	2♠	?

Now you only have one bid left below game — 3♥. However, the responsive double can help here too. With this hand, where you want to offer an invitation to game, bid 3♥ directly. If you just want to compete over 2♠, say with

♠ 5 4 2   ♥ A J 6 5   ♦ 9 6   ♣ K 10 7 3

start with a responsive double, and bid 3♥ over partner's minor suit. This sequence says "I want to play in 3♥; do not raise unless you are very strong."

What happens when RHO redoubles?

If RHO has enough to redouble, you will usually have a bad hand — opener has 12+ points, partner has 12+ points, and RHO has 10+ points. Even if each of them is minimum, there is not much left for you. More likely, you will have something like the following collection:

♠ 9 7 4   ♥ J 7 4   ♦ 8 6 4   ♣ 10 7 4 2

LHO	Partner	RHO	You
1♦	dbl	redbl	?

Yuk! It looks like you are about to get doubled. The penalty will be substantial, but the opponents can probably make game. What is important is that you find some kind of fit at the lowest possible level. If you were to bid 2♣, partner might well show up with something like:

♠ A K 7 5   ♥ Q 10 8 3   ♦ 8 6   ♣ A 8 3

That is a perfectly respectable takeout double but, opposite your hopeless collection, playing in 2♣-doubled will be a disaster. Indeed, there is no guarantee that you will make more than the three obvious winners. Perhaps you will also come to a long trump, but even if you do you will still be four down. That means either -800 or -1100 depending on the vulnerability

A much better strategy is for you to pass the redouble. All this says to partner is, "I have no strong preference among the unbid suits." It also gives the opponents a chance to bid themselves before partner must.

On this hand, if opener passes, partner will bid 1♥ (his cheapest four-card suit) and the opponents will either bid their game or they will double. If they double, you will come to five tricks (♠AK, ♣A and two trumps) — two down. Not only does hearts play a trick better, but you are playing a level lower.

Of course, you will sometimes have a preference, and if you do, you should express it:

♠ 9 5   ♥ J 8 7 6 4   ♦ 9 6 4 2   ♣ 9 3

LHO	Partner	RHO	You
1♦	dbl	redbl	?

After the same start to the auction, you must bid 1♥ now. This is not a 'free bid' (it is assumed that you have no values), but merely expresses a distinct preference for hearts over either of the other two unbid suits, and therefore guarantees at least five of them. If you pass, and partner happens to have a 4-3-2-4 shape, he will bid 1♠ — his lowest four-card suit. After that, you are in deep trouble. You can choose between playing in a six-card trump fit, or venturing into hearts at the two-level. Neither choice is particularly appealing.

BY THE WAY

Sometimes you may want to preempt the opponents:

LHO	Partner	RHO	You
1♦	dbl	redbl	?

♠ J 9 7 6 5 3 2   ♥ 8   ♦ 9 7 5   ♣ 10 3

Surely the opponents can make game. They have been good enough to tell you that. Maybe they should be playing in 4♥, perhaps 3NT, or even 5♦ or 5♣. What is important is that you do not allow them the room to investigate. Bid as high as you dare. We suggest a jump to 4♠ on this particular hand, especially if you are not vulnerable against vulnerable. Jumps after RHO has redoubled do not show high-card values, just a long suit facing a known fit — partner can tell from the opponents' bidding that you have 0-5 HCP.

Summary

✓ You must respond to a takeout double, no matter how weak your hand, except on the rare occasion that you actually want to defend their doubled contract.

✓ Making the minimum response in your longest suit does not show any values — i.e. you could hold zero points.

✓ With 9-11 points (including distribution), jump in your longest suit.

✓ With 12+ points, you can force to game by cuebidding opener's suit or you can just jump to game if you have a five-card major.

✓ Notrump responses to a takeout double show positive values. 1NT shows 8-10 HCP, 2NT 11-12, and 3NT 13+. You must also have at least one stopper (and preferably two) in the opener's suit — remember that partner will be short in that suit.

✓ If RHO intervenes over partner's double, you can pass with a bad hand. Making a free bid therefore shows some values (8+ points including distribution).

✓ If you double a new suit bid by RHO, you are showing length in that suit and some values. If RHO raises opener's suit, you can use a responsive double to describe certain types of hands.

✓ Bids after RHO has redoubled do not show values, just a long suit. Jumps are preemptive, rather than showing values.

RESPONDING TO A TAKEOUT DOUBLE

What is your next bid with each of these hands?

1   ♠   4 2
  ♥   8 6
  ♦   J 8 6 5 2
  ♣   9 7 3 2

LHO	Partner	RHO	You
1♦	dbl	pass	?

2   ♠   K 8 7 5 3
  ♥   A 6
  ♦   9 7 6 3
  ♣   Q 5

LHO	Partner	RHO	You
1♦	dbl	pass	?

3   ♠   K 9 8
  ♥   A 8 3
  ♦   Q 10 9 8
  ♣   9 7 2

LHO	Partner	RHO	You
1♦	dbl	pass	?

4   ♠   J 4 3
  ♥   J 7 3
  ♦   9 7 6 5 2
  ♣   K 5

LHO	Partner	RHO	You
1♦	dbl	pass	?

5   ♠   A Q 5 3
  ♥   7 2
  ♦   Q J 8 6
  ♣   K Q 7

LHO	Partner	RHO	You
1♦	dbl	pass	?

6   ♠   A J 6 4 2
  ♥   K 7 4
  ♦   A 8 3
  ♣   Q 9

LHO	Partner	RHO	You
1♦	dbl	pass	?

7   ♠   A 5
  ♥   K 8 4
  ♦   K J 9 8
  ♣   A J 5 3

LHO	Partner	RHO	You
1♦	dbl	pass	?

8   ♠   A 5
  ♥   9 3
  ♦   Q J 10 8 7 5
  ♣   Q 7 4

LHO	Partner	RHO	You
1♦	dbl	pass	?

9

♠	K 10 3
♥	8 5
♦	7 6 5
♣	J 7 5 3 2

LHO	Partner	RHO	You
1♣	dbl	1♥	?

10

♠	A Q 4 2
♥	9 6
♦	Q 5 2
♣	9 7 5 2

LHO	Partner	RHO	You
1♣	dbl	1♥	?

11

♠	A Q 2
♥	9 6 2
♦	J 7 2
♣	Q J 7 2

LHO	Partner	RHO	You
1♣	dbl	1♥	?

12

♠	Q J 5 2
♥	K 10 9 6
♦	10 9
♣	9 8 3

LHO	Partner	RHO	You
1♣	dbl	2♣	?

13

♠	K 10 9 2
♥	7
♦	A Q 5 2
♣	A 7 6 2

LHO	Partner	RHO	You
1♣	dbl	1♥	?

14

♠	J 10 3
♥	A J 10 7
♦	10 7 6 5
♣	A 5

LHO	Partner	RHO	You
1♣	dbl	1♥	?

ANSWERS

1   2♣   Be glad that you have four cards in one of partner's suits.

2   2♠   You have 9-11 points and five-card support for one of partner's suits. Jump in your best suit to tell him the good news.

3   1NT   You have positive values (8-10 HCP) and good stoppers in the opener's suit.

4   1♥   Bid your cheapest three-card suit when you have a bad hand and your only long suit is the one already bid by opener.

5   2♦   A cuebid. You may end up in 4♠ or 3NT (or even 5♣). Just tell partner that you have a game-going hand for now, leaving plenty of room to investigate the best contract.

6   4♠   You have enough values for game and at least an eight-card spade it. Why mess around when you already know where you want to play?

7   3NT   It seems unlikely that any other contract will be better. Partner is unlikely to hold a five-card major for his takeout double, and you have good stoppers in opener's suit.

8   pass   This is the only kind of hand on which you can pass a takeout double. You can look forward to collecting a large penalty with no guarantee that your side can make any contract. You need at least three sure trump tricks and at least one outside trick to pass a takeout double.

9   pass   With such a poor hand, you have nothing to say. RHO's bid removes your obligation to respond.

10   1♠   There is no need to jump to show your positive values. This is a free bid, since you could have passed, and thus it shows some strength.

11   1NT   This shows positive values and at least one stopper in opener's suit (clubs). You do not need a heart stopper to bid notrump, since partner has already said that he has some values/length in that suit.

12   dbl   You have enough to compete at the two-level (just!) and surely have a fit in one of the majors. But there's no need to guess which one — make a responsive double, and let partner tell you.

13   2♣   A cuebid. You cannot tell yet whether the best contract will be 4♠, 5♣ or 3NT.

14   dbl   Penalties, showing positive values and at least four hearts.

C H A P T E R

LATER BIDDING AFTER A TAKEOUT DOUBLE

 I have seen scores of persons whose art was perfection when it was a question of playing the dummy, and their team-work in defense was excellent — they never dropped a trick — but their team-work in bidding was atrocious!
Florence Irwin, Auction Highlights, *1913*.

Having read the previous two chapters, we are sure you are now confident that you will know when to make a takeout double of a one-level suit opening, and how to respond when partner does so. In this chapter, we move on to see how the auction might continue after these initial exchanges.

First, let us recap the three types of hand on which you would make a take-out double:

1. *A hand with support for all three unbid suits, shortness in the opponents' suit, and at least opening bid strength.*
2. *A single-suited hand that is too strong for a simple overcall.*
3. *A balanced hand that is too strong for a 1NT overcall (we're getting ahead of ourselves, but basically this is a good 18 HCP upwards).*

We're going to look at 'normal' doubles first.

What does doubler do after partner makes a minimum response?

First, remind yourself what partner's minimum response shows. He has 0-8 points (including distribution), and he will usually have at least four cards in the suit he has bid. It is not hard to realize that you will need a pretty good hand to make game when all partner could do was make a minimum response. A fair estimation would be around 16+ points to have any hope at all.

LHO	Partner	RHO	You
		1♣	dbl
pass	1♥	pass	?

Let's give partner a super-maximum for his 1♥ response. Say something like:

♠ Q96 ♥ AJ852 ♦ 93 ♣ 843

That is close to the best hand he could hold. Now let's give you a 16-count:

♠ A754 ♥ KQ93 ♦ K74 ♣ K5

You have a nine-card trump fit. You both have a ruffing value. However, even with all that, to make game you will need to find opener with both minor-suit aces (likely) and for the ♠Q to be worth a trick sitting under the opening bid (unlikely).

In order to try for game over a minimum response, you need at least 16 points.

LHO	Partner	RHO	You
		1♣	dbl
pass	1♥	pass	?

With 16-18 points:
Raise to 2♥. This invites partner to bid game with a maximum for his 1♥ response.

With 19-21 points:
Jump to 3♥. This invites partner to bid to game with anything except a useless hand.

With 22+ points:
Jump to game. You hope to find partner with a fifth trump or a useful jack or queen.

Even with such good hands as these, you may find that you are too high. Partner could easily be stuck with a worthless hand like:

♠ 864 ♥ 9753 ♦ 963 ♣ 642

The better your hand, the more likely it is that partner has a bust. Remember that he did not choose to bid 1♥ — you have forced him to do so.

Note that in the examples above, you always raised the suit that partner chose in response to your double. This is the only option when you hold a normal takeout double (unless you have such a monster hand that you are interested in slam even opposite a virtual Yarborough — see the discussion on cuebidding below). Doing anything other than raising partner's suit would show one of the other two types of takeout double.

Does it make any difference if opener bids again?

In all of the situations we have discussed so far, opener has passed partner's minimum response to your takeout double. With LHO having passed initially over your takeout double, it is likely that the hand belongs to your side. The question we have therefore addressed up to now is, 'How do we bid to our correct game or partscore?'

Alas, the opponents are not always this accommodating. Sometimes they also want a say in the outcome. If the opening bidder competes further over partner's minimum response, you must now find a way to compete for the contract.

Say you hold this hand:

♠ A 8 7 4 ♥ K J 8 5 ♦ 8 ♣ Q 8 6 4

LHO	Partner	RHO	You
		1♦	dbl
pass	1♥	2♣	?

You have the classic takeout double shape and so, even though you are not overburdened with high cards, you are not ashamed of your double. So, are you now thinking about raising to 2♥?

Many players would do so. "I have four-card support for partner's suit..." is the reasoning behind their choice. In fact, that is not true; what is true is that you have forced partner to bid. Remember, too, that when you doubled, you effectively bid clubs, hearts and spades all at the same time, and showed an opening bid. What do you have that you have not already shown?

You do not need to bid again on this minimum double. If partner has a hand near the top of his range (i.e. not 0 points, but 7-8), he will compete further, perhaps by bidding 2♥. He has heard you double, so he knows that you have a minimum of something like the hand above, and he knows you have hearts, because you doubled. He might have:

♠ K 3 ♥ Q 9 6 4 3 ♦ 9 7 5 3 ♣ J 10

If he does hold this hand, he will not sell out to 2♣. A likely auction is:

LHO	Partner	RHO	You
		1♦	dbl
pass	1♥	2♣	pass
2♦	2♥	all pass	

Of course, partner may be stuck with a much less suitable collection for his 1♥ response:

♠ 9 5 3 ♥ 9 7 2 ♦ K 10 7 5 3 ♣ J 10

Do you think he will be happy if you compete to 2♥ and put down the above hand as dummy? Indeed, LHO will probably be so happy that he does not have to pick between his two-card minors that he will double 2♥ on his four- or five-card trump holding. No indeed, partner will not be a happy camper in 2♥ doubled.

However, you can have a hand with extras, one that is still not good enough to invite game, such as:

♠ A 10 9 4   ♥ K Q 8 5   ♦ 8   ♣ K 10 9 4

LHO	Partner	RHO	You
		1♦	dbl
pass	1♥	2♦	?

If opener had passed at his second turn, this would not have been enough to invite game. So, you would have passed 1♥. However, your hand is also better than it might have been. We suggest that if your hand is in the 14-15 point range with four-card support for the suit partner chose, you can make a competitive raise *if the opponents bid again*. In this situation, then, a single raise of partner's minimum response shows some extra values, but is not a full-blooded invitation.

Remember that competitive bidding is not a science, and there is a certain amount of guesswork involved. You will not guess right every time; no one does. But by following these guidelines, you will certainly improve your success/failure ratio. Minimum responses to the takeout double cause the most problems; this is hardly surprising, since partner has a wide range (0-8 points).

What if partner shows some values over your double?

The rebid by the doubler after partner has shown more than a minimum 0-8 points is basically a question of adding the points partner has shown to those you hold. You can then raise to the appropriate level. Essentially, you do exactly as you would in hundreds of other bidding situations. A couple of examples should suffice:

LHO	Partner	RHO	You
		1♦	dbl
pass	1NT	pass	?

Partner's 1NT response shows 8-10 HCP. If you want to bid more notrump now, it is a simple matter of adding points. Remember though, that while you may have accounted for distributional points when deciding whether your hand was worth a double, you can only count HCPs now, since you are in a notrump auction. Thus:

with up to 14 HCP:	*pass*
with 15-16:	*invite with 2NT*
with 17+:	*raise to 3NT*

Of course, you may have enough to raise even higher than game, and we will leave you to work out how many points you need for a quantitative 4NT raise (you'll need about 33 between you for slam...). Bear in mind that if you are interested in a slam, you might want to investigate contracts other than notrump. As we mentioned earlier (when discussing partner's minimum response), you can create a game-forcing situation by cuebidding at your second turn.

The situation is very similar when partner has jumped in a suit over your double. Now he has shown 9-11 points including distributional values. Thus:

LHO	Partner	RHO	You
		1♦	dbl
pass	2♥	pass	?

This is not quite so easy as raising partner's notrump response, since it is possible that you do not have four cards in partner's suit — you will recall that you only guaranteed three-card support for every unbid suit when you doubled. However, when you know that you have found at least an eight-card fit, you can also add your distributional points to your HCP and evaluate your hand accordingly. Thus in the above auction:

up to 13 points:	*pass*
14-15 and four hearts:	*invite with 3♥*
14-15 , only three hearts and a diamond stopper:	*invite with 2NT (partner will choose among 2NT, 3NT, 3♥ and 4♥)*
16+ and four hearts:	*raise to 4♥*
16+, only three hearts:	*bid 3NT with a stopper, or cuebid without one; perhaps partner can bid 3NT, or has five hearts*

Similar calculations are possible when partner makes a free bid (8+ points including distribution) after LHO has bid over your takeout double. Remember though, that partner's free bid does not show quite as much as a positive response.

What about the really big hands?

You will recall that if you have a strong, single-suited hand that is too strong for a simple overcall, you start with a double. In Chapter 6, we gave the following guidelines for this kind of hand: 16+ points and a six-card suit, or 18+ points with a five-card suit. It's easy for partner to tell when you have this type of hand rather than a normal takeout double, because you will bid your own suit over his response.

♠ A K J 8 6 4   ♥ Q 3   ♦ A Q 5   ♣ 7 4

LHO	Partner	RHO	You
		1♣	dbl
pass	1♥	pass	?

This hand is a minimum for a double followed by bidding your own suit. Rather than just counting points, there is a better way to evaluate these distributional hands — count tricks. On the hand above, you can estimate that you have approximately five spade tricks and one or two diamonds, with additional values in both majors. In the auction shown, you should bid 1♠ on this hand. Yes, this simple, one-level change of suit shows a hand something like the one above. Doubling and then bidding a new suit should show approximately 6-6½ tricks in your own hand. In terms of points, you are likely to hold around 16-18 HCP with a six-card suit.

Now let's make your hand a little stronger:

♠ A K J 7 6 4   ♥ K 9 3   ♦ A K 5   ♣ 4

You can now count roughly 4-5 spade tricks, one heart trick and two diamonds. That makes a total of 7-7½, so this is worth a jump to 2♠ which tells partner to bid on with any excuse at all. Notice how important it is for you to be able to rebid only 1♠ on a fairly strong hand. If you had to jump to 2♠ to show that type of hand, you would immediately lose the ability to tell partner just how much help you need from him.

If we add another trick to your hand, you almost have game. You need very little from partner:

♠ A K J 7 6 4   ♥ K 9 3   ♦ A K 3   ♣ A

You need partner to have very little. Two small spades and the ♥Q may be enough, or the singleton ♠Q, or the ♦Q. Jump to 3♠ on this gold mine, asking partner to raise with any excuse.

Only when you actually have game in your own hand do you need to jump all the way to game. With a very strong hand and only a five-card suit, or with a hand that is too strong just to settle for game, there is one final option — to start with a double and then cuebid the opponents' suit. This creates a game-forcing auction, and effectively, this sequence is akin to an opening 2♣ bid. In fact, you should use this sequence only when you have a hand you would have opened 2♣. Having created a game-force, however, you will have plenty of room to describe your hand accurately and investigate the best contract, without worrying that partner will suddenly pass.

When partner shows positive values over your takeout double, for example by bidding notrump or making a jump response, you can simply introduce your suit at the minimum level. You do not need to jump, as you automatically force to game if you introduce a new suit having doubled and heard a positive response from your partner. The reason for this is not hard to see — you have a strong suit and 16+ points (with less, you would have overcalled instead of doubling), and partner has shown 8+ points. It is hard to imagine that you would want to stop short of game in these circumstances.

What about strong balanced hands?

There is still one more type of hand on which you need to start with a takeout double — the strong, balanced type. These hands are easy, however — you just count your HCP and bid the appropriate number of notrump in the same way that you do as the opener or responder in unopposed auctions. With 15-18 HCP, you would have overcalled 1NT immediately over the 1♣ opening bid (see Chapter 10). To double first and then rebid notrump automatically shows a better hand than that. Thus:

19-20 HCP	*double and then rebid the cheapest number of notrump*
21-23 HCP	*double and then jump in notrump*
24+ HCP	*double and then jump to game in notrump or cuebid opener's suit*

Responder now knows a great deal about your hand, and is usually well-positioned to place the final contract.

✓ Raising partner's minimum response (when the opening bidder passes) shows game interest facing 0-8 points — we suggest 16-18 points. A jump raise is even stronger as it shows game interest opposite a suitable 4-5 count.

✓ Bidding a new suit after partner's minimum response shows a single-suited hand too strong for an initial overcall — 6-6½ playing tricks, or 16+HCP and a good six-card suit. Jumping in a new suit shows the same type of hand, but even stronger.

✓ Bidding notrump over a minimum response shows a hand too strong for a 1NT overcall — around 19-20 points. Jumping in notrump shows even more.

✓ Cuebidding opener's suit at your second turn creates a game-forcing auction. It is like opening 2♣. You may have a single-suited or a balanced hand, or an exceptional three-suiter which has slam interest even facing 0-8 points.

✓ If opener intervenes over partner's minimum response, you can stretch to raise with 14-15 points and a four-card fit for partner's suit. With a minimum double, pass and let partner decide whether to compete for the partscore or to defend.

✓ When partner makes a positive response to your double (8+ points), simply add your points to those he has shown and pass or raise appropriately.

✓ Bidding a new suit after partner has made a positive response to your double (8+ points) shows a strong single-suited hand and creates a game-forcing auction.

LATER BIDDING AFTER A TAKEOUT DOUBLE

NOW TRY THESE...

What is your next bid on each of these hands?

1
- ♠ K 10 7 3
- ♥ A K J 7
- ♦ Q J 8
- ♣ 9 7

LHO	Partner	RHO	You
		1♣	dbl
pass	1♥	pass	?

2
- ♠ K J 9 7
- ♥ A 6 5 4
- ♦ A 7 6
- ♣ Q 5

LHO	Partner	RHO	You
		1♣	dbl
pass	2♣	pass	?

3
- ♠ K 9 8
- ♥ A Q 8 3
- ♦ K Q 9 8
- ♣ 9 7

LHO	Partner	RHO	You
		1♣	dbl
pass	1♥	pass	?

4
- ♠ A J 9 3
- ♥ A Q 7 3
- ♦ K J 10 2
- ♣ 5

LHO	Partner	RHO	You
		1♣	dbl
pass	1♥	pass	?

5
- ♠ A K 10 3
- ♥ K J 8 2
- ♦ K 8 7 6
- ♣ A

LHO	Partner	RHO	You
		1♣	dbl
pass	1♥	pass	?

6
- ♠ A Q 6 2
- ♥ A K 7 4
- ♦ A K 8 6
- ♣ 2

LHO	Partner	RHO	You
		1♣	dbl
pass	1♥	pass	?

7
- ♠ A Q 8 5
- ♥ K 4
- ♦ A J 9
- ♣ A Q 5 3

LHO	Partner	RHO	You
		1♣	dbl
pass	1♥	pass	?

8
- ♠ 9
- ♥ A K Q J 7 5
- ♦ K Q 3
- ♣ K 7 4

LHO	Partner	RHO	You
		1♠	dbl
pass	2♦	pass	?

ANSWERS

1 pass Partner had 0-8 points. Game is therefore very unlikely.

2 2♥ Partner made a forcing cuebid, so show him your cheapest suit. If he bids spades next, you will be happy to raise, while if he wants to try notrump, your ♣Q may turn out to be useful.

3 pass Your 15 points together with partner's maximum of eight will seldom produce game. It is far more likely that you will turn a small plus score into a minus by bidding on.

4 2♥ You have 17 points including distribution. Game is possible if partner has a maximum for his 1♥ response.

5 3♥ You have 20 points this time, but you still need partner to have some high cards if you are to make ten tricks. On a bad day, even the three-level will prove to be too high.

6 4♥ You may not make it, but you can hardly bid less.

7 1NT You have a hand too strong for a 1NT overall. Rebidding 1NT now shows 19-20. Don't worry that partner will pass when he has the smattering of values that you need to make game. Partner knows you hold a very good hand.

8 3♥ You have 8-8½ tricks. Even so, you still have six potential losers. If partner has a complete bust, you may lose them all unless LHO helps you with a club lead. Doubling followed by jumping in your own suit encourages partner to take a bid with any excuse — ♦J10xx and the ♣Q would probably be enough for you.

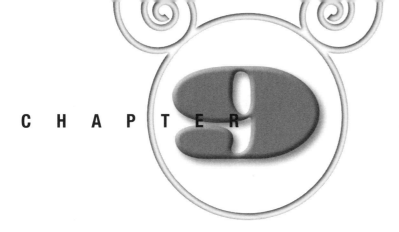

OTHER TAKEOUT DOUBLE SITUATIONS

I say that there are always ways to solve these difficulties, ways that
are delightfully delicate and that require thought and skill.
Florence Irwin, **Auction Highlights, 1913.**

So far in this section, we have concentrated only on auctions that begin with a
one-level suit opening bid and an immediate takeout double. However, there are
a number of questions that might occur to you in relation to takeout doubles
that we have carefully avoided answering so far. In this chapter, we'll try to tidy
up these points.

Can you make a takeout double as a passed hand?

One of the requirements in our definition of a takeout double was 'opening
bid strength'. So, what do you make of this auction:

LHO	Partner	RHO	You
	pass	pass	pass
1♦	dbl		

How can partner have a hand strong enough to make a takeout double and yet not have opened the bidding? Did he find an ace? Well, that is certainly one possibility, but there is a more practical answer to this apparent inconsistency. When you are making a takeout double, your distributional values are worth more once the opponent opens the bidding in your short suit, so a hand can become worth a double even though it was below par as an opener. Thus:

♠ K J 7 5   ♥ A J 9 6   ♦ 9   ♣ J 10 8 6

LHO	Partner	RHO	You
			pass
pass	pass	1♦	dbl

You should not even consider opening the bidding on this hand. However, it is a perfectly respectable takeout double of a 1♦ opening (whether you are a passed hand or not). Your singleton is a particularly valuable feature, as after revaluing, you have 12 dummy points including distribution. In fact, as a passed hand, you can afford to be quite frisky with your doubles, since there is no danger that partner will go crazy expecting you to have a really good hand.

♠ A 9 6 5   ♥ Q 10 8 5   ♦ —   ♣ Q 9 7 5 3

LHO	Partner	RHO	You
			pass
pass	pass	1♦	dbl

Please reassure us that you would not open this hand. Despite the attractive distribution, it would also be risky to make a takeout double of a 1♦ opening bid if you were not a passed hand. The danger is not that an opponent will be waiting with a big penalty double, but that partner will bid too much. However, you desperately want to compete for the partscore. If you have already passed as the dealer, you can feel quite happy about doubling once RHO opens 1♦. Remember — partner knows you do not have an opening bid.

What if both opponents are bidding?

So far in all our examples the opening bidder has always been on your right. Obviously, you will sometimes have a good hand when the opening bidder is on your left. We will deal with auctions that begin with an opening bid and two passes to you in Chapter 20. Right now, we're going to look at how you can get into the auction after the opener's partner responds. (This is called being in the 'sandwich seat', because you are sandwiched between two opponents who are both bidding.) Perhaps the auction begins like this:

LHO	Partner	RHO	You
1♣	pass	1♥	?

Here's a diagram that will help you see the 'sandwich' clearly:

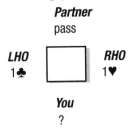

Partner
pass

LHO
1♣

RHO
1♥

You
?

With both opponents bidding, your side is not likely to have the majority of the HCP. If you have a good hand, then you can expect partner to hold very little. You should, therefore, be wary of entering the fray on marginal hands. Entering the auction in the sandwich seat is dangerous. Both opponents have already shown some values and, if you come in at the wrong time, they will find it easy to extract a large penalty. You may find yourself caught between them like a piece of pastrami. Responder's hand is essentially unlimited at this point — all you know is that he has at least six points.

You can still overcall in either of the unbid suits, but you should only do so with some expectation of buying the contract. You should always have a really good suit for an overcall in this kind of auction.

♠ K Q J 10 8   ♥ 9 6   ♦ 8 6 4   ♣ A K 5

LHO	Partner	RHO	You
1♣	pass	1♥	?

This hand is a reasonable 1♠ overcall in this auction.

You can also come in with a takeout double. However, in contrast to when you double in second seat, where you have a chance to find a fit in any of three suits, here you must have at least four-card support for each of the two unbid suits. Indeed, because of the exposed nature of the position, it is preferable to have nine cards in your two suits.

♠ K Q 9 7   ♥ A 7 3   ♦ Q J 9 7 5   ♣ 2

RHO	Partner	LHO	You
1♣	pass	1♥	?

Although you have only 12 HCP, most of your honors are in your own suits and this is a good hand for offense. Despite the dangers, your chances of competing successfully for the partscore make it worth taking the risk that entering the auction entails. Make a takeout double, showing good support for the two unbid suits (spades and diamonds in this case).

However, you should avoid coming in on hands with more questionable values.

♠ K J 8 5   ♥ Q J 3   ♦ A Q 7 3   ♣ J 4

RHO	Partner	LHO	You
1♣	pass	1♥	?

You have 14 HCP, but those queens and jacks in the opponents' suits are of doubtful value except (perhaps) on defense, and your suits are only four cards long with poor spot cards. The odds are that opener holds the missing honors over you in at least one of your two suits. You should resist the temptation to make a takeout double on hands like this — pass and let the opponents have the auction to themselves. You have defensive values and, with luck, you will be able to defeat the opponents' contract.

We cannot overemphasize the dangers of bidding in the sandwich seat. The primary reason for this is that the opponents have not yet discovered a fit. The biggest penalties tend to occur on hands where neither side has a decent trump fit. If opener happens to be sitting with length and strength behind your suits, and your partner's length is in the two suits the opponents have already bid (your short suits), then even the soundest of takeout doubles can lead to disaster.

Remember that the best you can hope for is about an even split of the forty high card points in the deck. (Of course, partner might hold a complete bust, no matter what your hand is.) On the second of our example hands, partner can have at most a six-count. On the first, your prospects are much brighter. Your high cards are well-enough placed that you might even make game if partner has something in both your suits — a hand like:

♠ J 8 5 4 3　♥ K 2　♦ K 10 3　♣ 9 6 4

What if you're 5-5 or even 6-5 in the unbid suits?

As we saw in Chapter 4, if you are using the Unusual Notrump (UNT) convention a jump to 2NT over RHO's opening bid shows a hand with at least 5-5 in the two lowest unbid suits. In the sandwich seat, a jump to 2NT still shows a two-suiter in the unbid suits, only this time both suits are known. Say you have this collection:

♠ K Q 9 4 3　♥ 9　♦ A Q 10 6 4 2　♣ 4

LHO	Partner	RHO	You
1♣	pass	1♥	?

You could make a takeout double, but it makes more sense to keep the double for the more balanced type of hand we have just discussed, with 4-4 or 5-4 distribution in the two unbid suits. Hands that are 5-5 or better are very powerful (five-five, come alive!) and if you have this much distribution then it is unlikely that the opponents have balanced hands either. How will you feel if the auction continues something like this:

LHO	Partner	RHO	You
1♣	pass	1♥	dbl
4♥	pass	pass	?

Are you going to bid game on your own? If so, which suit are you going to choose? Are you going to double again? A much better approach is to show your hand straight away and then to leave any further decisions to partner.

LHO	Partner	RHO	You
1♣	pass	1♥	2NT

This overcall of 2NT, then, is still Unusual; it shows at least 5-5 in the two unbid suits. Essentially, you are overcalling both spades and diamonds at the same time with only one bid. Note that with both opponents bidding, you should have a good hand to bid 2NT. You are forcing your partner, who is quite likely to hold almost nothing and may not have a fit with you, to bid at the three-level. Bidding 2NT on this next hand is quite wrong:

♠ 65　♥ A 10 9 6 4　♦ A 9 7 6 5　♣ 5

If RHO opened 1♣, you might elect to jump to 2NT with this hand (although doing so is highly questionable, and definitely wrong vulnerable). But if the auction starts 1♣ on your left and 1♠ by RHO, jumping to 2NT on this collection is suicidal. The opponents have at least 19 points (13+ for opener and 6+ for responder) and they quite possibly have appreciably more than that.. Do you really want to play this hand in 3♦ or 3♥ (doubled, of course) when partner has a balanced hand with 5-6 HCP? If you do, then perhaps you would enjoy some high-stakes rubber bridge — it will not be difficult to find willing opponents. Do remember to bring your checkbook, though. Jumping to 2NT is far too dangerous with both opponents bidding, and neither of your suits is sufficiently robust to justify what is effectively a three-level overcall (you are forcing partner to pick a suit at the three-level).

What if RHO bids 1NT?

Usually, doubles of notrump bids are for penalties, but there is an exception to every rule, and this is an exceptional case.

LHO	Partner	RHO	You
1♥	pass	1NT	dbl

Again, your side cannot have more than about 20 HCP at best, so why would you ever want to double 1NT for penalties? You wouldn't, of course, so as usual it makes sense for your double to mean something else. A double here shows a hand that would have made a takeout double of hearts if it had been RHO who opened that suit. Perhaps something like:

♠ K Q 8 6　♥ 9　♦ A J 10 7　♣ Q J 10 7

LHO	Partner	RHO	You
1♥	pass	1NT	dbl

After the auction starts like this, you have no way to get into the bidding sensibly unless a double shows this type of hand.

Our earlier comments about passing bare minimum hands with both opponents bidding still apply equally here. For example:

♠ K J 8　♥ 9 6　♦ A 8 6 4　♣ K J 6 4

If RHO opened 1♥, you *might* decide to make a takeout double with this hand, although you wouldn't be proud of it when you put it down as dummy. It does fit all of the basic requirements for a double, but only just! However, after a 1♥ opening on your left and a 1NT response from RHO, coming in with a takeout double would be asking for trouble. For a start, you are forcing partner to respond at the two-level, which is too high unless you are lucky enough to find a fit and he has seven or eight points. Also, with opener's strength poised over you, some of your black-suit honors are almost bound to be worthless. With a hand like this, you should just pass and hope the opponents get into trouble.

What if RHO raises opener's suit?

In the previous section we emphasized the danger of entering the auction in the sandwich seat. The reason it was so dangerous was that the opponents had not discovered a fit. Things change dramatically once the opponents have found a trump suit, since if they have a fit, it is much more likely that you also have one. If you do have a fit (even if you have not yet found out where it is) then you can enter the auction with a higher degree of safety.

As usual, you need to have support for all the unbid suits — you are offering partner a choice of three suits.

LHO	Partner	RHO	You
1♥	pass	2♥	dbl

♠ A J 5 3　♥ 8 6　♦ K Q 4　♣ A 10 5 2

Not only can you make a takeout double with this hand, but you certainly should. If you pass, and LHO passes, you're likely to end up defending 2♥ when it's really your hand. You don't expect partner to bid on his six-count when 2♥ is passed around to him, do you?

Can a takeout double help when they've bid your best suit?

We've all been there — you have a good hand, but RHO opens your best suit. What do you do with something like this when you hear a 1♦ opening on your right?

♠ A 8 6 4　♥ 9　♦ A K 7 5　♣ K J 9 7

LHO	Partner	RHO	You
		1♦	?

Few players would argue with a pass. You cannot make a takeout double since you have neither support for hearts nor shortness in opener's suit, and with a singleton heart, bidding notrump is out of the question. Not surprisingly though, the opponents choose to play not in diamonds, but in hearts, your short suit:

LHO	Pass	RHO	You
		1♦	pass
1♥	pass	2♥	?

Now the opponents have found a fit, and thus your side is also likely to have one. You can hardly overcall 2♠ or 3♣ though. Nor can you expect partner to bid 3♣ if 2♥ is passed around to him. His hand is likely to be something like:

♠ 9 7   ♥ A 10 6 3   ♦ 6   ♣ Q 6 5 3 2

If his hand looks like this, you might or might not be able to beat 2♥, but three clubs will be an easy make. You can, however, get into the auction now, by making a takeout double. Your double here still shows good support for the two unbid suits — however it also says you have shortness in the suit you are doubling (hearts), and implies some length and usually strength in diamonds (both possible reasons for your failure to double the first time round).

Summary

✓ You can still make a takeout double even though you are a passed hand. To do so, you should have shortness in the opener's suit, support for all three unbid suits, and something close to an opening bid in terms of high cards.

✓ Takeout doubles in the sandwich seat must be sound. Wait until you have at least nine cards in your two suits. Avoid sandwich seat takeout doubles if you have wasted queens and jacks in the opponents' suits or if your own suits are poor.

✓ Show big distributional two-suiters in the sandwich seat by jumping to 2NT.

✓ A double of a 1NT response to LHO's opening bid shows a hand that would have made a direct takeout double of opener's suit.

✓ Be prepared to make a second-round double if opener has bid your strongest suit first but then rebids your short suit. You still need good support for the two unbid suits, however.

OTHER TAKEOUT DOUBLE SITUATIONS

NOW TRY THESE...

What is your next bid on each of these hands?

1
- ♠ K 10 7 3
- ♥ Q 7
- ♦ A J 8 7
- ♣ K 8 4

LHO	Partner	RHO	You
1♣	pass	1♥	?

2
- ♠ Q 8 7 6 5
- ♥ K J
- ♦ A 6 3
- ♣ 9 7 5

LHO	Partner	RHO	You
1♣	pass	1♥	?

3
- ♠ A K J 8
- ♥ 3
- ♦ K Q 9 8 3
- ♣ 9 7 3

LHO	Partner	RHO	You
1♣	pass	1♥	?

4
- ♠ A 3 2
- ♥ 7 3
- ♦ A K J 10 6 2
- ♣ 5 3

LHO	Partner	RHO	You
1♣	pass	1♥	?

5
- ♠ A Q J 3
- ♥ A 9 8 2
- ♦ K Q J 6
- ♣ 3

LHO	Partner	RHO	You
1♣	pass	1♥	?

6
- ♠ Q J 9 8 7
- ♥ A 4
- ♦ K Q J 9 7 4
- ♣ —

LHO	Partner	RHO	You
1♣	pass	1♥	?

7
- ♠ 5
- ♥ A K 8 6
- ♦ K Q 9
- ♣ Q 8 5 3 2

LHO	Partner	RHO	You
1♠	pass	2♠	?

8
- ♠ K Q 7 5
- ♥ 9
- ♦ A Q 3
- ♣ K J 6 4 2

LHO	Partner	RHO	You
1♠	pass	2♠	?

9
- ♠ 5
- ♥ J 8 6 4
- ♦ A Q 5 2
- ♣ K 10 8 6

LHO	Partner	RHO	You
1♠	pass	1NT	?

10
- ♠ 5
- ♥ A 8 6 4
- ♦ A Q 5 2
- ♣ A K 10 8

LHO	Partner	RHO	You
		1♣	pass
1♠	pass	2♠	?

ANSWERS

1　pass　Your poor shape and minor honors in the opponents' suits suggest caution.

2　pass　You would risk a 1♠ overcall if the opening 1♣ bid had been on your right, since you might have been able to shut out responder's heart suit. It is too late for that now, and your suit is not strong enough to interfere in a 'live' auction.

3　dbl　You have good suits and no wasted values. Perfect!

4　2♦　If you are going to be able to buy the hand, it will surely be in your strong suit. Only if partner can bid spades freely (showing at least a decent five-card suit) do you want to play in that suit.

5　dbl　You have lots of high cards, but all that means is that partner will be virtually broke. However, all your honors are pulling their weight, so you should risk a double.

6　2NT　Tell partner you have this great two-suiter straight away, and then leave any future bidding up to him.

7　dbl　What are you afraid of? Since they have found a fit, it is much more likely that you have one. Don't fall into the trap of bidding 3♣ on that revolting suit — not only is it dangerous, but you don't want a club lead and partner could easily have five or six diamonds or four hearts.

8　pass　You know partner has short spades, and not many high cards. His best suit is likely to be hearts, for which you have no support. Do not try to buy the hand when you have length and strength in the opponents' suit. Let them play the hand and go down instead.

9　dbl　If RHO had opened 1♠, you would have made a takeout double; doubling 1NT sends partner exactly the same message.

10　dbl　You hated passing over 1♣, but what else were you supposed to do? You probably have the best hand at the table, and now they have found a spade fit too, but there's no need to go quietly. With good support for the unbid suits, you can come in with a double now. Partner is surely looking at several spades, so he will know that you passed first time around because you had good clubs.

NOTRUMP
OVERCALLS

 After the opening bid, no player should bid notrump unless he has the proper material, and never unless he has a stopper in the adversary's suit! *Florence Irwin,* **Auction Highlights,** *1913.*

Bidding balanced hands when you are the opening bidder is easy. It is simply a matter of counting up your HCP and either opening with a notrump bid, or opening with a suit and rebidding in notrump. The exact auction will be determined by the number of HCPs you hold and partner will have an accurate picture of your hand after one or two bids.

Bidding balanced hands when there is a one-level opening bid on your right is not much tougher. Here is a rough guide to bidding balanced hands within various point ranges — in all cases, you promise at least one stopper in the opener's suit, and preferably two.

15 to 18 HCP	*overcall 1NT*
19-20 HCP	*double, then rebid notrump at the minimum level*
21-23 HCP	*double, then jump in notrump*
24+ HCP	*double, then cuebid or jump to game in notrump*

In this chapter, we will concentrate on those hands that fall within the range for a 1NT overcall. Saying that you can overcall 1NT with a balanced hand in the 15-18 HCP range is somewhat simplistic. As we mentioned above, you also need a stopper in the opener's suit, and without it, you have to pass or find some other way to bid the hand. There will also be some 15-point hands that are not really good enough — if you have only 15 HCP, you should also have some additional feature such as a five-card suit or excellent intermediate cards (nines and tens).

Say your RHO opens 1♥. Do you overcall 1NT with this hand?

♠ Q 6 ♥ A K 7 ♦ K 8 6 5 ♣ K 6 4 3

You would open 1NT happily with this hand, of course, but as an overcall, it's not really worth 15 points. Sure, you have a double stopper in opener's heart suit, but your intermediates are non-existent — although the HCP count would be the same, the hand would be much better if your minor suits were ♦K1098 and ♣K1087. You have no real source of tricks — not even a five-card suit. It is easy to see how a fifth card in one of the minors would improve your playing strength. As it is, you are going to be scrambling to take even four tricks in 1NT unless partner puts down a very good dummy. Reluctantly, therefore, you should pass with this hand.

♠ Q 10 6 ♥ K J 9 ♦ A J ♣ A J 10 9 7

This hand, by contrast, is infinitely better. You almost certainly have a double heart stopper but relatively few of your high cards are expended in that suit. You have a potential source of tricks in clubs, and the ♠10 and ♦J will prove useful opposite any little goody in partner's hand, such as the ♠J or ♦10xx. You should be happy to overcall 1NT on this hand, but passing our first example is the prudent action.

Why do you need so much to overcall 1NT?

When you open 1NT (whatever range that shows in your favorite system), each opponent must decide whether to overcall or to double you without any clue as to how good his partner's hand may be. Bidding over a 1NT opening bid, as we shall see in a later chapter of this book, is very tricky and quite dangerous.

However, when you come in with a 1NT overcall, your LHO already knows that his partner has at least 12 points. If he has 10 HCP or upwards, he will know that his side has the balance of the high cards and he will double. If your partner happens to be completely broke, the penalty may be substantial, particularly if you have overcalled on a trickless collection such as the first hand above. That is why, even though you open 1NT with 15-17 HCP, you need about a point more to reduce the risk when overcalling.

As we have discovered in earlier chapters, it is important to get across the general nature of your hand as quickly as possible in a competitive auction. It is therefore often right to overcall 1NT even when you do not have classic notrump shape. For example:

♠ A J 10   ♥ K 5   ♦ K J 10 9 8 6   ♣ K 7

If you were the dealer, you would probably open 1♦. Opening 1NT with a good six-card minor, even when you are within the right HCP range, may lead to missed minor-suit slams because your partner underestimates your playing strength. But slams are rarely an issue when the opponents have opened the bidding — you want to reach good games or buy the partscore.

Whether RHO has opened 1♣, 1♥ or 1♠, this hand falls into the category of both 'strong' and 'relatively balanced' with a stopper in the opener's suit. It is a 15-count with some extras — a source of tricks or good intermediates. You should overcall 1NT on it.

Let's say instead that after a 1♠ opening bid on your right you decided to overcall 2♦. If LHO raises to 2♠ and this is followed by two passes, you may well feel that you need to bid again with this many high cards. Doing so could be disastrous, whether you repeat your suit (with 3♦) or make a takeout double. If you overcall 1NT, you will have got the message across to partner about the strength and general nature of your hand and you can happily leave any further moves to him.

In a competitive auction, whenever you can describe your hand more or less completely in one bid, is it is wise to do so. For that reason, you can be a little more cavalier about distribution when you overcall 1NT than you would be when you open the bidding 1NT.

How do you respond when partner overcalls 1NT?

Responses to a 1NT overcall are best played as identical to those you use after a 1NT opening bid — use 2♣ as Stayman and 2♦ and 2♥ as transfers. Although not played universally, this method (which is known as 'Systems On') is the most popular.

The most important thing to remember when responding to a 1NT overcall is that you should be very aggressive. Look at these two hands:

BY THE WAY

One alternative method of responding to a 1NT overcall, which is known as 'Systems Off', is to use a cuebid of opener's suit as Stayman, allowing for 'drop dead' bids in the other three suits.

If only your side has bid (i.e. the opponents have remained silent throughout the auction), would you like to play these two hands in 3NT?

	Partner		You
♠	A 10 8 3	♠	J 9 7
♥	A Q 2	♥	8 5
♦	A 9 4 2	♦	Q J 10 7 3
♣	J 7	♣	A 10 4

You probably would, but it will be a touch and go affair. You have no clue where the missing high cards lie. However, notice the difference if the bidding has been opened by your LHO, say with a 1♥ call. There are only 17 HCP missing, so the opener is an odds-on favorite to hold both red-suit kings, and he is likely to hold both the king and queen of at least one of the black suits. Now bidding game is an excellent move. With partner's good hand sitting over most of the enemy's high cards, your finesses are much more likely to succeed.

Not only that, but it is always easier to be declarer when you know where most of the high cards are located. Those nasty two-way finesses are always less troublesome when you know in advance which defender holds the queen!

With a good 8 HCP (particularly if you have a five-card suit) you should go ahead and bid game facing a 1NT overcall. Don't mess around making an invitational raise on a hand such as the one shown above.

Summary

✓ A 1NT overcall shows a relatively balanced hand in the 15-18 HCP range, although you should prefer to pass or perhaps double with a poor 15-count containing no potential source of tricks.

✓ You must have at least one stopper in opener's suit to overcall 1NT — preferably two.

✓ Prefer to overcall 1NT if you are within the range and you have a stopper, even if your hand is not quite a classic notrump shape. Overcalling 1NT gets across the general nature and strength of your hand in one bid.

✓ If you agree to play 'Systems On' responses to a 1NT overcall, then you respond in exactly the same way as you would if partner had opened 1NT.

NOTRUMP OVERCALLS

NOW TRY THESE...

What is your next bid on each of these hands?

1 ♠ K Q 3
   ♥ A J 7
   ♦ Q J 8 7
   ♣ Q J 4

LHO	Partner	RHO	You
		1♦	?

2 ♠ K 7 6 5
   ♥ A K 6 3
   ♦ K 3
   ♣ Q 7 5

LHO	Partner	RHO	You
		1♦	?

3 ♠ K J 8 4
   ♥ A Q 8 7
   ♦ K Q 9
   ♣ J 3

LHO	Partner	RHO	You
		1♦	?

4 ♠ A 3 2
   ♥ K 7 3
   ♦ A 6 2
   ♣ A 8 5 3

LHO	Partner	RHO	You
		1♦	?

You are playing 'Systems On' after a 1NT overcall — Stayman and Jacoby Transfers. What is your next bid on each of these hands?

5 ♠ J 10 4
   ♥ Q 9 8 2
   ♦ J 6
   ♣ K J 10 3

LHO	Partner	RHO	You
1♦	1NT	pass	?

6 ♠ Q J 9 8 7
   ♥ A 4
   ♦ Q 7 5
   ♣ 10 4 2

LHO	Partner	RHO	You
1♦	1NT	pass	?

7 ♠ K J 7 5 3 2
   ♥ Q 7 6
   ♦ 2
   ♣ 10 8 3 2

LHO	Partner	RHO	You
1♦	1NT	pass	?

8 ♠ 7 5
   ♥ Q J 7 6 5 3
   ♦ 7 5 2
   ♣ 10 8

LHO	Partner	RHO	You
1♦	1NT	pass	?

ANSWERS

1   **1NT**   You have a balanced 16-count with solid stoppers in opener's suit. Perfect!

2   **dbl**   This 15-count has poor playing strength in notrump — poor spotcards and no obvious source of tricks for you to develop. Remember, in notrump, you usually need to establish small cards and, with no long suits, that is not easy. You also have only a single stopper in opener's suit, two four-card majors, and support for the third unbid suit. A takeout double is the best option.

3   **1NT**   Even though you have four-card support for both majors, a 1NT overcall describes your hand better than a takeout double. If partner has some values and is interested in finding a major-suit fit, he can use Stayman in response to your overcall.

4   **pass**   A 1NT overcall on this featureless collection would be ill-advised. Yes, you have 15 HCP, but there are very few prospects for developing any long-card tricks. The 4-3-3-3 shape also makes this hand unattractive for a takeout double. What do you do, then? Pass and hope you have enough defense to beat your opponents' contract.

5   **2♣**   Start with Stayman. Whatever partner's response, you should go straight to game (4♥ if he responds 2♥, and 3NT over a 2♦ or 2♠ response). You have some help in diamonds, good intermediate cards, and a potential source of tricks in clubs. Remember too, that partner will know where most of the missing high cards are located, so he will have an easy time playing the hand.

6   **2♥**   Transfer to spades and then bid 3NT to offer partner a choice of games.

7   **2♥**   You intend to raise partner's 2♠ bid to 3♠, inviting him to bid on to game with a good hand.

8   **2♦**   This not a cuebid, but a transfer to hearts. Your hand will be useless in 1NT, but 2♥ should be safe enough.

C H A P T E R 11

RHO BIDS OVER
A 1NT OVERCALL

 A notrump hand is always either easy or impossible, and there is nothing quite so sad in life as a notrump hand gone wrong. *Florence Irwin,* **Auction Highlights,** *1913.*

In the previous chapter, we looked at how the auction normally continues after partner overcalls 1NT and your RHO passes. To complete this discussion, we need to consider the problems caused by further enemy action. There are three possibilities we shall examine here — RHO may double 1NT, he may raise opener's suit, or he may bid a suit of his own. We're going to look at how you should handle each of these possibilities, but there's a very simple way to deal with these auctions that works every time: just do what you would in the same auction if partner had opened 1NT. Just pretend the opening bid never happened, and bid as you would in that auction! We'll come back to that, but just tuck it away in the back of your mind for now.

What should you do if RHO doubles?

If RHO doubles partner's 1NT overcall, it is a penalty double. The chances are that you will have a bad hand. Think about it — LHO has 12+ points for his opening bid, partner has 15-18 for his 1NT overcall, and RHO has 10+ for his double. There are not many points left for you, are there?

Most of the time you will have a hand with fewer than 4 HCP. The chances are high that your side does not have the majority of the points. Since you are outgunned, you have two options — you can pass, suggesting a weak hand without a five-card suit to run to, or you can remove yourself to a long suit at the two-level.

After this penalty double by RHO, all your bids have the same meaning as they would have if partner had opened 1NT. In other words, 2♣ is still Stayman, and you have transfers available if you normally play them. Redouble can be used to force partner to bid 2♣, so you can escape to a minor suit.

Remember that partner's 1NT overcall has been doubled for penalties. You should usually choose to rescue partner if you hold a five-card or longer suit. Thus:

♠ 8 ♥ Q J 9 6 4 ♦ 7 6 3 2 ♣ 8 6 2

LHO	Partner	RHO	You
1♣	1NT	dbl	?

Bid 2♦, a transfer to hearts. Your hand will be useless to partner in 1NT, but if you catch partner with three or more hearts, 2♥ will be playable, and they may not even double it.

LHO	Partner	RHO	You
1♣	1NT	dbl	2♣

Even here, your 2♣ bid is not a forcing cuebid of the opponent's suit — it is Stayman. A typical hand for you is something like:

♠ 9 8 7 3 ♥ J 1 0 6 3 ♦ 8 7 5 4 ♣ 3

You plan to pass whatever partner bids, even 2♦. Whatever he bids, it won't be worse than 1NT doubled opposite this dummy, and they may not double you!

You do have one other option with a weak hand. With a six-card or longer suit, you can choose to make a preemptive jump. For example:

♠ 8 ♥ Q J 1 0 7 5 3 2 ♦ 7 6 ♣ 8 6 2

LHO	Partner	RHO	You
1♠	1NT	dbl	?

Jump to 3♥ (transfers only apply at the two-level). Perhaps RHO has foolishly doubled 1NT holding a three- or four-card spade fit. Of course, 3♥ may get doubled and you may lose a penalty when the opponents cannot make game, but there are significant advantages to taking preemptive action on such a one-suited hand. Which of these auctions do you think is better for your side?

LHO	Partner	RHO	You
1♠	1NT	dbl	2♦
pass	2♥	2♠	3♥

LHO	Partner	RHO	You
1♠	1NT	dbl	3♥
pass	pass	3♠	

Clearly, you are much better placed in the second auction. In the first, RHO has limited his hand and opener now has the choice of competing to 3♠ or of doubling you in 3♥, knowing exactly what his partner holds. In the second auction, RHO has been forced to bid in order to show his spade fit. Opener does not know if his partner has stretched to bid 3♠, or whether he would have jumped to 3♠ if you had bid only 2♥.

Any time you can make the opponents guess, you give them a chance to do the wrong thing, which can only be good for your side. Bidding as high as you dare immediately is likely to achieve that goal.

So far, we have only discussed bad hands, but it is just about possible for you to have as many as 7 HCP. Perhaps LHO opened the bidding on a shapely 11-point hand. Maybe RHO decided to chance a double with what he considered a nice 7-count.

When you have 6-7 HCP facing a 1NT overcall, you should tell partner that the hand belongs to your side. How do you do that? Redouble!

LHO	Partner	RHO	You
1♥	1NT	dbl	redbl

RHO has made a mistake. Your redouble says to partner, "We have the balance of the points. Let's either play the hand in 1NT redoubled or, if the opponents take it out, let's try to double them and collect a nice penalty."

Remember our discussion in the last chapter — we said that you should raise aggressively after a 1NT overcall. One of the reasons for this is because your partner's strong hand is sitting over the opener, who will hold most of the enemy's strength. Your side's honors will therefore be worth more than the enemy's. Remember also that your partner will have a good holding in opener's suit. If the opponents run there is a good chance that the suits will lie badly for them and you will collect a substantial penalty.

How do you continue if RHO bids a suit?

Remember what we said at the start of this chapter — try to play exactly the same system after a 1NT overcall as you do after a 1NT opening bid. A primary reason for this is that you already know and understand that system. Why try to remember another one for a situation that will occur only rarely?

Just as is the case after an opening 1NT bid and a suit overcall by RHO, Stayman is no longer available, and transfers are off. This makes sense because usually not all transfers are available. For example, in this auction

LHO	Partner	RHO	You
	1NT	2♦	?

you need to have natural 2♥ and 2♠ bids both available. The same thing applies here; with 5-7 points and a decent five-card suit do not be afraid to compete:

♠ J 6 3　♥ K Q 10 9 5　♦ 6 4 3　♣ 8 2

LHO	Partner	RHO	You
1♣	1NT	2♦	?

Bid 2♥, natural, but not suggesting any interest in game.

If you have read our previous book, *25 Bridge Conventions You Should Know*, then you will already be familiar with the Lebensohl convention which is commonly used when partner opens 1NT and your RHO overcalls. However, it is equally useful when partner's 1NT was an overcall and RHO bids a suit.

Assuming that you are already playing Lebensohl after an opening 1NT bid and an overcall, continue to do so in this auction too. Here is a very brief recap, beginning with the situation when RHO raises opener's suit:

LHO	Partner	RHO	You
1♠	1NT	2♠	?

If you have an invitational hand (i.e. enough high-card values to want to invite game facing a 15-18 1NT) then you can bid your five-card or longer suit at the three-level. Perhaps your hand is something like:

♠ 6 3　♥ K 4　♦ K J 10 7 6 3　♣ 7 4

Invite game — bid 3♦ directly over LHO's 2♠.

If you just wish to compete in your long suit, with a weakish hand, then you start by bidding 2NT, which simply asks partner to bid 3♣. Over his forced response, you can pass (if clubs is your suit) or you can correct to 3♦ or 3♥, which partner will then pass. For example:

♠ 6 3　♥ 7 4　♦ K 10 9 7 6 3　♣ 7 4

You are not interested in bidding game, but you also do not want to defend 2♠. Bid 2NT (Lebensohl), which will force partner to bid 3♣. When you then correct to 3♦, partner will know to pass.

You can also force to game using Stayman if you wish — 3♠ (a cuebid of the opponents' suit) tells partner that you have enough high cards to bid game and that you have four cards in the other major (hearts here). Something like:

♠ 6 3　♥ A J 7 4　♦ Q 10 3　♣ K 5 4 3

Note that there are fewer Lebensohl sequences needed after a 1NT overcall than when partner's 1NT is an opening bid. You do not need to be able to show a stopper in the opponents' suit, since partner has already promised one of those with his overcall. The auction is a little more complicated though, if RHO bids a new suit.

LHO	Partner	RHO	You
1♦	1NT	2♠	?

When you have a suit of your own, you can use Lebensohl just as you did above. Thus, an immediate 3♣ is invitational, but with clubs and a competitive hand you bid 2NT (asking partner to bid 3♣) and pass his response. The same idea also works when you have hearts:

♠ 8 ♥ Q 10 8 7 6 5 ♦ Q 7 3 ♣ 8 7 4

LHO	Partner	RHO	You
1♦	1NT	2♠	2NT
pass	3♣	pass	3♥

You do not want to sell out to 2♠. Neither do you want partner raising you to game. Partner will know that you do not have enough to invite game — you are simply competing for the partscore. If you wanted him to raise, you would have bid 3♥ immediately over 2♠.

Things are a little more complicated if you want to force to game. Remember, partner has already said that he has diamonds stopped, but he may not hold a spade stopper. The meaning of the game-forcing Lebensohl bids are therefore the same in this auction as they would be if partner had opened 1NT and RHO had overcalled in spades:

3♠:	*Game forcing, four hearts, no spade stopper*
3NT:	*GF without four hearts or a spade stopper*
2NT, then 3♠ over partner's 3♣:	*GF with four hearts and a spade stopper*
2NT then 3NT over partner's 3♣:	*GF with spade stopper but not four hearts*

When your RHO has bid a new suit and you cuebid, either directly or after using the 2NT relay, you show four cards in the other major, and when you bid 3NT you deny interest in the other major. Remember the saying 'Slow Shows Stopper'. If you start with the 2NT relay and then force to game (with 3NT or a cuebid) over partner's 3♣ response, then you also promise a stopper in the opponent's suit — Slow Shows Stopper. This is the same as the Lebensohl convention that you may already be playing after an opening 1NT and an overcall (see *25 Bridge Conventions You Should Know*, Chapter 18).

What does it mean if you double RHO's suit?

There are different opinions on the meaning of double in these auctions. As is so often the case in competitive bidding, there is no absolute right or wrong here, but we're going to recommend doing whatever you would do in the same situation if partner had opened 1NT. At least it's easy to remember!

LHO	Partner	RHO	You		LHO	Partner	RHO	You
	1NT	2♥	dbl		1♦	1NT	2♥	dbl

If you play the double in the first auction as penalties, then it is easy to remember that the second one is also for penalties. Play whatever you and your partner are most likely to remember. Playing penalty doubles here will enable you to collect some nice penalties when RHO has stuck his oar in when he should not have done so. Unfortunately, there will also be some hands on which you have to guess.

What does 'double' mean after RHO raises opener's suit?

LHO	Partner	RHO	You
1♦	1NT	2♦	dbl

Again, you have choices, and it is certainly not very likely that you will hold a penalty double. Think about it — opener has diamonds, partner's 1NT overcall shows diamonds, and RHO has diamonds. What are the chances that you will also have enough diamonds to make a penalty double? Not high, are they?

However, these situations don't come up that often, and our advice is therefore to err on the side of simplicity rather than introducing complicated exceptions that are hard to remember. So if you normally play double of an overcall of partner's 1NT opening as penalties, then by all means do so here.

Summary

✓ The simplest set of methods is to pretend the opening bid did not happen, and treat the auction as you normally would if partner had opened 1NT.

✓ If RHO doubles, Stayman and transfers are on (if you normally play them). Jumps are natural and preemptive.

✓ A redouble tells partner that the hand belongs to your side. You expect partner to pass and, if the opponents bid, partner is invited to double for penalties with a suitable trump holding. If RHO bids a suit (whether a new suit or a raise of opener's suit) Lebensohl applies just as it would if partner's 1NT had been an opening bid.

✓ Doubles of RHO's suit bids (even if RHO raises openers' suit) can be played as penalties or takeout, and you must agree in advance with your partner which you prefer. We recommend you do whatever you would do in the auction if the opening bid had not occurred and partner had opened 1NT.

RHO BIDS OVER A 1NT OVERCALL

NOW TRY THESE...

What is your next bid on each of the following hands? After opening 1NT, you play Stayman, Jacoby Transfers, Lebensohl, and Penalty Doubles of overcalls.

1
- ♠ 9 7 6 3
- ♥ 8 7 3
- ♦ 8 7
- ♣ J 8 6 4

LHO	Partner	RHO	You
1♦	1NT	dbl	?

2
- ♠ 8 7 6
- ♥ J 9 8 6 3
- ♦ 10 7 3
- ♣ 5 3

LHO	Partner	RHO	You
1♦	1NT	dbl	?

3
- ♠ 8 4
- ♥ 8 7
- ♦ Q 10 7 6 4
- ♣ J 8 6 3

LHO	Partner	RHO	You
1♦	1NT	dbl	?

4
- ♠ A 3 2
- ♥ 10 8 7 3
- ♦ J 9 8
- ♣ 10 5 3

LHO	Partner	RHO	You
1♦	1NT	dbl	?

5
- ♠ J 10 9 8 6 5 4 3
- ♥ 7 3
- ♦ 9
- ♣ 10 8

LHO	Partner	RHO	You
1♦	1NT	dbl	?

6
- ♠ Q 10 7 5 4
- ♥ 8
- ♦ J 6 3 2
- ♣ Q 10 9

LHO	Partner	RHO	You
1♥	1NT	2♦	?

7
- ♠ 8 7 3
- ♥ 7
- ♦ J 5 3
- ♣ K 10 8 7 4 2

LHO	Partner	RHO	You
1♥	1NT	2♦	?

8
- ♠ Q 5
- ♥ 7
- ♦ K J 7 6 5 4
- ♣ J 10 8 3

LHO	Partner	RHO	You
1♥	1NT	2♥	?

9
- ♠ K 8 7 3
- ♥ 7 4
- ♦ K J 3
- ♣ Q 10 8 7

LHO	Partner	RHO	You
1♥	1NT	2♥	?

10
- ♠ K J 7
- ♥ 7 3
- ♦ K J 5
- ♣ J 10 8 3 2

LHO	Partner	RHO	You
1♥	1NT	2♦	?

ANSWERS

1   pass   There is no guarantee that you have a fit. Why venture to the two-level? Just hope that partner can scramble enough tricks in 1NT doubled to avoid a complete disaster.

2   2♦   There is no guarantee that 2♥ will play better than 1NT. Indeed, 2♠ might be the best contract. However, there is no way to find out. Our recommendation is that you should always remove 1NT with a five-card major. The advantage of doing so is that if the opponents double and you find partner with a nice fit, you might even make 2♥ doubled. Even when 2♥ is the wrong spot, that may not be clear to the opponents, who will be wary of doubling you into game, and thus you may either escape undoubled, or the enemy may bid a contract of their own.

3   pass   Unfortunately, 2♦ would be a transfer to hearts. Diamonds may be your best spot even though it is opener's suit, but there is no way to get there if you are playing transfers. As usual, when you play a convention, you give up a natural bid, and this might be one time that you get hurt. *C'est la vie.*

4   redbl   Tell partner that this is your hand. If the opponents pass, the chances of making 1NT redoubled (which is game!) are excellent. If they bid, then the penalty should be worth getting.

5   3♠   Who knows what anyone can make? Perhaps the opponents can make 4♥ or 3NT. Maybe you can make 3♠. You cannot tell, so make life as tough as you can for the opponents.

6   2♠   You could elect to defend 2♦, and you might be right. However, the odds strongly favor trying to play the hand in 2♠. Partner will not raise, as 2♠ is neither forcing nor invitational.

7   2NT   Lebensohl. Partner will respond 3♣ and you will pass.

8   3♦   Invitational. You could just blast 3NT and hope, but for this to be a success you will need partner to hold some kind of diamond fit, so consult him. If he passes, 3♦ should be fairly safe.

9   3♥   Cuebid. This is like using Stayman. This tells partner that you want to play in game and that you have four spades. He will either bid 3NT (if he does not have four spades) or he will set spades as trumps.

10   2NT   Lebensohl. You're not going to be happy defending 2♦ doubled if RHO turns out to have six small ones and the ♦AQ are on your left! Over partner's forced 3♣ response to Lebensohl, you plan to bid 3NT, reassuring him that you have diamonds stopped. Slow Shows Stopper!

CHAPTER 12

COMPETING
OVER 1NT

 A notrump opening will force the adversaries to two of anything, and it will debar them from bidding notrump themselves.
Florence Irwin, **Auction Highlights, *1913.***

The kind of 1NT openings you encounter will vary enormously depending on where you live. In days gone by, just about everyone in North America (with the exception of the odd Kaplan-Sheinwold or Precision Club pair) stuck to the strong notrump. They used either the traditional 16-18 range or the more modern 15-17. Meanwhile, players in the UK and various other Acol strongholds seldom came across opponents who were not playing the weak notrump (12-14). Nowadays, there are considerably more weak-notrumpers in North American tournaments, while many regular partnerships in the UK are playing either 14-16 or 15-17 1NT openings. We have also seen the growth in popularity of another weapon much loved by ultra-aggressive pairs — the mini (10-12) 1NT opening.

Not surprisingly, the strategy you should adopt when defending a 1NT opening will depend to some extent on its strength. Always be sure to check your opponents' 1NT range in advance. For the rest of this chapter, we're going to assume that you are playing against a 15-17 notrump.

When should you bid over a 1NT opening?

Your motives for entering the auction over 1NT, considering the dangers involved, will vary depending on the strength of the opening bid and, to some extent, the vulnerability and the form of scoring. The reason for this is not so difficult to understand.

As soon as RHO opens a 15-17 HCP 1NT, the likelihood that it is your hand becomes fairly small, while the chances that you can make a game are practically non-existent. Think about it. Barring some wildly distributional hand or a great deal of luck, you normally need around 24+ points to bid (and expect to make) game. The chances of your side holding that many points once RHO has 15-17 are very small. You are therefore on the defensive immediately, and your motivation for entering the auction is primarily obstructive. You want to make life difficult for your opponents — a perfectly respectable reason to get into the auction if you can do so safely.

Most pairs have fairly sophisticated and well-worked-out bidding structures that they use after they open 1NT. Some variant of Stayman (which can be highly complex), transfers in two, three or four suits, and a whole host of other gadgets are at their disposal. But what if your side removes some of that precious bidding space?

LHO	Partner	RHO	You
1NT	2♠	?	

Most of the machinery that the enemy have for constructive bidding has suddenly gone out of the window. In order to invite game in hearts, RHO has to go through something like Lebensohl. He has to commit the partnership to the three-level, and he no longer has any way to invite in notrump — 2NT as a natural bid is history.

If you are familiar with Lebensohl, you will know that it can be used to compete at the three-level, to invite game, or to force to game, while at the same time enquiring about major suits and stoppers. Very useful, but by the same token therefore, the Lebensohl 2NT bid will be used on quite a wide variety of hands. Consider the devastating effect of a gentle raise from you:

LHO	Partner	RHO	You
1NT	2♠	2NT	3♠
pass	pass	?	

What a nightmare! Now the three-level has gone, and RHO is reduced to guessing what to do. He may bid on and go down, when he should just have defended 3♠. He may pass when they had a good contract. He may bid on and fail to guess what the right contract is.

You won't always be this successful, but this simple example should help to convince you of the enormous benefits of overcalling a 1NT opening bid.

What do you need to overcall a strong notrump opening?

We mentioned earlier that your chances of bidding and making game are slight after RHO opens a strong 1NT. It is possible that you can make a partscore, but primarily your bidding should be geared to obstruction. If you are considering overcalling on a less than perfect hand, ask yourself how much damage your intervention might do. The more room you take away from your opponents, the more inclined you should be to bid. With a suitable shape, feel free to come in on fairly marginal values without worrying that partner will carry you too high because he expects you to have a good hand.

As always, though, you must bear in mind how easy it is for LHO to double an overcall. Often he will know that opposite a 15-17 notrump he does not have enough for game but he has enough to defeat your contract handily. That is especially true if he has trump tricks, so the quality of your suit is one of the most important factors when you decide whether or not to overcall. Obviously, the vulnerability will affect your decision, too. You will need to be even more cautious when vulnerable.

In Chapter 14, we will look at some of the conventional defenses you can choose to employ against a 1NT opening. For the purposes of the discussion here, we will just assume that all two-level overcalls are natural.

♠ K Q J 8 6 3   ♥ 3   ♦ Q 10 8 4   ♣ 6 3

This is a perfectly respectable 2♠ overcall at just about any form of scoring, and at any vulnerability. So too is:

♠ Q J 10 9 8 6   ♥ A K 2   ♦ J 8 6 4   ♣ —

Sure, you might get doubled and go three down when the opponents cannot make a slam, but that is just about the worst-case scenario.

♠ K Q J 7 5   ♥ 5   ♦ 3 2   ♣ Q 10 9 8 5

This time you have only a five-card suit, but with 5-5 distribution you cannot afford to allow the opponents an easy ride to their 2♥, 4♥ or 6♥ contract. When you have a 5-5 (or better) hand, you can afford to be very aggressive. Remember, 'five-five, come alive!'

Switch the black suits and this would still be a 2♠ overcall.

♠ Q 10 9 8 5   ♥ 5   ♦ 3 2   ♣ K Q J 7 5

Yes, you may buy the hand, but the primary reason for choosing to bid a queen-high spade suit rather than the clubs headed by KQJ is the obstructive nature of bidding spades. If the opponents do shoot 3NT over you, they may get a nasty shock when you lead the ♣K rather than a spade!

Remember, you are not trying to outbid the opponents. You are assuming that you are outgunned. You are trying to make life tough for your opponents. Partner will not go crazy. He heard the strong notrump opening too. The only time he will carry you higher than you think you want to go is with a super fit for your suit.

Would you ever make a jump overcall over a strong 1NT?

Jump overalls of a strong notrump are preemptive. You would usually have a good suit but little else. For example:

♠ K Q J 9 8 6 5 ♥ 7 ♦ 3 2 ♣ Q 4 2

Jump to 3♠ except at unfavorable vulnerability. You have approximately six tricks and no defense to speak of. How badly wrong can things go?

What about bidding in fourth seat?

It is a widely-held misconception that when your LHO's 1NT opening is followed by two passes, you can overcall at the sniff of an oil rag. Actually, the opposite is a more accurate assessment. In this auction

LHO	Partner	RHO	You
1♦	pass	pass	?

you usually can and should bid on a fairly weak hand if you have the right distribution (see Chapter 20 for more discussion on this). LHO can have as little as 12 points, while RHO, who could not scrape up a response, has fewer than 6 points and probably has no more than a king or so. But an opening 1NT creates an entirely different situation:

LHO	Partner	RHO	You
1NT	pass	pass	?

When the opening bid is 1NT, responder will pass on quite a good hand. All we know about responder's hand is that he does not have enough high cards to invite game (so he has less than a good 8 HCP if the opening showed 15-17), and he probably does not have a five-card major or a six-card minor either. That suggests a relatively balanced hand, i.e. enough trumps to double you if you enter the fray and find him with 6-7 HCP. The danger of entering this auction isn't lessened if the 1NT bidder only has 12-14 HCP. Now responder will pass smoothly with anything up to a balanced 10 HCP, hoping you will come in.

You may also recall, when we discussed raising a 1NT overcall, that we recommended doing so aggressively since your side's strength was well positioned over most of the opponents' high cards. When 1NT is followed by two passes, the reverse of the same argument suggests that, if anything, you should tend to err on the side of caution. This time, it is the opponents who have the strong hand sitting over you.

Summary

✓ Make sure that your overcall is based on a good suit, to reduce the chances of a penalty double on your left. Be more aggressive with distributional hands (5-5, for example).

✓ If you have a close decision as to whether to overcall, consider how much space you consume (i.e. be more inclined to stretch to overcall 2♠ but tend to stay out when your suit is a minor).

✓ Beware of overcalling on relatively balanced hands (eg. 5-3-3-2 shape).

✓ Do not bid in the passout seat just because it is your turn. If you would not have made an overcall in second seat, you probably do not have one in fourth either.

✓ A jump overcall over 1NT shows a good suit and little in the way of defensive values.

COMPETING OVER 1NT

NOW TRY THESE...

Your opponents are playing a 15-17 1NT. What is your next bid on each of the hands below?

1
♠ A 9 7
♥ K 7 5 4 3
♦ 8
♣ A J 6 4

LHO	Partner	RHO	You
		1NT	?

2
♠ Q 6
♥ 8 2
♦ A K 10 9 6
♣ Q 10 8 4

LHO	Partner	RHO	You
		1NT	?

3
♠ K Q J 9 5 4
♥ 8
♦ 10 7 6 4
♣ J 8

LHO	Partner	RHO	You
		1NT	?

4
♠ A Q J 3 2
♥ 7 3
♦ 8
♣ Q 10 5 3 2

LHO	Partner	RHO	You
		1NT	?

5
♠ K Q J 9 8 6 5
♥ 3
♦ 9 3
♣ 10 8 3

LHO	Partner	RHO	You
		1NT	?

6
♠ K Q J 9 8 6 5 3
♥ 3
♦ 9
♣ 10 8 3

LHO	Partner	RHO	You
		1NT	?

7
♠ A J 7 6 4
♥ K 5 4
♦ Q 7
♣ K J 3

LHO	Partner	RHO	You
		1NT	?

8
♠ A 9 7
♥ K 7 5 4 3
♦ 8
♣ A J 6 4

LHO	Partner	RHO	You
1NT	pass	pass	?

ANSWERS

1   pass   Your suit is not good enough and you have a good defensive hand. If partner has nothing then 2♥ may be very expensive. If he has a few scattered honors, you may have enough to beat the opponents' contract.

2   2♦   Although 2♦ does not take up much room, it does prevent LHO from using Stayman. With a doubleton in both majors, it is very likely that the opponents have a fit in one of them. If you pass, they will surely find it. Your overcall may give LHO a problem if he has two four-card majors but not enough values to force to game.

3   2♠   Your good suit and distribution, combined with the preemptive nature of the spade suit make it worth the risk. Partner will not go crazy just because he has a few high cards. He can add.

4   2♠   Your excellent offensive shape make this hand well worth an overcall. You would also bid 2♠ if your black suits were reversed.

5   3♠   The hand is very likely to belong to the enemy. Make it hard for them to find their best spot.

6   4♠   You would have opened a preemptive 4♠ as dealer. Knowing that RHO has a good hand makes it even more important to eat up the opponents' bidding space.

7   pass   Why turn a plus score into a minus? You have no source of tricks, a poor suit, and your defensive cards are sitting over the enemy's strength.

8   pass   This wasn't an overcall in second seat (see Problem 1) and it isn't one now. In fact, since the strong hand is now on your left, things have become considerably worse.

C H A P T E R **13**

DOUBLING
1NT

 You want the strong hand on your right — so you can play after it.
Florence Irwin, Auction Highlights, *1913*.

A double of a 1NT opening bid is always for penalties. Think about it — how can you make a takeout double when the opponents have not bid a suit? A takeout double, by definition, shows shortness in opener's suit and support for the other three. Of which suit would a double of 1NT be a takeout? As we'll see in the next chapter, some conventional methods of defending against 1NT use a double for something other than showing a very strong hand. Although popular with some tournament players, these methods are best avoided. As regular rubber bridge players will tell you, doubling 1NT, even a strong notrump, can often be extremely profitable.

What do you need
to double 1NT?

As a double of 1NT is for penalties, it says to your partner, 'I have a better hand than the one shown by the opener.' Note though, that a double of 1NT does not necessarily show a balanced hand, although it may do so.

Basically, if RHO's opening 1NT shows 15-17 HCP, you need 17+ to double. If the 1NT opening shows 12-14, then you need 15+. (If you happen to come up against opponents who are playing a mini 1NT opening, showing 10-12 points, you should also wait until you hold 15+ points to double.)

That seems fairly black-and-white, but things are never quite that simple, are they? Remember, if 1NT doubled becomes the final contract you will be on lead. If you have a good opening lead, you can happily double on a hand with fewer HCP. For example:

♠ A 3 ♥ 6 5 4 ♦ K Q J 10 9 5 3 ♣ A

You can double any strength 1NT opening with this 14-HCP hand. Why? Because if your double ends the auction (as it often will) you can lead the king of diamonds. This will drive out the opponents' ace. Declarer will be able to cash some heart tricks but, when he leads a black suit, you will be able to win and cash the rest of your diamonds — fundamentally, you can beat 1NT two tricks without needing any help from partner.

Now think about this hand:

♠ K J 8 5 ♥ A Q 7 ♦ K 6 5 ♣ A J 4

Your RHO opens 1NT showing 15-17 points. You have a nice 18-count and you should double; however, we're going to warn you not to be overly surprised if you find that the contract cannot be beaten. The odds are just in your favor, since your honors are well placed, sitting over declarer, but the hand is likely to depend on whether it is partner or LHO who turns up with a key jack or queen. On a bad day, partner has nothing, and every time you get the lead you will have to give declarer a trick because you have to lead away from your honors. Unlucky.

The same principle also applies if the opponents open a 12-14 1NT:

♠ A J 7 ♥ K J 5 3 ♦ Q 9 7 ♣ A 3 2

Most players would double but it is very close. You have 15 points. Let's say opener is in the middle of his range, with 13. That leaves 12 points to be shared between LHO and your partner. If your partner has 8+ of those missing 12 HCP, you will collect a nice penalty from 1NT doubled (or against some doubled two-level contract if the opponents run). If LHO is the one with the points then you may run into a redouble. In that case, it will be your side that has a choice of ways in which to concede a large minus score.

♠ K 10 5 ♥ A 3 ♦ K Q J 9 7 5 ♣ J 10

Although only 14 HCP, this is a much better double, no matter what strength the 1NT opening shows. Certainly things might go awry, but the chances are that 1NT doubled will fail provided that partner shows up with his share of the missing points and that you do not find declarer with ♦A10832. Sure, you might still give away a trick on the opening lead — maybe partner has the singleton ♦A and RHO holds ♦10832, but you are far more likely to give away a trick leading from the balanced hands with more high-card points that we saw earlier in this chapter.

What do you need to double in fourth seat?

It is worth mentioning briefly the subject of doubles in the fourth seat, after 1NT is opened on your left and the next two players pass. As we shall see in Chapter 20 (Balancing), when a suit opening bid is passed around to you, you can bid on much less than you would need for the same action in second seat. This is not the case when the opening bid is 1NT.

There are partnerships that play fourth seat doubles as weaker than those in the direct seat. This caters for those rare hands on which the 1NT opener steals the contract when both of his opponents hold balanced hands in the 10-13 point range. It is poor strategy, though, and for every good result it produces, there will be a handful of disasters.

We strongly recommend that a fourth seat double should show at least as good a hand as a direct seat double of 1NT. There are two reasons why this should be the case. Bear in mind that when you double in fourth seat, you will not be on lead if the auction proceeds no further. The fact that you have a good suit, therefore, may not help, unless your partner happens to lead it. Also, your high cards are poorly positioned in that they are under the opener, who will hold most of the opponents' strength. This may mean that your honors do not pull the same weight they would if they were sitting over the opening bidder.

What do you do when partner doubles 1NT?

This is an important question, and one to which even many fairly experienced players do not understand the answer. What would you bid here?

♠ K 6 4　♥ 9 8 7 3 2　♦ Q 10 6　♣ 10 6

LHO	Partner	RHO	You
1NT	dbl	pass	?

If you decided to retreat to 2♥, you would have company, but you would also be wrong. Let's examine why.

Remember that your partner has said, by doubling, that he has a better hand than the opener. Irrespective of the strength of the 1NT opening, that does not leave many HCP to share between you and your RHO. Partner only needs you to hold a couple of stray honors in order for your side to have the balance of the strength. Besides, your partner is on lead against 1NT doubled, which puts your side ahead in the race to set up your tricks before the opponents can establish theirs. You should therefore look upon hands such as the one above as being exactly what partner is hoping you hold.

It is remarkable how rarely a 1NT opening suffers a large penalty in practice, even a weak notrump opening. One of the reasons for this is that most players go wrong on the kind of hand we gave you above. Partner has made a penalty double. Add the points he has promised to your five and you can see that the opponents are outgunned. Indeed, partner may have appreciably more than his minimum, whereas the opening 1NT bidder will never have lots of extras. Your RHO may easily have a 4333 zero-count. If he does, what do you think of declarer's chances in 1NT doubled? We suspect that four down is not an unreasonable expectation. That is a substantial penalty, and one you will miss if you pull partner's double to 2♥.

Irrespective of the notrump strength, you should pass partner's double of a 1NT opening bid whenever you have as much as an ace or a balanced hand of any strength. (The only exception is with a distributional hand when you expect to bid and make game yourself — and even then only when you are vulnerable and they are not). Of course, 1NT doubled will sometimes make. Sometimes, it will even make an overtrick. That's hardly a disaster though — it isn't game.

When your LHO has opened with 1NT and partner has doubled, there is a case for passing no matter what your hand is. Opener has 15-17 HCP and partner has 18+. How many are left for you and your RHO? Not many! Partner already knows you have a bad hand when he doubles. He does not need you to remove his double to tell him that. Much of the time, he will not need you to have much — perhaps even a well-positioned jack will be enough. Sometimes, he will be able to beat 1NT on his own. Just pass the double and you will start to collect some nice penalties.

Of course, there are always exceptions...

♠ 7 3   ♥ 10 8 7 5 3 2   ♦ 3   ♣ 8 6 4 3

LHO	Partner	RHO	You
1NT	dbl	pass	?

Your hand is likely to be completely useless unless hearts are trumps, so you should pull the double to 2♥. Not that you will always be right to do so. For openers, perhaps partner has seven or eight cashing diamond tricks against 1NT doubled. If he also has short hearts, then your bid will have turned a sizable plus score into a minus, perhaps a large one. However, partner will often have a strong balanced hand. Then the chances are that 1NT doubled will make and, who knows, you might even make 2♥ if the hands fit well.

Should you ever remove partner's double with a good hand?

If you have a strongish, distributional hand, with a reasonable expectation of making game, you can think about removing partner's double. This is particularly true when you are vulnerable and the opponents are not, since the penalty from 1NT doubled may not be enough to compensate for your game bonus. Typically, you will have a one-suited hand, so you can simply jump in your suit:

♠ 3　♥ K Q 10 7 6 5　♦ Q 4 3　♣ 5 4 2

LHO	Partner	RHO	You
1NT	dbl	pass	?

Jump to 3♥. Partner will usually raise your suit, but he may also choose to play in 3NT if his double was based on a solid minor suit, a few scattered high cards, and a heart shortage.

What happens if RHO runs?

♠ K 7 5　♥ Q 8 6 5　♦ Q J 9 5　♣ 4 3

LHO	Partner	RHO	You
1NT	dbl	2♦	?

Obviously, you want to defend 2♦ doubled. That is okay — a double from you is now for penalties. This is not a takeout double; as your side has already doubled the opponents for penalties, all subsequent doubles are for penalties too.

So, how do you get partner to bid a suit instead? Say your hand is something like:

♠ K Q 6 4　♥ K 9 6 4　♦ 4　♣ 10 9 6 5

Now you have to bid 3♦ — a cuebid of the opponents' suit. This says to partner, 'I have enough values for game and shortness in RHO's suit.' Effectively, it is a takeout double of diamonds.

✓ A double of a 1NT opening bid is for penalties.

✓ If you hold a balanced hand, then your double shows more than opener's maximum. Thus, if the opening bid shows 15-17 HCP, then you need 17+ to double. A double of a 12-14 1NT opening bid shows at least 15 HCP.

✓ You can shade the point-count requirement slightly if you have a good suit to lead. The better your suit, the fewer HCPs you need for a double.

✓ Doubles in fourth seat (after 1NT is followed by two passes) show at least as good a hand as a direct-seat double.

✓ Do not remove partner's double of a 1NT opening when you hold a balanced hand, whatever your strength.

✓ With a weak, distributional hand, you can remove the double, but even then you will not always be right to do so.

✓ You can consider removing the double with a good hand if you expect to make game, particularly at unfavorable vulnerability. Jumps to the three-level are natural and forcing to game.

✓ If your RHO runs from the double, a double by either of you is for penalties. A cuebid of the opponents' suit is like a takeout double — it shows the values for game and asks partner to bid his best suit (or to bid notrump with a good holding in the enemy's suit).

DOUBLING 1NT

NOW TRY THESE...

A. The opponents are playing a 15-17 1NT. What is your next bid on each of the following hands?

1 ♠ A J 9 7
    ♥ 4
    ♦ K 9 7 3
    ♣ A Q 6 4

LHO	Partner	RHO	You
		1NT	?

2 ♠ A Q 6
    ♥ A 6
    ♦ K 10 7 3
    ♣ Q J 6 5

LHO	Partner	RHO	You
		1NT	?

3 ♠ K Q J 10 5 4
    ♥ A
    ♦ 10 7 6 4
    ♣ A 8

LHO	Partner	RHO	You
		1NT	?

4 ♠ A J 3 2
    ♥ A 3
    ♦ K Q 7
    ♣ A J 7 6

LHO	Partner	RHO	You
		1NT	?

B. Your LHO opens a 15-17 point 1NT and your partner doubles. After RHO passes, what do you bid on each of these hands?

5 ♠ K J 10 8 6 4
    ♥ 3
    ♦ Q J 3
    ♣ 10 8 3

LHO	Partner	RHO	You
1NT	dbl	pass	?

6 ♠ 9 8 6 5
    ♥ J 7 3 2
    ♦ 9
    ♣ 10 8 3 2

LHO	Partner	RHO	You
1NT	dbl	pass	?

7 ♠ J 7 6
    ♥ K 5
    ♦ 9 7 6 5
    ♣ Q 8 6 3

LHO	Partner	RHO	You
1NT	dbl	pass	?

8 ♠ J 7 6
    ♥ K 5
    ♦ 9 7 6 5
    ♣ Q 8 6 3

LHO	Partner	RHO	You
1NT	dbl	2♣	?

9 ♠ J 7 6 4
    ♥ K 5 3 2
    ♦ K J 7 6
    ♣ 3

LHO	Partner	RHO	You
1NT	dbl	2♣	?

10 ♠ 9 7 4
    ♥ K Q 10 6 5
    ♦ 9
    ♣ J 8 6 3

LHO	Partner	RHO	You
1NT	dbl	2♦	?

ANSWERS

1   pass   You cannot overcall on a four-card suit, and you are not even close to being strong enough for a double.

2   pass   You still do not have enough for a double — you have only a 16-count and no playing strength. Indeed, if partner has almost nothing, you might even get to defend 2NT or 3NT if you pass now.

3   dbl   Despite having only 14 HCP, you fully expect 1NT doubled to go down after you lead the ♠K.

4   dbl   With 19 HCP the odds are somewhat in your favor. Even so, you will not always beat 1NT — partner will have next to nothing, and you are likely to give away a trick on the opening lead.

5   3♠   If you pass, it is quite possible that declarer will be able to score an ace and four or five tricks in one of your weak suits. You can surely make game though, with 4♠ being your most likely spot. Show your good hand and your six-card suit by jumping to 3♠.

6   pass   Your partner has 18+ HCP and LHO 15-17, so you do not have to remove the double to tell partner you have a weak hand — he can count, so he already knows that. Pass, and hope partner can cash seven diamond winners. If he cannot, then hope your ♥J is the help he needs to beat the contract. Sure, 1NT doubled will make sometimes, but that is hardly the end of the world and besides, if you bid, which of your four-card suits are you going to choose? There is no guarantee that you will find your best fit, so pass and hope.

7   pass   And expect to collect a large penalty. Your RHO must have a virtual bust.

8   dbl   This tells partner that you have some values and at least four clubs. Now he may be in a position to double if they run to another suit.

9   3♣   Cuebid the opponents' suit and ask partner to do something intelligent. You don't want to defend 2♣ doubled on this hand, and you can probably make a game somewhere.

10   2♥   You have no particular interest in defending 2♦ even if partner can double it, so ignore them and bid your own good suit. Since you would not bid at all on a weak hand (partner will, after all, get another turn to bid even if you pass), this shows some values, and partner can bid on with a heart fit or extra strength.

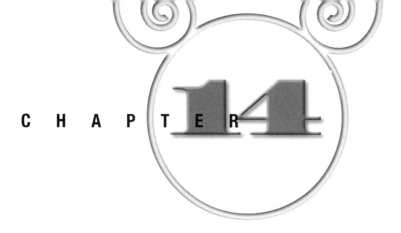

CONVENTIONAL DEFENSES TO 1NT

A thing that works beautifully in theory may fail utterly in practice. If this were not true, there would be fewer suicides at Monte Carlo.
Florence Irwin, Auction Highlights, *1913*.

We have seen that after a 1NT opening, since opener's hand is a known commodity, it is fairly easy for opener's partner to make the right decision about doubling an overcall. Thus we have emphasized that it is somewhat dangerous to overcall a 1NT opening. This is especially true of a strong notrump opening, since the chances that your side can make a game are very small once one opponent has so much strength. There are many players, therefore, who feel more comfortable overcalling a 1NT opening if they can offer partner a choice of two suits.

There are very many conventional ways to do this, all of which give up something (as does any convention — the difference here is that often you are giving up something you may not be able to afford to lose). It is up to you whether you choose to bid naturally over the opponents' 1NT opening or whether you decide to play one of the many conventional defenses available. When choosing a conventional method, be aware that some are designed primarily for use against a strong notrump while others are more suited to bidding over a weak notrump. Indeed, many serious partnerships play more than one defensive method, depending on the opponents' notrump range.

In this chapter, we offer a basic description of three popular defensive systems — Landy, Cappelletti, and DONT. We'll point out the strengths and weaknesses of each of these methods, but we're not going to recommend any particular one. We'll return to this point at the end of the chapter.

What is Landy?

This is one of the simplest conventional defenses to 1NT, but it is one that is easy both to remember and to understand. One reason is that there is only one artificial bid involved. The following overcalls show the suit you bid and say nothing about any other suit.

LHO	Partner	RHO	You
		1NT	2♦

shows diamonds, and

LHO	Partner	RHO	You
		1NT	2♥

shows hearts, and

LHO	Partner	RHO	You
		1NT	2♠

shows spades. There is only one artificial overcall when you play Landy:

LHO	Partner	RHO	You
		1NT	2♣

Playing Landy, this 2♣ overcall shows a hand with both majors. In Alvin Landy's original description of this method, 2♣ only promised at least 4-4 in the majors but we strongly recommend that you promise at least nine cards between the two suits. To see why having a single bid to show both majors can be useful, consider these two hands:

Partner	You
♠ K J 9 5	♠ A Q 8 4
♥ 3	♥ K J 8 7 4
♦ A 8 6 5 2	♦ K 4 3
♣ 10 7 6	♣ 4

Playing no conventional defense to 1NT, the auction is likely to go this way:

LHO	Partner	RHO	You
		1NT	2♥
all pass			

You can expect to make around 6-8 tricks in a heart contract. Now see how much better things proceed if you are playing Landy:

LHO	Partner	RHO	You
		1NT	2♣
pass	3♠	pass	4♠
all pass			

Your 2♣ bid shows at least 5-4 (either way around) in the majors. Partner has a reasonable hand and a good fit for one of your suits so he invites game by jumping to the three-level. With a little to spare for an overcall you are happy to accept the invitation. Most of the time you will make ten tricks in a spade contract. What a difference!

What happens next?

After a Landy 2♣ overcall, there is no standard set of responses by the overcaller's partner. However, one significant improvement on how the system was originally played is the introduction of 2♦ as a kind of relay response. Consider these two hands:

	Partner		You
♠	J 3	♠	K Q 10 8 4
♥	Q 4	♥	K J 9 2
♦	K 8 6 2	♦	9 7 5
♣	J 9 7 5 3	♣	A

Assuming you decided to come in over 1NT, which contract would you prefer (and expect) to reach? Obviously, 2♠ is your best spot. However, after your Landy 2♣ overcall showing both majors, you might think that your partner will simply choose his better major — in this case, hearts. Not so...

LHO	Partner	RHO	You
		1NT	2♣
pass	2♦	pass	2♠
all pass			

Partner's 2♦ response says nothing about diamonds. It simply says, 'I have no preference between the majors. You pick one.'

Knowing that your partner has equal length in the majors (perhaps a doubleton, as here, but perhaps three- or even four-card support for both majors), it is not difficult to select spades.

So what's wrong with Landy?

Nothing at all, in many ways. It's simple to remember, and works well as far as it goes. However, it doesn't go very far, because it only works when you have the majors. If you have spades and diamonds, for instance, all you can do is overcall spades and hope that partner doesn't have a big diamond fit. Because of this, many of today's tournament players have abandoned Landy in favor of conventions that allow them to describe a wider range of two-suited hands.

How strong should you be to overcall with a two-suited hand?

The strength requirements for a two-suited overcall are not that different to those needed for a natural bid as discussed in Chapter 12. Vulnerability and the strength of the 1NT opening are still factors when overcalling with a two-suited bid, but playing strength is more important than high-card points. Consider these two hands:

♠ K J 10 7 5   ♥ K Q J 4   ♦ 6   ♣ J 10 5

♠ Q 7 6 4 3   ♥ K 6 5 3   ♦ A Q   ♣ K 5

BY THE WAY

You can also use all these conventions in the balancing seat, and as usual, we don't advise bidding over 1NT on a hand where you wouldn't bid in the direct chair.

Playing a convention that enables you to show both majors, such as Landy, you might decide to overcall 2♣ over a 1NT opening on either of these hands, but which do you think is the better hand? The first has 11 HCP and the second 14, but the concentration of honors in the long suits and the good intermediate cards give the first hand much more playing strength.

There is no real upper limit for a two-suited overcall. However, if your hand is stronger than opener's maximum, you will normally start with a penalty double unless your distribution is particularly wild.

What is Cappelletti?

This is easily the most popular defense to 1NT throughout North America. As your circle of bridge-playing friends grows, you are likely to find partners who cannot survive without it and you will certainly meet plenty of opponents playing it. You therefore need to know at least something about how it works, if only so that you know what is going on when your opponents use it against you.

The basic structure is as follows:

LHO	Partner	RHO	You
		1NT	?
dbl		*penalties*	
2♣		*a single-suited hand, suit unknown —*	
		partner normally bids 2♦ (artificial) to	
		discover the suit.	
2♦		*both majors*	
2♥		*hearts and a minor*	
2♠		*spades and a minor*	

A double is for penalties while most of the two-level overcalls show a two-suited hand. The distinguishing feature of the Cappelletti defense to 1NT is the 2♣ overcall, which is used to show any single-suited hand that is not good enough to double. This is how it works:

♠ K Q 10 8 6 5   ♥ 3   ♦ A 6 5   ♣ J 5 4

LHO	Partner	RHO	You
		1NT	2♣
pass	2♦	pass	2♠
all pass			

Your 2♣ overcall showed a single-suited hand, and partner's 2♦ asked you to bid your suit. You bid 2♠, and that ended the auction.

What else can happen when you bid 2♣?

If you have diamonds, you simply pass partner's forced 2♦ bid; with hearts or clubs, you bid them over 2♦ just as you did your spades in this example. So far so good — but what if partner has a good hand? Suppose he has

♠ J 5 2   ♥ J 7   ♦ K Q 7 4 2   ♣ A 6 3

LHO	Partner	RHO	You
		1NT	2♣
pass	2♦	pass	2♠

With 11 HCP, a ruffing value and a three-card fit, he would like to invite you to bid game if you have a good overcall. And he can — partner is allowed to raise your suit with some values and fit, so on this hand he bids 3♠.

♠ J 5 2   ♥ A 7 4   ♦ K 10 4   ♣ A J 6 3

LHO	Partner	RHO	You
		1NT	2♣
pass	?		

Here he is a little stronger, and his 12 points are enough that he wants to force to game. On this type of hand, he simply refuses to bid 2♦ over 2♣ in case you have diamonds and pass! Instead, he either bids his own suit, or if he doesn't have a good five-card suit, as here, he bids 2NT. Once partner has bypassed 2♦, the auction proceeds naturally until a game is reached.

BY THE WAY

This conventional defense to 1NT is called Cappelletti in most of North America, although in parts of the USA and Canada it is also known as Hamilton, and players in the UK are familiar with it as Pottage.

What about the other two-bids?

The 2♦ overcall works just like Landy, except that you no longer have room for the neat relay that asks the overcaller to bid his better major — this time, you're going have to guess which to bid as responder, and you won't always be right.

In order for the 2♥ and 2♠ overcalls to work well, you must have five cards in the major suit you are bidding, so partner can pass with a bad hand. Many pairs allow the second (minor) suit to be only four cards long, but since you will be at the three-level if you do play in it, it would certainly be preferable to have five of them.

♠ J   ♥ 9 7 4 2   ♦ K 10 4 2   ♣ Q J 6 3

LHO	Partner	RHO	You
1NT	2♠	pass	?

Here you have an easy decision — bid 2NT and ask partner to bid his minor. Then you pass. But this example is more difficult:

♠ J 6   ♥ 9 7 4 2   ♦ K 10 4   ♣ Q J 6 3

LHO	Partner	RHO	You
1NT	2♠	pass	?

This is why you need to be confident that partner has five spades. Unless he guarantees a five-card minor, you had better pass. At least you'll have seven trumps between you here, and no one's doubled — yet. If you bid 2NT knowing partner's minor may only be four cards long, you take your life in your hands. Yes, he might bid 3♣ next, but if your luck is running that well you should be at the race track. The odds are he will bid diamonds, and you may well be in a seven-card fit at the three-level. RHO could be licking his chops, just waiting to double.

So what's wrong with Cappelletti?

Cappelletti has gained wide popularity because it allows you to bid on quite a large number of hands with a fair degree of safety, it still lets you double 1NT for penalties, and it's easy to remember. It is also quite playable against either a strong or a weak notrump opening. So is it the answer to all your problems?

Possibly, but only provided that the opponents are kind enough to pass throughout after opening 1NT. In the real world they are less likely to do so. The 2♣ bid that allows you to introduce all your one-suiters, as well as getting in there on two-suiters, is the Achilles heel of the convention. Not only have you lost much of the preemptive advantage that overcalling directly (especially in a major) produces but you may also never discover what partner's suit actually is. Consider this auction:

♠ J 5 ♥ Q 8 7 5 4 ♦ K 8 6 ♣ 7 3 2

LHO	Partner	RHO	You
1NT	2♣	2NT	pass
	3♣	pass	pass
?			

Your partner's 2♣ overcall shows an undefined one-suited hand but RHO intervenes with a Lebensohl 2NT bid. The most likely explanation for the auction is that your partner has spades. Would you want to compete to the three-level with this hand facing a natural 2♠ overcall? Of course not. But actually, this is partner's hand:

♠ A Q 5 ♥ A J 10 9 6 3 ♦ Q 4 ♣ 9 4

He doesn't have spades at all; instead your side has an excellent play for 4♥! Yet you couldn't bid, and he certainly wasn't going to come in at the three-level. The situation would have been rather different if partner had overcalled with a natural 2♥ bid, though, wouldn't it? You might well think about jumping straight to 4♥ and you certainly don't want to defend 3♣ with your 6-5 heart fit.

What is DONT?

DONT is an acronym for 'Disturb Opponent's NoTrump', and was invented by US expert Marty Bergen. Its philosophy is that the opponents should rarely be allowed to play in 1NT, unless you or your partner both have flat hands. The theory is that your side is likely to have an eight-card fit, and if you can find it, the Law of Total Tricks (see Chapter 24) says you will be safe at the two-level. If the opponents open a strong notrump, DONT players tend to take the attitude that your side does not have a game, and that in fact, it probably isn't even your hand. In its original and simplest form, then, DONT is an obstructive system, designed to get in the opponents' way.

Here's how it basically works:

LHO	Partner	RHO	You
		1NT	?
dbl	single-suited hand (not spades)		
2♣	clubs and a higher-ranking suit		
2♦	diamonds and a major		
2♥	hearts and spades		
2♠	spades (six-card suit)		
2NT	both minors (optional)		

We recommend that, until you have a lot of experience with this convention, you play that the overcaller promises at least five cards in the suit he bids, and at least one other higher-ranking four-card suit.

How do you respond to a DONT overcall?

Bidding opposite a 2♠ overcall is straightforward; it is made on hand that looks like a good Weak Two-bid, something like

♠ K Q 10 9 8 5 ♥ A 6 3 ♦ 7 5 ♣ 6 4

Responder knows exactly what overcaller's hand is, and can bid accordingly.

The 2♥ bid, which shows both majors, is similar to a Landy 2♣ or the Cappelletti 2♦. The difference is that you may have 5-4 shape, and your five-card suit could be either hearts or spades. This makes it hard always to land in the right spot — even if you are lucky enough to find partner with three cards in each major.

With both minors you can simply bid 2♣, or optionally use a 2NT overcall. If 2NT is your choice, you should be a least 5-5, since you are committing your side to the three-level, just as you are when you use the Unusual Notrump.

Playing DONT, the double of 1NT shows a single-suited hand just as the Cappelletti 2♣ overcall does. In DONT, however, your six-card suit is usually hearts or a minor — if it is spades, you can deal with that hand by bidding 2♠ instead of doubling. (Since you could have overcalled 2♠, doubling first then later bidding spades shows a fairly strong hand.) The double forces partner to bid 2♣ (just as the Cappelletti 2♣ forces a 2♦ response), and overcaller now passes with clubs, or bids his suit. Remember, the rationale of this whole system is that it is probably not your hand — the assumption is that you don't need constructive bidding methods, you just want to get the opponents out of 1NT without incurring too much risk yourself.

Where it gets really tricky is when the overcall is 2♣ or 2♦. Remember, what you're trying to do here is find your eight-card fit, if you can, and not get doubled (both these objectives are equally important); the premise as always is that it is probably not your hand. As responder, you have to decide whether to pass the overcall, or try to find partner's other suit in the hope that it will play better. Sometimes your decision will be easy:

♠ Q 8 6 4 ♥ Q 8 6 4 ♦ Q 8 6 4 ♣ 4

LHO	Partner	RHO	You
1NT	2♣	pass	?

Whatever partner's second suit is, you want to play in it. (Note that if you have a good major suit of your own, you are allowed to bid it now.) Here, however, you bid 2♦, which implies diamonds but doesn't necessarily promise good ones; it simply says you don't want to play in clubs. If partner doesn't have diamonds he will bid his other suit, and you will pass. Mission accomplished.

But it isn't always like that:

♠ Q 8 ♥ Q 8 6 4 ♦ Q 8 4 3 2 ♣ 6 4

LHO	Partner	RHO	You
1NT	2♣	pass	?

Should you pass 2♣ or bid 2♦ again? Bidding will work very well if partner has a red suit, but if his second suit is spades, you're going to wish that you had passed 2♣. If partner' second suit is hearts or diamonds, 2♣ surely will not be your best spot. So what do you do? Again, recall that you're just trying to get them out of 1NT, and reaching a making partscore yourself is a secondary objective. The best plan here is probably to pass until you get doubled, then run like a rabbit.

As you can see when you play DONT, it involves a lot of judgment, which is the expert term for guessing. Of course, the experts do tend to guess right more often than most of us, which is perhaps why they are experts!

Are there any other options if you don't like these defenses?

There sure are — how much time do you have? We're not going to get into any others, since those we've described are far and away the most popular. However, you will come across dozens of conventions with names like Brozel, CRASH, Suction, Astro, Aspro, and so forth, all of which have their adherents. They all involve methods of overcalling two-suited hands over 1NT. Some of them, like DONT, give up the ability to make a penalty double in order either to show all the possible two-suiters, or to be able to show single-suited hands more conveniently. We do not recommend giving up the penalty double, especially against the weak notrump, but other than that we take no position. By all means, research the alternatives, and if you find something to your liking, play it — it will probably be as good as anything else!

With so many conventional methods available, selecting the right one(s) for your partnership is not easy. Adding new conventions to your armory is exciting but also comes with a warning. You need to be confident that you will both remember them when they come up. A new convention may come up not today or tomorrow, but a month or two after you agree to play it. Are you sure that neither of you will forget the new toy? It is also important that you have discussed all the important sequences that are likely to arise.

With any convention, you will have to give up a natural bid in order to adopt an artificial one. Always consider whether the value of that natural bid is worth the advantage you gain from the artificial bid. We think it is worth giving up a natural overall in clubs in order to be able to show a hand with both majors, but we would not give up penalty doubles. If we are to be objective here, we should point out that some people disagree with this view. It is a decision that, eventually, you and your partner will have to make for yourselves.

Summary

✓ Avoid systems that mean giving up penalty doubles of 1NT.

✓ Stick with a system that you are confident you will remember.

✓ Before adding a convention to your system, consider the value of the natural bid that you must give up in exchange.

✓ Knowing what the first bid in the convention means is not enough. Before starting to play a convention, discuss responder's options and consider how you will handle further bidding by the opponents.

CONVENTIONAL DEFENSES TO 1NT

NOW TRY THESE...

The 1NT opening shows 15-17 HCP; in Problems 1-4 you are playing Landy, in Problems 5-8, Cappelletti, and Problems 9-12, DONT.

1
- ♠ A J 9 7
- ♥ K Q 8 7 3
- ♦ 6
- ♣ Q 6 4

LHO	Partner	RHO	You
		1NT	?

2
- ♠ Q 8 6 3
- ♥ A 6
- ♦ 10 7
- ♣ A Q J 6 5

LHO	Partner	RHO	You
		1NT	?

3
- ♠ K Q J 10 5 4
- ♥ J 8 6 4
- ♦ 4
- ♣ A 8

LHO	Partner	RHO	You
		1NT	?

4
- ♠ A 10 7
- ♥ K 10 3
- ♦ 7 3
- ♣ K 6 4 3 2

LHO	Partner	RHO	You
1NT	2♣	pass	?

5
- ♠ A J 9 7
- ♥ K Q 8 7 3
- ♦ 6
- ♣ Q 6 4

LHO	Partner	RHO	You
		1NT	?

6
- ♠ Q 8 6 3
- ♥ A 6
- ♦ 10 7
- ♣ A Q J 6 5

LHO	Partner	RHO	You
		1NT	?

7
- ♠ K Q J 10 5 4
- ♥ J 8 6 4
- ♦ 4
- ♣ A 8

LHO	Partner	RHO	You
		1NT	?

8
- ♠ A 10 7
- ♥ K 10 3
- ♦ 7 3
- ♣ K 6 4 3 2

LHO	Partner	RHO	You
1NT	2♣	pass	?

9
- ♠ A J 9 7
- ♥ K Q 8 7 3
- ♦ 6
- ♣ Q 6 4

LHO	Partner	RHO	You
		1NT	?

10
- ♠ Q 8 6 3
- ♥ A 6
- ♦ 10 7
- ♣ A Q J 6 5

LHO	Partner	RHO	You
		1NT	?

11
- ♠ K Q J 10 5 4
- ♥ J 8 6 4
- ♦ 4
- ♣ A 8

LHO	Partner	RHO	You
		1NT	?

12
- ♠ A 10 7
- ♥ K 10 3
- ♦ 7 3
- ♣ K 6 4 3 2

LHO	Partner	RHO	You
1NT	2♣	pass	?

ANSWERS

1 2♣ You have 5-4 in the majors. Perfect!

2 pass You no longer have the option of making a natural 2♣ overcall. That is the price you must pay for being able to show both majors with a single bid.

3 2♠ This is not a hand on which to show 'both majors'. If partner has a singleton spade and two or three hearts, he will give preference to hearts, but spades will still be a much better spot. Do not use Landy when one of your suits is so much stronger than the other — you do not want partner to choose his longer or better major. You already know which suit you want to play in.

4 2♦ You want partner to bid his better major, and you plan to raise it to the three-level, inviting him to bid game.

5 2♦ You have 5-4 in the majors. Perfect!

6 pass You cannot bid 2♠, showing spades and a minor, since you need to have five spades for that bid. You could bid 2♣, intending to rebid 3♣ over partner's 2♦ bid, but the three-level is a touch high for this hand.

7 2♣ Treat this as a single-suiter, since your spades are much better and longer than your hearts. You have to hope that LHO doesn't get into the auction, since bidding 3♠ later on is not appealing.

8 3♣ You are too good just to bid 2♦, which it is all too likely partner will pass. If he has a major suit, you can raise to game; if he bids 3♦, you will try 3NT.

9 2♥ You have 5-4 in the majors. Perfect!

10 2♣ This shows clubs and a higher suit. If partner is weak and passes with a doubleton club for fear of not finding a better fit elsewhere, you will be fine.

11 dbl This hand is just too good to overcall 2♠, which some would do without the ♣A. Again, this hand should not be treated as a major two-suiter, since the spades are much better and longer than the hearts.

12 3♣ Invitational. If partner does have at least nine cards in two suits, 3NT is probably not the right place to play this hand. However, 5♣ is not out of the question, and 4♣ would not be an outrageous bid here.

CHAPTER 15

TAKEOUT DOUBLES OF WEAK TWO-BIDS

♥ The preemptive bidder does atrocious team-work. He says to his partner, 'Do not interfere with me, I don't care one iota what you have. I'm going to play this hand, whether it combines well with yours, or not.' *Florence Irwin,* **Auction Highlights,** *1913.*

Let's start by recapping the requirements for a takeout double at the one-level:

1. *Opening bid strength*
2. *Support for all the unbid suits*
3. *Shortness in the opener's suit*

You will also recall that you start with a takeout double on very strong hands even though they do not necessarily fit the requirements of (2) and (3) above.

The same constraints also affect takeout doubles at higher levels, except that you must be even more disciplined. Marginal hands on which you might risk a one-level takeout double will have to be passed when your RHO preempts. For example:

♠ K4 ♥ KJ5 ♦ Q8753 ♣ QJ4

BY THE WAY

All of the things you learned about takeout doubles earlier in this book still apply when the bidding is opened above the one-level. Remember, though, that you are committing your side to playing at a higher level, even if your partner has very little.

If your RHO opened with a 1♠ bid, you might chance a takeout double (although you would prefer to have four hearts). Sometimes it will not work out, but you will probably not get too badly burned. If instead RHO has opened with a weak 2♠ bid, it might still turn out to be right to double, but doing so is just too dangerous.

Why, you might wonder, is it more dangerous to come in when RHO has made a bid showing 6-10 HCP than when he has announced 12-19? There are two primary reasons: it is easier for opener's partner to double you, and the auction is more difficult for your partner.

Why is it easy for opener's partner to double you?

Let's consider LHO's problem when you make a takeout double of 1♠. The wide range of an opening 1♠ bid will often leave him uncertain how to proceed. For a start, he may not be sure which side owns the majority of the high cards. Even if he has a good hand, it may not be clear that he should seek a low-level penalty in exchange for a likely game, or perhaps a slam. Bear in mind that when opener bids 1♠, he often holds a second suit, perhaps one for which his partner has a good fit. This all means that although your takeout double of 1♠ has brought your side into an auction in which you are heavily outgunned, the opponents will frequently not realize that they should be penalizing you until it is far too late for them to do so.

None of these factors come into play after a Weak Two-bid. Responder knows opener's range within a very narrow margin. He also knows that his partner has a good six-card suit and probably no other four-card suit. As a result, LHO will often know immediately that you are out of your depth. Look at this auction:

LHO	Partner	RHO	You
		1♠	dbl
?			

This is your LHO's hand:

♠ 9 ♥ Q 10 8 6 4 ♦ K J 5 ♣ A K 7 5

LHO knows that his partner has 12-19 HCP and at least five spades. Opener may also have four or five hearts, or perhaps five clubs. He may have four diamonds, or none. If he is close to a maximum with 5-5 in the black suits and perhaps three hearts too, will it be best to defend 2♦ doubled or play a slam in clubs? Who knows?

It is too early for LHO to commit to defending because too little is known about opener's hand. (Sure, he can redouble, but the chances are that your partner will bid 2♦. When that is passed back to LHO, he will be no better placed.) Compare that with this auction:

LHO	Partner	RHO	You
		2♠	dbl
?			

This is now your LHO's hand:

♠ 9 ♥ A 10 8 6 4 ♦ A Q 6 ♣ A K 7 5

Although LHO has an extra 4 points, opener now has only 6-10, instead of 12-19. Opener also has a good six-card spade suit but probably no other four-card suit, and certainly not four hearts. Do you think that your LHO will choose to defend a doubled contract at the three-level or bid to a contract of his own?

It is not even close, is it? He will redouble and choose to defend every day of the week, and on at least seven of those he will be right. There is no guarantee that his side can make anything. The prospect of your side playing in 3♣, 3♦ or 3♥, doubled of course, is frightening. The chances are that the penalty will be at least 800.

There is another reason why doubles of Weak Two opening bids should be played as showing sound values with shape...

Why is it more difficult for your partner?

You need to think about the problems a takeout double of a Weak Two might create for your poor partner.

As we have seen, when you make a takeout double at the one-level, he has a wide range of bids available to show a poor hand, an invitational hand or a game-going hand. When you make a takeout double of a Weak Two (particularly 2♠), he probably has to start bidding at the three-level, meaning that he has far fewer options.

When he has a good hand, 3NT will frequently be the best contract. He must therefore find a way to describe his hand and to stop in time, without having very much room to do so.

How do you respond to a takeout double of a Weak Two?

Does it seem impossible? It isn't easy, but help is at hand. You will recall that in Chapter 11, we discussed the Lebensohl convention. At that time, we used it to show hands of various strength after RHO had intervened over your partner's 1NT overcall. Well, a similar convention is also very useful when responding to partner's takeout double of a Weak Two opening.

♠ 8 6 ♥ J 8 6 5 3 ♦ J 10 7 5 ♣ 7 4

LHO	Partner	RHO	You
2♠	dbl	pass	?

Give your partner a minimum double, say 13-16 points, with short spades. Where do you want to play the hand? Right — you want to play in hearts at as low a level as you can manage, which in this case is going to be 3♥. At the same time, when you bid 3♥, you do not want partner to think about going to game just because he has 15-16 points rather than 13-14, do you? So, you bid 3♥, yes? Before deciding, consider what you would do with this hand:

♠ 8 6   ♥ K Q 8 6 5   ♦ Q 10 7 5   ♣ 7 4

LHO	Partner	RHO	You
2♠	dbl	pass	?

This time, you have quite a good hand. But it is not quite good enough to undertake game in hearts opposite a 13-14 count. However, if partner has just a little more than a minimum takeout double, say 15-16 points with four hearts, then you want to play in 4♥.

The problem is that there is very little room to maneuver. You want to play both of these hands in hearts, and you have only one way to tell partner that — by bidding 3♥. Or do you?

You will remember from our previous discussion of Lebensohl, that a bid of 2NT can be used as a relay, asking your partner to bid 3♣. So in this auction too, with a weak hand (0-8 points) you start by bidding 2NT, the Lebensohl relay. There are various ways in which the auction might continue.

When your hand is

♠ 8 5   ♥ 9 6   ♦ 9 7 6 4   ♣ Q 9 8 7 5

you clearly want to play in clubs at the lowest possible level. That's easy enough to achieve:

LHO	Partner	RHO	You
2♠	dbl	pass	2NT
pass	3♣	all pass	

You bid 2NT (Lebensohl), and pass once partner has obediently responded 3♣ as you asked him to.

When you hold a red suit, you bid it at your second turn. Thus:

♠ J 9 7   ♥ Q 9 6   ♦ J 8 7 5 3   ♣ 4 3

LHO	Partner	RHO	You
2♠	dbl	pass	2NT
pass	3♣	pass	3♦
all pass			

Since you reached 3♦ via the 2NT Lebensohl relay, partner will know that you have a weak hand, and he will pass 3♦. Similarly, with the first hand that we saw above:

♠ 8 6　♥ J 8 6 5 3　♦ J 10 7 5　♣ 7 4

LHO	Partner	RHO	You
2♠	dbl	pass	2NT
pass	3♣	pass	3♥
all pass			

The operation is a success — the patient is still alive. You have reached 3♥ and partner knows not to raise.

When you actually have an invitational hand (9-11 points), such as the one we saw earlier, you show this by bidding your suit directly over partner's takeout double, without using the Lebensohl 2NT relay. Thus:

♠ 8 6　♥ K Q 8 6 5　♦ Q 10 7 5　♣ 7 4

LHO	Partner	RHO	You
2♠	dbl	pass	3♥

If partner has a minimum hand for his original double, then he will decline the invitation by passing 3♥. With a little extra, he will accept and go to game.

In our previous discussion of Lebensohl, we also talked about the various ways of bidding stronger, game-forcing hands (12+ points). While much of the time when you use a Lebensohl 2NT you will have a weak hand, if you bid strongly on the next round you are now showing a much stronger hand. Therefore, by using a cuebid of the opener's suit and 3NT, either in conjunction with the 2NT Lebensohl relay or by bidding directly over the double, you have four strong sequences. These can be used to differentiate between hands with four cards in the unbid major and those without, and those with or without a stopper in the opener's suit. With five cards in the unbid major and a good hand you can just bid game, since partner has promised at least three of the suit.

These auctions are complicated, and for a full summary of how everything works, you should refer back to Chapter 11, but here are a couple of examples of how the game-forcing Lebensohl sequences work after a Weak Two opening:

♠ K Q 3　♥ J 5　♦ K J 4 3　♣ Q J 9 7

LHO	Partner	RHO	You
2♠	dbl	pass	2NT
pass	3♣	pass	3NT
all pass			

Do you remember the saying we gave you in Chapter 11 — 'Slow Shows Stopper'? That still applies when the opponents have opened with a Weak Two bid. By making a game-forcing bid (3NT or a cuebid) after using the 2NT Lebensohl relay, you show a stopper in the opponent's suit. Bidding 3NT immediately, without using Lebensohl, denies four cards in the unbid major.

♠ A J 4 3 ♥ 7 3 ♦ K Q 8 5 ♣ K 5 4

LHO	Partner	RHO	You
2♥	dbl	pass	3♥

This time, you have no stopper in the opponents' suit, but you do have four cards in the unbid major. You show your four-card spade suit by cue bidding the opener's suit, and by doing so directly (without using the 2NT Lebensohl relay) you also deny a heart stopper.

If there are two unbid majors, a cuebid shows four cards in at least one. Thus:

♠ Q 10 7 6 ♥ 7 4 ♦ A J 9 ♣ A Q 8 5

LHO	Partner	RHO	You
2♦	dbl	pass	2NT
pass	3♣	pass	3♦

By cuebidding, you show at least one four-card major. Before doing that, you used the 2NT Lebensohl relay so partner knows that you have a diamond stopper.

Summary

✓ Apply the same principles as you would to making a takeout double at the one-level, but be aware that you must not enter the auction at such a high level on a less than perfect hand.

✓ When responding to a takeout double of a Weak Two, use 2NT as a Lebensohl relay to 3♣ (followed by bidding your own suit if it is not clubs) on weak hands (0-8 points), and bid your suit directly at the three-level with invitational values (9-11 points).

✓ With a game-going hand, cuebid opener's suit to show four cards in an unbid major (and 3NT to deny) — just bid game with five cards in the unbid major. Using the 2NT relay before bidding 3NT or making a cuebid shows a stopper in the opener's suit.

TAKEOUT DOUBLES OF WEAK TWO-BIDS

NOW TRY THESE...

What is your next bid on each of the following hands?

1
- ♠ A J 9
- ♥ 8 3
- ♦ K 10 6
- ♣ Q J 6 5 4

LHO	Partner	RHO	You
		2♥	?

2
- ♠ A Q 8 6
- ♥ 6
- ♦ K 10 7 3
- ♣ K 9 7 6

LHO	Partner	RHO	You
		2♥	?

3
- ♠ A K 5 4
- ♥ 4
- ♦ A Q J 8
- ♣ A J 10 8

LHO	Partner	RHO	You
		2♥	?

4
- ♠ 9 4
- ♥ 8 3
- ♦ K 10 8 6 3
- ♣ Q 8 6 4

LHO	Partner	RHO	You
2♠	dbl	pass	?

5
- ♠ 8 6
- ♥ J 6
- ♦ K 10 3
- ♣ A J 9 6 5 4

LHO	Partner	RHO	You
2♠	dbl	pass	?

6
- ♠ 5 4
- ♥ K Q 8 4
- ♦ A J 8
- ♣ A J 10 8

LHO	Partner	RHO	You
2♠	dbl	pass	?

7
- ♠ A J 10
- ♥ K 6 3
- ♦ K Q 8 7
- ♣ J 7 6

LHO	Partner	RHO	You
2♠	dbl	pass	?

8
- ♠ A J 10
- ♥ K Q 8 7 4
- ♦ K 6
- ♣ J 7 6

LHO	Partner	RHO	You
2♠	dbl	pass	?

ANSWERS

1   pass   You might have risked a takeout double of 1♥, but coming in at a higher level on this very marginal hand is asking for trouble.

2   dbl   You have perfect takeout double shape as well as sound, although minimum, values. Do not allow the 'fear factor' to keep you out when you have a legitimate takeout double. Sure, you will get into trouble sometimes. All we can say is that you can't be perfect over preempts!

3   dbl   There is no upper limit for a takeout double. There is no guarantee that you will go plus even with this huge hand, but you can hardly pass, can you?

4   2NT   You do not want to invite game, so start with a Lebensohl 2NT. When partner responds 3♣, convert to 3♦ and partner will know to pass.

5   3♣   If partner has some extras, you want to play in game. By bidding 3♣ without using the Lebensohl 2NT relay, partner will know you have an invitational hand.

6   3♠   You want to play in game, but should it be 3NT, 4♥, or perhaps even five of a minor? You cannot tell, so you cuebid the opener's suit (to show four cards in the other major), and since you do so without going via the Lebensohl 2NT, you deny a spade stopper. (Remember — Slow Shows Stopper.)

7   2NT   The chances are that 3NT is where you want to play. You do not have four hearts, so you intend to rebid 3NT (rather than cuebidding 3♠) at your second turn. Remember though, that if you bid 3NT directly over partner's double that would also deny a spade stopper. Slow Shows Stopper — start with 2NT and then rebid 3NT over partner's 3♣.

8   4♥   Partner has promised at least three hearts, so this time you know where you want to play the hand.

C H A P T E R 16

OVERCALLING WEAK TWO-BIDS

♥ In a former book, I described the frequent danger and the absolute futility of preemptive bids. They do not preempt. If the adversary has a better hand than you, he will win the contract anyhow.
Florence Irwin, Auction Highlights, *1913.*

It may seem that coming in with an overcall over a Weak Two is not that different from bidding over a one-level opening. In some respects, that is true, but you are much more exposed after a preemptive opening bid on your right. Remember that your LHO knows his partner's hand within fairly well-defined parameters when he has opened with a preempt. The reasons for overcalling are also very different.

BY THE WAY

LHO will have no problem making a penalty double when you make a poor overcall of a Weak Two opening bid.

Why is overcalling a Weak Two more dangerous?

♠ A J 10 7 5 ♥ 8 6 ♦ K 7 6 5 ♣ Q 4

If RHO opened 1♥, it would be fairly normal to overcall 1♠ with this collection. The major benefit of a 1♠ overcall is that your side may be able to compete for the partscore, or you may be able to push the opponents too high if partner has some kind of fit. You would also prefer a spade lead if your LHO becomes declarer, perhaps in a notrump contract. It is unlikely that the 1♠ overcall will be necessary if your side has a game — partner will need a pretty good hand opposite this, and the chances are that he will be able to bid himself if you pass.

What is the downside to a 1♠ overcall? Yes, partner might bid too much. You are not really worried about being doubled in 1♠, though. Say your LHO holds this hand:

♠ K Q 8 3 ♥ 5 ♦ A J 9 ♣ A K 6 3 2

LHO	Partner	RHO	You
		1♥	1♠
?			

Do you think he will choose to defend 1♠ doubled? For all he knows, opener may have an 18-19 count, perhaps with a four-card club fit. A slam in clubs or notrump, or even diamonds, could easily be cold. He can be virtually certain of making at least game. He expects to defeat 1♠ by two or three tricks perhaps but, depending on the vulnerability, electing to defend 1♠ doubled could be disastrous. Even +500 will look rather sick if he could have had +920 in six clubs. The correct action for LHO is to ignore your 1♠ overcall and bid 2♣, the bid he would have made if you had passed.

Now let's give LHO the same hand but change the auction slightly.

♠ K Q 8 3 ♥ 5 ♦ A J 9 ♣ A K 6 3 2

LHO	Partner	RHO	You
		2♥	2♠
?			

How do you think LHO will assess his prospects this time?

Typically, opener will have something like a 1-6-3-3 hand with ♥AKxxxx or perhaps ♥AQxxxx and a minor-suit queen. He might have a doubleton spade, or even three of them. Can LHO be certain that his side will make game? No — far from it. If opener's shape is 2-6-3-2, they do not even have an eight-card fit anywhere. Game is unlikely on the combined points if opener has his minimum six.

Do you think LHO will expect to beat 2♠? For sure — it rates to go down at least two, and on a good day, it will go down three and possibly even four. The defense might well score two clubs and a club ruff, two top hearts, two diamond tricks and two trump tricks. Most of the time, defending 2♠ doubled will be their best spot.

What's more, LHO does not even need any help from opener in the bidding. A double of your overcall after opener has preempted is for penalties, and not a negative double. LHO will simply double 2♠ and that will, in all likelihood, end the auction.

Note the difference:

LHO	Partner	RHO	You
		1♥	1♠
dbl			

This is a negative double — it is for takeout.

LHO	Partner	RHO	You
		2♥	2♠
dbl			

This is a penalty double. It says that LHO expects to beat 2♠. Negative doubles apply only after partner has opened with one of a suit and there has been an overcall on your right. After a preemptive opening (a Weak Two or higher) doubles of overcalls are for penalties.

To come in with an overcall over a Weak Two, then, you need both a fairly good suit and a reasonable expectation that the hand belongs to your side — opening bid values. Even when you have a good hand, it will sometimes be wrong to bid — partner may have nothing and you will go for a large penalty when the opponents could not even make game. However, you can't afford to pass strong hands and allow the Weak Two bidder to buy the contract cheaply. The following hand is a reasonable overcall of a weak 2♥ bid.

♠ A Q J 10 6　♥ A 4　♦ K 10 7 4　♣ 7 4

Your suit is sufficiently robust to make it unlikely that LHO has a really strong holding in it. You have enough high-card strength to expect that your side can make game if your partner has a fair share of the missing HCP. (You have 14 HCP and RHO has an average of about 7, which leaves 19 to share between partner and LHO.) Overcall 2♠.

♠ A J 4　♥ 9 7　♦ A Q 10 7 5 4　♣ A 4

When making a three-level overcall in a minor, your objectives are twofold. Firstly, to buy the contract in a making partscore rather than defending a low-level contract that might also make. Secondly, to try to get to game yourself. If game is on for your side, it will probably be in notrump. You need partner to value stoppers in the opponent's suit and fitting cards in yours. This hand is strong enough that you will be able to make game if partner has a smattering of high cards provided they are well placed. Overcall 3♦.

How do you respond to an overcall of a Weak Two?

When responding to a one-level overcall, you have plenty of room to show your hand — you can make a defensive raise of partner's suit, show an invitational raise, bid a suit of your own, or make a limited bid in notrump.

When your partner's overcall is at the two- or three-level, you have very little room for anything. This is a second reason why an overcall of a Weak Two must show a decent hand — responder must be able to tell right away whether your side is just competing for the partscore, close to bidding a game, or clearly in the game zone. There is no room for delicate maneuvering.

When partner overcalls in a major, you will usually have three options — to make an invitational raise, to introduce a good suit of your own, or to bid notrump.

♠ K J 4　♥ 9 6 5　♦ K J 6 5 4　♣ Q 3

LHO	Partner	RHO	You
2♥	2♠	pass	?

Opposite a wide-range one-level overcall, this hand would be below the range for a cuebid raise. Opposite a two-level overcall, with a much higher lower limit, you have a clear game try. Cuebid 3♥ to show an invitational spade raise.

♠ J 6　♥ Q 7　♦ A K J 7 6 4　♣ K 5 3

LHO	Partner	RHO	You
2♥	2♠	pass	?

You have a good hand, but it is unclear which, if any, game you might be able to make. You do not really want to support partner's spades with only a doubleton. Neither can you bid 3NT with only ♥Qx in the opener's suit. Bid 3♦ (forcing, as usual) and see where partner leads you. Perhaps the only game your can make is 5♦, but you will never get there if you do not bid the suit now.

Here's another example:

♠ Q　♥ K Q 9 7　♦ A Q 7 5　♣ K 10 7 5

LHO	Partner	RHO	You
2♥	2♠	pass	?

Partner has a good hand with spades, and it is odds on that you will be able to make game. Bid 3NT and hope it is the right spot — it rates to be as good as anything else. Of course, there is the risk that 5♣ or 5♦ might be better, and you might be able to make a slam in one of the minors, but there is no room to find out.

Having seen how difficult things are for responder when he has to start bidding at the three-level, it is perhaps now more obvious why it is important that an overcall of a Weak Two opening bid show sound opening bid values.

Can you make a jump overcall over a Weak Two?

Yes, but doing so does not show the weak hand type that a jump overcall of a 1-level opening promises. Remember this rule — **do not preempt over a preempt.** When the opponents open with a Weak Two-bid (or any preemptive bid) an overcall is constructive rather than obstructive and always guarantees full opening bid values. Jump overcalls also show strong hands — there are no weak jump overcalls (preempts) once the opponents have preempted. When an opponent preempts, it is because he thinks the hand belongs to your side. Much of the time, he will be right and, since you have much less space to bid constructively after a preempt, all of the available bids are needed to show good hands.

♠ K J 10 7 4 3 2　♥ 8 6　♦ K 4　♣ 5 4

If RHO opens 1♥, you might decide to jump to 3♠. The primary reason is to try to stop the opponents from reaching their best spot. This is an effective ploy because there is such a wide range of possible hands for opener, both in terms of strength and distribution. Your preemptive overcall forces LHO to an immediate decision, and it is one that he will often get wrong.

After a 2♥ opening bid, LHO already knows his partner's hand within fairly narrow limits, and he will do the right thing most of the time. With much of the destructive force of the jump overcall removed, it is best to use the bid to show a different hand type — a strong single-suited hand. Perhaps something like:

♠ A Q J 10 7 6　♥ 5 4　♦ A K 4　♣ K 5

It is easy to see why it is useful to be able to show this hand immediately, rather than having to double 2♥, intending to bid spades at your next turn. This is not an unlikely auction:

LHO	Partner	RHO	You
		2♥	dbl
4♥	pass	pass	?

Now you have little choice but to bid 4♠. The opponents' preemptive tactics have railroaded you into making the decision without consultation with your partner. You have been forced to make the last guess.

Your bidding will be much more accurate if you can show this hand by jumping to 3♠ directly over the 2♥ opening. Then, irrespective of what LHO does, your partner will be able to make a sensible decision based on your combined holdings.

Can you show a two-suiter after a Weak Two opening?

The short answer to this is "Yes you can," but it's not quite as easy as over a one-level opening. (We seem to be saying that a lot, don't we?) To begin with, the Unusual Notrump convention does not apply over a Weak Two opening. After a Weak Two opening bid from RHO, a 2NT overcall is natural. It shows 15-18 HCP, a relatively balanced hand, and at least one stopper in opener's suit. After a 2NT overcall, we recommend that you play whatever system you would use after an 2NT opening — Stayman, transfers, and so forth. Similarly a jump to 3NT is natural — either you have a very strong balanced hand, or something like:

♠ K 4   ♥ A 6   ♦ A K Q 10 6 3 2   ♦ K 4

LHO	Partner	RHO	You
		2♠	3NT

With eight tricks in your own hand, you are hoping partner or the opening lead will provide the ninth.

In Chapter 18, we will look more closely at notrump overcalls of Weak Twos and other preemptive opening bids. The problem arises on hands such as this next example. How would you bid this hand after RHO opens a weak 2♠?

♠ 7   ♥ A Q J 8 6   ♦ A 6   ♣ K Q J 10 5

If the opening bid had been 1♠, then you could have used a Michaels Cuebid of 2♠ to show a two-suited hand with hearts and minor. Here you can bid 3♠ over the 2♠ opening bid to show the same type of hand. Remember, though, that you are forcing partner to bid at the four-level in this auction, so if you are only 5-5, you had better have a pretty good hand.

That takes care of two-suited hands including the other major. What about hands with both minors? After a one-level opening bid, you can overcall with an unusual 2NT and then, with a particularly strong hand, bid again if you wish. Once the opponents up the ante with a Weak Two, there is no room for such a subtle approach. Your lowest available Unusual Notrump bid is at the four-level, as both 2NT and 3NT overcalls are needed as natural bids. With such a wide range of hands to show, how can partner hope to do the right thing with any regularity?

LHO	Partner	RHO	You
		2♠	4NT

You might have either of the following hands:

♠ 8   ♥ 4   ♦ A Q J 7 5   ♣ K J 7 6 5 4

♠ —   ♥ A 8   ♦ A K Q J 6   ♣ A J 10 9 8 4

Bidding 4NT on the first example will not always work out, but you can hardly pass. You may be able to make five of a minor, or it may be a good sacrifice against 4♠. Where is the heart suit? Probably with partner (as usual), but if

LHO has a whole raft of hearts, 4♥ may be the best spot for the enemy. Don't give them room to find out.

On the second hand, while on a bad day you might not beat 4♠, you are more worried about whether or not your side is making a slam. In the end, you have to trust partner. He will look at the vulnerability, and make a judgement about how good a hand you are likely to have. He will also look at his hand and value minor suit honors and major suit controls — aces, singletons, voids. The question he should ask himself is, "How much worse could my hand have been?" And on all these hands, after asking that question, he should bid more than just 5♣:

$$♠ A 5 3 2 \quad ♥ Q 6 4 \quad ♦ 4 2 \quad ♣ K 6 3 2$$

$$♠ 5 3 2 \quad ♥ K 6 4 2 \quad ♦ 4 2 \quad ♣ K 6 3 2$$

$$♠ 7 5 3 2 \quad ♥ 7 6 4 \quad ♦ 4 2 \quad ♣ K Q 3 2$$

Yes, we did pick these hands so that they fitted rather well with yours, didn't we? In fact, you'll make a grand slam opposite all three of them! Which just goes to show, once again, that it's very hard to be perfect over preempts. Sometimes you have to settle for the best result possible, not the best possible result.

Summary

✓ You should have both a decent suit and sound opening bid values for an overcall of a Weak Two opening.

✓ When you overcall a Weak Two opening with a minor, partner will often judge whether to bid on by how well his cards seem to fit in terms of a notrump game. The emphasis will be on fitting cards in your suit and on stoppers in opener's suit. If that is not what you need from him, then a three-level minor-suit overcall is probably not the best action.

✓ A jump overcall to three-of-a-major shows a strong single-suited hand.

✓ When responding to high-level overcalls, you will have little room to describe your hand. When raising partner's major, remember that his minimum is significantly higher than it would be if he had made a one-level overcall.

✓ A three-level cuebid is similar to Michaels, and shows a good two-suited hand (at least 5-5).

✓ To show a minor two-suiter, you have to commit to at least the five-level. 4NT is the lowest notrump bid available for this purpose.

OVERCALLING WEAK TWO-BIDS

NOW TRY THESE...

What is your next bid on each of the following hands?

1
- ♠ K J 9 7 4
- ♥ 8 3
- ♦ K 10 6
- ♣ Q J 6

LHO	Partner	RHO	You
		2♥	?

2
- ♠ A Q J 9 7
- ♥ K 6
- ♦ A 10 7 3
- ♣ J 6

LHO	Partner	RHO	You
		2♥	?

3
- ♠ A 4
- ♥ J 4
- ♦ A Q J 8 7 5
- ♣ A 10 8

LHO	Partner	RHO	You
		2♥	?

4
- ♠ A K J 9 7 4
- ♥ 8 3
- ♦ A K 10
- ♣ Q 6

LHO	Partner	RHO	You
		2♥	?

5
- ♠ A 7 4 3 2
- ♥ 8 6
- ♦ A K 3
- ♣ A 6 4

LHO	Partner	RHO	You
		2♥	?

6
- ♠ 7 4
- ♥ 3
- ♦ K Q 10 7 6
- ♣ Q J 6 5 4

LHO	Partner	RHO	You
		2♥	?

7
- ♠ 4
- ♥ 4
- ♦ K Q J 8 7
- ♣ A J 10 8 3 2

LHO	Partner	RHO	You
		2♥	?

8
- ♠ A Q J 9 7
- ♥ 6
- ♦ A Q 10 7 3 2
- ♣ J

LHO	Partner	RHO	You
		2♥	?

9
- ♠ Q 9 7
- ♥ K 6
- ♦ K 10 7
- ♣ 9 8 6 5 3

LHO	Partner	RHO	You
2♥	3♦	pass	?

10
- ♠ J 9 7
- ♥ 6
- ♦ A Q 10 7
- ♣ J 8 6 5 4

LHO	Partner	RHO	You
2♥	2♠	pass	?

11
- ♠ Q 7
- ♥ 6 3
- ♦ A Q 10 7 3
- ♣ K J 6 2

LHO	Partner	RHO	You
2♥	2♠	pass	?

12
- ♠ A J 9 7
- ♥ 6 3 2
- ♦ A Q 10 7
- ♣ J 5

LHO	Partner	RHO	You
2♥	2♠	pass	?

ANSWERS

1   pass   Coming in at the two-level with this offers LHO a choice of winning options. If he was going to bid game, expecting it to make, he already knows enough about his partner's hand that you will not be able to talk him out of doing so. If he has a marginal hand on which he *might* have tried game, particularly one with no heart fit, he will simply double and collect a large penalty. Do not overcall a Weak Two-bid without sound opening values.

2   2♠   Do not worry that partner will fail to raise when you can make game. He knows that you have a hand not far from this strength.

3   3♦   You want your partner to try 3NT if he has a heart stopper and a fitting card (the ♦K). A heart stopper and one of the black-suit kings is of far less use.

4   3♠   Show your strong single-suited hand immediately, and then leave the rest to partner. Whether LHO passes or raises hearts, your partner will be well-placed to make the correct decision.

5   dbl   Don't overcall with this kind of anemic suit. With 15 HCP you can't really afford to pass, so you just have to risk missing a spade fit if partner has only three of them.

6   pass   This is not the right hand for a 3♦ overcall (you do not have enough points), and you certainly do not want to force your side to the five-level by bidding 4NT.

7   4NT   Ask partner to pick a minor. You have no idea who can make what, but there is a fair chance that playing game in one of your long suits will be a good result no matter whose hand it is.

8   3♥   Show both your two suits immediately with a Michaels cuebid. Thereafter, having given an accurate description of your hand, you can happily leave any further decisions to partner.

9   3NT   Go for it! You don't have much, but it is well-placed. The ♥K is a stopper, and the ♦K107 give you pretty good assurance of six diamond tricks. Even the ♠Q is probably a good card.

10   3♥   A solid invitational spade raise; you certainly want partner to bid on if he has anything extra.

11   3♦   You have a good hand, but it's not yet clear what the right contract is going to be, so for now just start describing your hand. Your bid is forcing, so partner cannot pass. If he bids 3NT you will pass; if he rebids his spades, you can raise to 4♠. Who knows, maybe he'll bid 4♣!

12   4♠   Bridge is such an easy game. Sometimes.

BIDDING OVER 3-LEVEL OPENINGS

 The only opening bid that could surely deprive an adversary of his bidding privileges is 7NT.
Florence Irwin, Auction Highlights, 1913.

In the previous chapter, we examined two reasons for keeping overcalls of Weak Two openings up to strength — to avoid punishing penalty doubles, and to enable partner to judge his hand when he has little room for investigation. Exactly the same principles are needed when deciding whether to come in over a three-level opening bid, since your partner has almost no room at all.

How do you know when to bid over a preempt?

The simple answer to this question is that you don't. There will be times when you pass, only to find that you have missed an easy game. Other times, you will bid only to find LHO with a good hand and a penalty double waiting for you. Sometimes you will avoid the double, but your vulnerable contract will go down three undoubled for -300 when you would have gone plus on defense. Bridge is a game of probabilities, and when your opponent decided to open the bidding at the three-level, he started the dice rolling. You have to take the action that will be right more often than not, and accept that sometimes it will be wrong and that occasionally, it will be catastrophically wrong.

How do you know what to bid over a preempt?

Just as you will sometimes pass when bidding would have worked better, or bid when passing would have been the right thing to do, you will sometimes make the 'wrong' bid without actually doing anything wrong. For example:

♠ A Q 7 5 ♥ K 3 ♦ K 6 5 ♣ A Q 5 4

RHO opens 3♦. What do you bid?

If you gave this hand to a large number of experts, an overwhelming majority would vote to overcall 3NT. On a bad day, partner will show up with something like:

♠ J 8 6 3 2 ♥ 6 ♦ A 3 2 ♣ K 9 6 3

Partner will put down dummy, perhaps with a comment that he thought he was close to raising and that he hopes he does not have too much for you. Unfortunately, the defenders lead a heart and since the spade finesse doesn't work your contract goes two down, with both 4♠ and 5♣ an easy make. Should one of you have done something different? On this hand, yes! Clearly, making a takeout double would have worked much better. And yet on another occasion you will make exactly the same bid, and it will be the right thing to do, because partner will have

♠ J 8 6 ♥ 6 5 2 ♦ A 3 ♣ K 9 6 5 2

You can't be perfect over preempts!

There are essentially four types of hand that you might want to show after RHO opens with a three-level preempt. Here are the hand types and the normal action:

1-suited hand	*overcall*
2-suited hand	*cuebid or bid 4NT (Unusual)*
3-suited hand	*takeout double*
Balanced hand	*bid notrump*

In this chapter, we shall look at the whys and wherefores of the first three of these. We will deal with natural notrump overcalls of all kinds of preempts in the next chapter. You must understand though, that you will frequently have a hand on which you have a choice of actions. As we saw from the illustration above, you will sometimes choose the one that does not work. There is no easy rule to learn. There is no black and white.

When should you overcall after the opponents have preempted?

Basically, a three-level overcall in a major suit invites partner to raise with some kind of fit and some scattered high cards. It does not particularly invite him to bid a suit of his own. Ideally, you should therefore have a good suit and a pretty good hand too.

♠ A K 9 8 4 3   ♥ 8 6   ♦ A Q   ♣ K 6 5

LHO	Partner	RHO	You
		3♥	?

This hand is about a middle-of-the-road 3♠ overcall. You do not really want to play in game unless partner has a spade fit (or an exceptionally good hand). You have a good hand, but certainly not one too good for a simple overcall. Remember how exposed you were when you came in over a Weak Two? The same dangers are present when you bid over a three-level opening, but more so — you are a level higher. If partner has very little, you could easily go for 800 or 1100 even with a hand this good. By the same token, you clearly cannot afford to make a wimpy pass, as you do not need much from partner to make game.

Suppose you hold this hand with both sides vulnerable. Passing and collecting +100 from 3♥ when you could have made 4♠ is no better than bidding 3♠ and losing 1100 when they were making 4♥. As multiple World Champion Bobby Wolff once said, 'The fact that bidding is dangerous is not a reason for passing — passing can be just as dangerous as bidding.'

When you have a strong hand with a good minor suit, you will usually aim to play in 3NT. When RHO preempts, however, you often have to bite the bullet and give up that target.

♠ A 6   ♥ 7 3   ♦ A K J 10 8 6 5   ♣ A J

LHO	Partner	RHO	You
		3♥	?

You have two choices, neither of them particularly appetizing. You can overcall 4♦ and bypass 3NT or you can bid 3NT and hope that your partner has a heart stopper. The second choice is not overly realistic, although it will occasionally be the winning action. Even if partner does have something like ♥Kx, his hand will be in the dummy and the opening lead will come right through his stopper. By bidding 4♦, you at least have a chance that you will get to a making game in your long suit, or at least get a plus score at the four-level.

It may seem that a simple overcall does not do justice to this hand. You do, after all, have almost nine tricks in your own hand. However, remember that you are committing your partnership to make ten tricks without having any idea if partner has anything at all. But your choices are severely limited. Do you really want to commit to the five-level, where you will need partner to hold two or three of the right cards? If you overcall 4♦, partner will know you have a good hand and if he has enough to make game opposite this collection, he will raise.

You can make a jump overcall over a preempt, but remember the rule you learned in the previous chapter: do not preempt over a preempt. Thus, a jump overcall shows a good hand.

♠ A Q J 10 8 6 5   ♥ 9   ♦ A Q 7   ♣ K 4

LHO	Partner	RHO	You
		3♥	?

It would be a reasonable to overcall 4♠ on this hand. Don't worry that you have such a good hand and that partner might pass when you have a slam. Partner will expect you to have a good hand.

How do you respond to partner's overcall?

As you have no doubt realized, when partner overcalls a three-level opening bid, there are no invitational sequences available – there simply isn't any bidding space left.

LHO	Partner	RHO	You
3♦	3♠	pass	?

You can no longer show an invitational spade raise. Sometimes, you would like to bid 3½♠, but that would be frowned upon. Assuming that you are not interested in a slam, you have only two choices — pass 3♠ or raise to 4♠. So, how much strength do you need to raise?

The general theory is that, when he bids over a preempt, partner expects you to have around 7 points. This is easy to remember: **when the opponents preempt, expect partner to have ESP (Exactly Seven Points).**

If that is all you have, then it is probably right to pass partner's overcall unless you have an exceptional fit for his suit. With a little better hand than partner was expecting, you can raise to game. Obviously, you should discount queens and jacks in the opener's suit, as they will rarely be of any use.

♠ J 7   ♥ J 5 3   ♦ K 8 7 6 4   ♣ Q J 7

LHO	Pass	RHO	You
3♥	3♠	pass	?

On this hand, you have nothing more than partner was hoping for when he overcalled. You could raise, and doing so will sometimes be right, but on balance this hand will not produce game. Pass 3♠.

♠ Q 7   ♥ 9 5 3   ♦ K J 7 6 4   ♣ A J 7

LHO	Pass	RHO	You
3♥	3♠	pass	?

You have much more than partner had a right to expect, and game is probably a decent proposition. Raise to 4♠.

Place these two hands opposite the example of a 3♠ overcall that we gave earlier in this chapter:

	Partner		You
♠	A K 9 8 4 3	♠	J 7
♥	8 6	♥	J 5 3
♦	A Q	♦	K 8 7 6 4
♣	K 6 5	♣	Q J 7

	Partner		You
♠	A K 9 8 4 3	♠	Q 7
♥	8 6	♥	9 5 3
♦	A Q	♦	K J 7 6 4
♣	K 6 5	♣	A J 7

You will see that game has little chance opposite the first hand, but has a very good play opposite the second.

If you think you are close to a raise, always remember that suits are unlikely to break well once an opponent has preempted. If one player has a seven-card suit, it is unlikely that everyone else has a flat hand. (Bidding a game that needs a 3-3 break or two 3-2 breaks is heavily odds against after a preemptive opening bid. By the same token, partner is sitting over the preemptor, which means under the preemptor's partner, who is likely to have most of their side's high cards outside the preempt suit. Err on the side of caution if the decision is a close one.)

If you still cannot decide whether you are worth a raise, consider the degree of fit you have for partner's suit. High cards alone are not enough to justify a raise. On a bad day, even a hand as good as the one we told you to raise on may not produce game. Running into a 5-0 trump break, although a little unlucky, is certainly not wildly unlikely after the preempt.

Now let's make your hand significantly better.

♠ Q J 7 ♥ 9 5 ♦ A Q 7 6 4 ♣ K Q 5

Once again, partner bids 3♠ over LHO's 3♥ opening bid. This time, you are interested in a slam. You need partner to hold fairly specific cards, but there aren't that many honors missing, so he is not unlikely to hold the right hand. For example, slam will be excellent if he has ♠AK, ♦K, ♣A and a singleton heart.

The same principles that we have used after lower overcalls still apply. A cuebid of opener's suit shows an invitational raise of partner's suit. Even though you would be cuebidding at the four-level, a 4♥ bid in this auction says nothing about your heart holding. It simply tells partner that you are too strong to raise to 4♠.

When should you double a preempt for takeout?

Doubling a preempt for takeout is not that different from doubling a one-level or two-level opening bid. When we discussed takeout doubles of Weak Twos, we established that you should pass with those not quite perfect hands on which you might risk a one-level double. The same is obviously true when you have to enter the fray at the three-level, but at higher levels the correct shape is as important, if not more so, than how many HCP you hold.

Always remember that partner has no room to maneuver when you double at the three-level. He will often have to choose immediately between settling for a partscore or bidding game in his best suit. If he cannot be sure that you will hold proper support for whichever suit he chooses, he will tend to tread too cautiously, with the inevitable result that you will miss game with great regularity.

So, what would a takeout double of a 3♦ opening bid look like? Actually, not that different from a classic takeout double of a 1♦ opening — perhaps something like:

♠ K J 9 7　♥ A J 10 7　♦ 6　♣ K 10 9 7

BY THE WAY

There is a bridge maxim that it is better to play in the right suit at the wrong level than the other way around. It sounds strange when you first hear it, but it doesn't take a lot of thought to see why it's correct. If you are in the wrong suit, you are probably booked for a minus score, and one or both of the opponents will have enough trumps that they'll be quite happy to have you play there. But find a fit, and it may be as hard for the opposition as it is for you to determine whose hand it is and how high you should be. They may bid more, and either give you a second chance, or go down when you were already too high. So the crucial thing over a preempt is to find a good fit.

Of course, making a three-level takeout double on a bare 12 HCP is not completely without risk, but there are few experts who would even consider passing. You have excellent support for whichever suit partner chooses. If he jumps to game in one of the majors and it proves to be too high, then so be it, but there is too much chance that if you pass, LHO will also pass, and partner will be stuck with nowhere to go on his balanced 12-14 point hand. Partner is unlikely to have all three unbid suits, so he will find it much harder to bid if you don't take the pressure off him by getting in now.

How do you decide whether to overcall or double?

♠ A Q 10 8 6　♥ K Q 10 6　♦ 4　♣ A J 4

LHO	Pass	RHO	You
		3♦	?

Should you make a takeout double or overcall 3♠? Either could be the winning action. If you double, do you think partner will bid 4♠ when he holds

♠ K J 3　♥ J 7 2　♦ 9 7 4　♣ K 9 6 3

Of course not. He will bid 4♣, and you will pass and, in all probability, partner will go down — perhaps quite a lot down if the trumps misbehave. Yet 4♠ needs little more than a 3-2 trump break and no heart ruffs, and will even survive a 4-1 trump division quite a lot of the time. All in all, it is a game you certainly want to reach.

Had you overcalled 3♠, you would at least have played in the right suit, whether partner passed or raised. Of course, if you overcall 3♠, then partner may well turn up with something like:

♠ 3 ♥ A 9 8 7 5 ♦ 9 7 4 ♣ Q 6 3 2

Of course, he will pass 3♠ and you will almost certainly go down. And yet, 4♥ is just about unbreakable.

So, as you can see, there is no 'right' answer to this type of hand. As a general rule though, the question is whether your hand is such that your five-card suit offers the best chance of a game contract. Thus you should tend to double if you are 5-4 in the majors unless there is a great disparity between your two suits (e.g. ♠AKQJ4 and ♥10764). Even then, double might be right, but you should pretend you have six spades and only three hearts and bid accordingly.

With a decent five-card major and only three cards in the other major, the overcall is probably the safer bet. Doubling will result in playing a 4-3 fit too often, and although there are certainly times when you will have to double with only three cards in one of the majors, it is risky to do so. If you have a sensible alternative, such as overcalling a good five-card major, that will probably turn out to be the winning choice more often than not.

You will also sometimes have a close decision between doubling or bidding 3NT, or between overcalling and bidding 3NT. As we shall be looking at notrump overcalls in the next chapter, we will address this point there, but suffice it to say that once again there is no surefire winner available.

How do you respond to partner's takeout double?

The same principles discussed earlier when judging whether to raise an overcall also apply when responding to a takeout double. Partner has already assumed that you have ESP — 7 points. If that is all you have, then make a minimum response to the double.

♠ A 6 4 2 ♥ Q 6 5 ♦ Q 7 ♣ J 6 3 2

LHO	Partner	RHO	You
3♦	dbl	pass	?

You have only seven working HCP (discounting the ♦Q, which rates to be worthless); also, you have no five-card suit. Certainly, it is easy enough to construct normal takeout doubles of 3♦ opposite which 4♠ will be cold. It is equally possible to construct quite strong doubles opposite which even 3♠ may be too high, particularly if partner happens to hold only three spades. Bid 3♠.

While it is true that you might have had much less than this, partner has to be able to play you for some values when he decides whether or not he should enter the auction. Think about it — if he has to wait for a hand that is worth bidding on at the three-level even if you had nothing, then you will end up passing out the preempt on a large number of hands when you both hold a minimum opening bid.

Of course, as usual, you are allowed to jump to game in response to a take-out double:

♠ A 10 6 4 2 ♥ K 6 5 ♦ 7 5 3 ♣ Q 6

LHO	Partner	RHO	You
3♦	dbl	pass	?

You still only have 9 HCP, but this time they are all working and the fifth spade assures you of at least eight trumps and probably nine. That's worth a couple of extra points! Bid 4♠. Put this hand opposite the 12-HCP takeout double from the last section:

You can see that game is a good contract even though partner has a minimum hand.

Partner	You
♠ K J 9 7	♠ A 10 6 4 2
♥ A J 10 7	♥ K 6 5
♦ 6	♦ 7 5 3
♣ K 10 9 7	♣ Q 6

There will be times when you don't know which suit to pick. For example:

♠ K J 6 5 ♦ A 10 8 7 ♦ 7 6 4 ♣ Q 4

LHO	Partner	RHO	You
3♦	dbl	pass	?

You have a good enough hand (just) to go to game, but in which of the majors? The answer is that you would rather not jump to either 4♥ or 4♠, since partner might have made a takeout double with only seven major-suit cards. In that case, picking a seven-card fit (particularly when suits do not rate to split evenly) could be disastrous.

However, you can consult partner. A cuebid at the four-level (4♦ in this auction) simply says to partner, 'I have both majors — please choose one'. It does not show slam interest, or a hand too good just to jump to game. Do you remember what we said earlier about the importance of playing in the right suit? In a crowded auction, it is worth giving up the ability to make a slam try below game level in order to make sure that you reach the best fit. Bid 4♦ — a cuebid to get partner to pick his best major.

Can you show a two-suited hand over a preempt?

You can show some two-suiters directly over a preempt, by using a variant of Michaels and the Unusual Notrump.

Over a minor-suit preempt, a direct cuebid is used to show a two-suiter with both majors. For example:

♠ A Q 10 7 5　♥ A K 7 5 4　♦ 8 5　♣ 4

LHO	Partner	RHO	You
		3♦	4♦

This would be about a minimum hand on which you could cuebid 4♣ over a 3♣ opening or 4♦ over a 3♦ opening. Partner will simply pick his better major unless he is very strong, with slam interest opposite this type of hand.

After a major-suit preempt at the three-level, the cuebid is used in the same way that you use a regular Michaels cuebid after a one-level opening bid — i.e. it shows a two-suiter with the other major and an unspecified minor. But remember that you are driving partner to the five-level if the opponents' suit is spades:

LHO	Partner	RHO	You
		3♠	4♠
pass	?		

Partner will have to bid five of something now!

With both minor suits, you can show your two-suiter by bidding 4NT directly over a 3♥ or 3♠ opening bid.

Summary

✓ High-level suit overcalls are effectively game invitations, so they must be sound.

✓ When partner overcalls, he is assuming that you have ESP — Exactly Seven Points. If that is all you have, you should pass unless you have an exceptional fit for his suit. With more than that, accept his game invitation.

✓ Cuebidding in response to an overcall shows a slam try and agrees partner's suit.

✓ Takeout doubles at the three-level are not that different from those at lower levels except that it is even more important that you have adequate support for all unbid suits. If you have classic takeout double shape, you can elect to enter the fray even if you only have minimum opening bid strength in terms of high-cards.

✓ Responding to takeout doubles is like responding to overcalls. Partner has already assumed that you have 7 points. If that is all you have, make a minimum response, even though you have a better hand than you might have. Ignore minor honors in the opener's suit. Be particularly cautious when you have only four-card suits in which to respond, as you are not guaranteed an eight-card fit. With extra values you can jump to game in your best suit.

✓ After partner has doubled a minor-suit preempt, you can cuebid with equal length in both majors (4-4 or 5-5) and sufficient values to go to game. This cuebid is not a slam try, but simply asks partner to choose his best major.

✓ A direct cuebid shows a two-suited hand. If the opening was a minor, then cuebid shows both majors, at least 5-5. After a major-suit preempt, a cuebid shows the unbid major and an undefined minor. 4NT over a major-suit preempt shows both minors.

BIDDING OVER 3-LEVEL OPENINGS

NOW TRY THESE...

What is your next bid on each of the following hands?

1
- ♠ K J 9 7
- ♥ Q 8 3
- ♦ Q 8 6 5 3
- ♣ A

LHO	Partner	RHO	You
		3♣	?

2
- ♠ A Q J 9 7 3
- ♥ K 6
- ♦ A 10 3
- ♣ J 6

LHO	Partner	RHO	You
		3♣	?

3
- ♠ A 4
- ♥ A K J 10 9 3 2
- ♦ A J 8
- ♣ 8

LHO	Partner	RHO	You
		3♣	?

4
- ♠ K J 9
- ♥ A K J 3
- ♦ A K 10 3
- ♣ Q 6

LHO	Partner	RHO	You
		3♣	?

5
- ♠ K 10 3 2
- ♥ A J 8 6
- ♦ Q J 10 7 3
- ♣ —

LHO	Partner	RHO	You
		3♣	?

6
- ♠ A J 10 7 4 2
- ♥ A Q 8 7 3
- ♦ —
- ♣ 5 4

LHO	Partner	RHO	You
		3♣	?

7
- ♠ K J 8 6
- ♥ Q 7
- ♦ J 8 7
- ♣ J 10 8 3

LHO	Partner	RHO	You
3♦	dbl	pass	?

8
- ♠ A J 9 7
- ♥ Q J 9 3
- ♦ 7 3 2
- ♣ Q 6

LHO	Partner	RHO	You
3♦	dbl	pass	?

9
- ♠ Q 10 8 6 4
- ♥ A 3
- ♦ 8 7 3 2
- ♣ Q 6

LHO	Partner	RHO	You
3♦	dbl	pass	?

10
- ♠ Q 10 8
- ♥ A J 3
- ♦ K 10 3 2
- ♣ J 6 3

LHO	Partner	RHO	You
3♦	dbl	pass	?

ANSWERS

1 pass Your suit is not good enough for 3♦, so that is not an option. A takeout double might be the winning action, but there are too many downsides — you risk playing in a 4-3 heart fit and your offensive potential is damaged since your honors are not concentrated in your own suits. If the ♣A were in a different suit, this hand would be just worth a double. As it is, that is four points that will only win one trick, and will do nothing to help promote lesser cards for you.

2 3♠ A good suit and a strong enough hand to invite partner to raise. Perfect!

3 4♥ This may not make, but you cannot afford to bid less. You need very little from partner, and he will pass on many hands where game is easy if you bid only 3♥.

4 dbl The shape is not perfect, but your significant extra strength easily compensates for that. Not that your problems on the hand are over. If partner makes a minimum response, you will then have to decide whether to raise him to game.

5 dbl Although it is only 11 HCP, the distribution on this hand gives you good compensation. If partner jumps to game, he will almost certainly make it, even though you may not have the balance of the high cards. Perhaps you will even get doubled. If you do, expect to score +790 or more.

6 4♣ Partner will choose his best major. What more can you ask?

7 3♠ You have no more than partner expected, and you may not even have an eight-card fit. Even *thinking* about bidding game is a gross overbid.

8 4♦ At least make sure of playing in the right major. If 3♥ or 3♠ is the limit, so be it, but you almost have game values and it would not be a surprise to find that you had ten easy tricks in one of the majors.

9 4♠ You have 8 HCP, just as you did on Problem 7, but this hand is infinitely better. You have a fifth spade and all your honors are likely to be working.

10 3NT If partner has doubled on shape not high cards, you may not make this. However no one is likely to double, and nothing else is attractive. Did you think about passing? Your trumps aren't good enough, sitting under the diamond bidder; you might beat it a trick or even two on a good day, but those will be the hands where partner has enough that you can make game yourselves.

BIDDING NOTRUMP OVER A PREEMPT

 If my pen were sufficiently persuasive to induce players to give up preemptive bids, I should rest content.
Florence Irwin, **Auction Highlights,** *1913.*

In the last three chapters, we have seen how you should bid distributional hands after RHO opens with a preempt at the two- or three-level. We have thus far ignored balanced hands. As we have already discovered, the higher the level of the opening preempt, the more difficulty we have finding room to do everything we want to do. Sometimes, it must be confessed, we are reduced, if not to guessing, at least to playing the probabilities.

How do you bid balanced hands over a Weak Two opening?

♠ A Q 6 ♥ K 6 ♦ A 10 7 5 ♣ K 10 7 5

LHO	Partner	RHO	You
		2♠	?

If RHO opened 1♠, you would overcall 1NT on this hand. You are within the 15-18 HCP range for the bid and you have a stopper in opener's suit. In this auction, you can overcall 2NT to show roughly the same hand. 'Roughly?' we can hear you asking. You will recall that we said you should avoid overcalling 1NT on a 15-HCP hand with little or no playing strength, because it is easy for LHO to double you when he, and not your partner, has the balance of the missing points. It is also easier for partner to judge when to raise if he knows that you will deliver a full value hand. When making a 2NT overcall over a Weak Two-bid, both of these reasons are even more important. Now, partner has no room even to invite game. He must either pass 2NT or raise to game — there is no in-between. (We wish there was such a bid as 2½NT!) Moreover, if LHO doubles 2NT, the penalty will probably be huge. You could easily go four or five down if partner has a bust.

The range for a 2NT overcall over a Weak Two has a lower end of an excellent 15 HCP (a hand with a decent five-card suit and good intermediate cards) and goes up to a good 18 HCP.

How do you respond to a 2NT overcall?

Back in Chapter 10, we said that you should play the same system after your 1NT overcall that you use after a 1NT opening bid. The simple reason for this is that you already know that system, and it is therefore easy to remember. Our advice is therefore to treat a 2NT overcall just like a 2NT opening bid (except with a slightly lower range, of course). If you play Stayman and transfers when partner opens 2NT, then ignore the opening bid and play them in exactly the same manner when he overcalls 2NT in this kind of auction.

What if you have a balanced hand and aren't sure whether or not to raise to game? You could easily have a balanced 8 HCP, let's say. Over a 1NT overcall, you would have happily raised to 2NT; partner would have gone on with 17-18, and passed with the lower end of his range. But partner has already bid 2NT, so you have no way to invite. So, what is the answer? We are sorry to say that there really isn't one. The effect of the preemptive opening is to make you guess. When you have this type of hand, it works — you have to guess and you will not always guess right. Our advice is to assume partner has 17 HCP (about the middle of his range, because if he only has 15 it will be a 15-count that is worth 16 anyway), and bid accordingly. Raise with a working 8 HCP, and pass with less.

Can you overcall 3NT?

LHO	Partner	RHO	You
		2♠	3NT

It may seem that we are telling you to guess a lot in this section. We admit it. We are, but that's what preempts do to you. Jumping to 3NT over a Weak Two opening bid by the opponents basically says to partner, 'Please put down a dummy with enough high cards that I can make nine tricks.' It does not invite partner to bid. You have made the decision for the partnership.

There are many reasons why you might bid 3NT. Perhaps you have a strong semi-balanced hand with no suitable bid. Say RHO opens 2♣ and your hand is:

♠A84 ♥7 ♦AKQJ4 ♣AKQ4

What do you do?

Your obvious action is to overcall 3♦ — which partner will pass many times when game is cold. You can hardly overcall 2NT (showing about 15-18 HCP) as, again, partner will often pass when you have nine easy tricks. You could make a takeout double, but will you be happy when partner jumps to 4♥? Of course not. Perhaps you intend to bid 4NT over a 4♥ response, but we suspect that if you do that then your partner will tell you how many aces or key cards he holds, and he will be quite right to do so — 4NT in that auction is Blackwood agreeing hearts.

This is not a time for pussyfooting around making delicate attempts to find the optimum contract — the preempt has taken away any space you had for delicate probing. Jump to 3NT and hope that the defense cannot (or do not, which comes to same thing) cash the first five heart tricks. Remember what we said earlier: when the opponents preempt, try to get the best result possible rather than the best possible result. Of course, you might be able to make game or slam in a minor, but most of the time 3NT will be your best spot. Play the percentages and bid what you think you are most likely to be able to make.

Your hand might be even quite unbalanced for a 3NT overcall. Perhaps something like:

♠K4 ♥A ♦J5 ♣AKQJ9763

Again, RHO opens 2♠ (or 2♥). The odds are that 3NT is your best spot. Perhaps it will even make because LHO does not find the best opening lead. There is no way for you to investigate the various alternative contracts scientifically. You have to make a decision right now. Jump to 3NT and hope it makes.

Note that when you overcall 3NT you are not inviting partner to bid his weak six-card heart suit. If you wanted to consult him about where to play, you would have started with a takeout double. Even if you get doubled in 3NT, partner is expected to pass, no matter what his hand may be. If 3NT is doubled, the decision to sit or to run (to 4♣ on this hand) is yours, and yours alone.

How do you bid balanced hands after a three-level preempt?

Curiously, it is sometimes easier to bid after a three-level opening bid than it is over a Weak Two. Think about it — when you overcall 2NT you may be worried that partner will not raise when he has the right scattered 7-8 points, and perhaps you will miss a game. There are no such worries when you have to bid over a three-level opening. You will find out what partner has when he puts his hand down in dummy, and either it will be enough for you to make nine tricks or it will not. There is nothing you can do about it — you just have to guess whether to bid or pass. Those are your only options.

♠ K Q 5 ♥ K J 4 ♦ A Q 8 5 4 ♣ K 4

LHO	Partner	RHO	You
		3♥	3NT

You have no idea whether you can make 3NT. If partner has a few scattered points you might have ten top tricks. If he has nothing, you might go for 1100 when the opponents cannot even make game. But it's still the right bid now.

A 3NT overcall over a preempt has a very wide range. For example, you might decide to try your luck with 3NT over a 3♦ opening on as little as

♠ Q J 5 ♥ 9 3 ♦ K J 5 ♣ A K Q 10 7 5

Sometimes, it will be the right thing to do, since the only real alternative is to pass. Bidding 4♣ has very little upside as, if you can make a game, it is likely to be 3NT. Doubling will get you into deep trouble far too often to make it worthwhile.

Of course, you might also hold a real monster. Perhaps something like

♠ A K J ♥ A Q J 7 ♦ K Q 10 ♣ A K 10

What else can you bid over a 3♦ opening but 3NT? Do you really want to start with a double and have to rebid 4NT over a 4♣ response? Going minus in 4NT with 27 HCP will not impress your partner.

Of course, you could also hold anything in between these two extremes when you bid 3NT. You might also hold a completely different hand type. Something like

♠ A 3 ♥ Q 4 ♦ K 4 ♣ A K Q J 10 7 5

You hope to get a diamond lead and, even if partner does not have any help there, they may not find a heart switch. It's a gamble, but a reasonable one in the circumstances. After all, if partner holds as little as the ♥A or the ♥K, 3NT will be cold.

Of course there will be many balanced hands on which the question is not "Do I bid?" but, "What should I bid?" For example:

♠ A K 7 4 ♥ K Q J 6 ♦ A Q 4 ♣ Q 6

LHO	Partner	RHO	You
		3♦	?

Should you overcall 3NT or make a takeout double? Doubling will work out well if partner bids a major, although you will still have to decide whether to pass a 3♥ or 3♠ response or raise to game. If he bids 4♣ though, you will wish you had bid 3NT. Bidding 3NT may also work poorly though — perhaps the opponents can cash the first five tricks in clubs, or set up four club tricks to go with the ♥A, when game in a 4-4 major-suit fit would have made easily.

There is no right or wrong answer on these hands. With 4-4 in the majors, the odds favor doubling, but if you were 4-3 in the majors with a similar hand, then 3NT is slightly more likely to work. You will guess wrong with some regularity though. Hey, as we keep saying, that's why people preempt.

The other choice that you will often have to make is between overcalling your own suit and bidding notrump.

♠ A Q J 8 6   ♥ K 3   ♦ A Q 4   ♣ Q 10 8

LHO	Partner	RHO	You
		3♦	?

This time you have only two hearts, so a takeout double is not an option, but you still have a choice — 3♠ or 3NT. If you choose 3NT, then you may find partner with a spade fit and short clubs, meaning that 3NT is hopeless while 4♠ is unbreakable. If partner does not have a spade fit, then you probably want to try 3NT. However, do you think that partner will have a diamond stopper? Of course not. So if you overcall and find partner with no spade fit, two bad things might happen. Firstly, he might pass, leaving you to struggle in a 5-1 fit when 3NT is an easy make. Secondly, he might introduce his own suit, thus carrying you beyond the only making game.

Again, there is no secret formula that will enable you to guess right all of the time. One way to make these decisions is to do so on the basis of the quality of your stopper in the opener's suit. With only a single stopper, the lead of opener's suit might well place 3NT in danger, so you might opt to double or to overcall in a suit. With at least a double stopper in opener's suit, you should tend to lean towards 3NT if the decision is a close one.

How do you respond to a 3NT overall?

Usually, you pass and hope that 3NT is the right spot. Even if you have a moderate six-card major, pulling 3NT to your suit will only be the winning action some of the time. Sometimes, partner will have nine easy tricks in notrump because he has a source of tricks (usually a long minor suit) of his own, although if he does have a balanced hand, the suit game may easily prove to be superior.

You can raise to 4NT, inviting partner to bid a slam if he is significantly better than he might have been. You need about 13-14 points, as that should be enough to ensure that partner can make ten tricks even if he has a minimum. You can also choose to play 4♣ as Stayman and 4♦ and 4♥ as transfers over a natural 3NT overcall, although that is something that you would need to prearrange with your partner.

Summary

✓ A 2NT overcall over a Weak Two shows an excellent 15 to18 HCP with a stopper (preferably two) in opener's suit.

✓ Continuations should be the same as those you normally play over an opening 2NT bid (Stayman, transfers, etc.).

✓ A jump to 3NT over a Weak Two asks partner to put down dummy. It is done either on a strong balanced hand or a hand with a source of tricks.

✓ You might choose to bid 3NT over a three-level preempt on many different hand types. You may have a balanced hand on which you risk an overcall hoping to find partner with enough bits and pieces to allow you to make nine tricks, or you may have a powerhouse with virtually game in your own hand. You could also have a running suit (usually a minor) and a stopper in opener's suit.

✓ When choosing between doubling and bidding 3NT or between overcalling in a suit or in notrump, weigh up the possible gains and risks of each action.

✓ Pre-arrange with partner whether 4♣ is Stayman and whether transfers apply after a 3NT overcall.

BIDDING NOTRUMP OVER A PREEMPT

NOW TRY THESE...

What is your next bid on each of the following hands?

1
- ♠ K J
- ♥ A 4 2
- ♦ K 8 6 3
- ♣ A 9 7 4

LHO	Partner	RHO	You
		2♥	?

2
- ♠ A Q 7 3
- ♥ K Q 10 6
- ♦ A 10 3
- ♣ K 6

LHO	Partner	RHO	You
		2♥	?

3
- ♠ K 4
- ♥ K J 2
- ♦ A K J 8 7 5
- ♣ 8 3

LHO	Partner	RHO	You
		2♥	?

4
- ♠ J 9
- ♥ K 3
- ♦ A K Q 10 9 7 6 3
- ♣ A

LHO	Partner	RHO	You
		2♥	?

5
- ♠ K 10 2
- ♥ A J 8
- ♦ Q J 10 7 3
- ♣ A Q

LHO	Partner	RHO	You
		3♣	?

6
- ♠ A J 10 7 2
- ♥ Q 8
- ♦ K J 4
- ♣ A K 4

LHO	Partner	RHO	You
		3♣	?

7
- ♠ A Q J 6
- ♥ A K 7 5
- ♦ K
- ♣ K J 8 7

LHO	Partner	RHO	You
		3♣	?

8
- ♠ A 10 6 4
- ♥ A 10 7 5
- ♦ K
- ♣ K J 8 7

LHO	Partner	RHO	You
		3♣	?

ANSWERS

1   pass   It may work out to overcall 2NT, but doing so regularly on such a moderate hand will get you to a great many games that drift two or three down.

2   2NT   You have a balanced hand with heart stoppers in the right HCP range. Don't worry about missing 4♠, as partner can use Stayman if he is interested in that suit.

3   2NT   Despite being only 15 HCP, this is a much better hand than Hand 1. If partner raises on a scattered 8-count, you will almost certainly have play for your game. You could choose to overcall 3♦, but you have good heart stoppers too, and you need black-suit cards from partner. If he has no help in either red suit, he will be inclined to pass 3♦ even when he holds enough high cards to make game a reasonable proposition.

4   3NT   It may not make, but you have no room to conduct a careful investigation. Take a stab at game and pray that it is the right contract.

5   3NT   It may not make, but you don't need partner to produce much to give it play, and it might just have nine top tricks.

6   3NT   Bidding 3♠ may work better. However, you know that partner will not be able to bid notrump as he cannot have a club stopper. If partner cannot raise spades, he will therefore either pass (missing an easy game) or bid diamonds or hearts (bypassing 3NT).

7   3NT   A major-suit game may be better, but you cannot afford to start with a takeout double. If partner responded 3♦ you could still bid 3NT, but what if he jumped to 4♦ in response to your double? Bidding 4NT would now be Blackwood.

8   pass   Sometimes you get preempted. No, you're not happy passing, but you can't double with a singleton diamond, and you don't have nearly a good enough hand to shoot 3NT. Take away your club cards (which are really only useful on defense) and discount the singleton ♦K, and what have you really got here? Two aces.

 I delight in having my adversaries make preemptive bids — I love to know all they are willing to tell me.
Florence Irwin, **Auction Highlights, 1913.**

We have already seen that coming in over a two-level or three-level opening bid often involves an uncomfortably high level of guesswork. As you can imagine, you might just as well be playing roulette when the bidding starts at the four-level.

What do you need to overcall a four-level opening?

Let's begin at the bottom, with a 4♣ or 4♦ opening bid. Entering the fray after these openings is not that different to coming in over 3♣ or 3♦ except, of course, that you have even fewer options because you are one level higher. Anything you do is highly unilateral. There is no room for delicate investigative auctions. You either bid game or you elect to defend — there is no middle ground.

In general it pays to be aggressive, although not suicidal. You would not risk a 4♥ overcall of a 4♣ opening bid with

♠ A J 5 ♥ K Q 9 6 4 ♦ K J 6 ♣ 5 4

Not that it will always prove to be the wrong thing to do, but it will be wrong more often than not and sometimes horribly wrong. For one thing, you might run into a double. Losing 1100 to save against -130 is not the way to fame and fortune. Worse, partner may pass your 4♥ overcall when he has

♠ K Q 10 6 3 2 ♥ 3 ♦ A Q 5 2 ♣ 7 3

If you had quietly passed over 4♣, he would have tried 4♠ when it came around to him, and been just delighted with the dummy you put down. Instead of scoring an easy game in spades, you will go a few down in 4♥.

The most important thing when deciding to overcall at the four-level is your suit quality. This is even more important than the number of high cards you hold. Compare the two hands above. The first one has 14 HCP and a poor five-card suit, and an overcall would be terrible. The second has only 11 HCP and yet it is a routine 4♠ overcall.

When you decide to bid, you are hoping that partner will have a reasonable share of the remaining high cards. You will probably need that no matter what your hand is. You cannot expect him to have excellent trump support too. Remember also, that after RHO opens at the four-level, suits are very unlikely to split, even more so than after a three-level preempt. If your LHO is looking at A-Q-10-x-x in your suit, he is not hard pressed to double you. If he has only J-x-x it is much tougher for him.

Sometimes it will be right to bid even when you cannot make ten tricks. Facing a four-level preempt, particularly at favorable vulnerability, LHO does not need a great deal of encouragement to sacrifice at the five-level if you bid a game that he thinks you can make. If he is not sure who can make what, he is likely to take insurance and bid one more.

What about takeout doubles?

Your other option after a 4♣ or 4♦ opening bid is to make a takeout double. This does not differ greatly from making a takeout double of a three-level opening. You should have at least reasonable (strong three-card) support for both majors. Beyond that, you pay your money and you take your chances.

After a 4♣ opening, both of these hands would be reasonable takeout doubles:

♠ A Q J ♥ K J 9 8 ♦ A Q 8 6 ♣ A 6

♠ K J 10 6 ♥ A J 8 4 ♦ K Q 7 4 ♣ 6

You might wonder how partner is supposed to judge what to do when you could hold such a wide range of hands. The answer is that he can't. He will bid his best suit (preferably a major if he has one) and hope it is the right contract. He might also guess to pass. Remember that it is usually easier to take four tricks than it is to take ten, a philosophy to which we will return in a few moments.

Remember, you are trying to get the best result possible, rather than the best possible result. What this means is that you must make the best of it once the opponents preempt. If you don't think you have enough to bid, pass and don't worry about it. You will not get it right every time. No one does.

What about competing over opening bids of 4♥ or 4♠?

Now there is even more guesswork involved. There are two schools of thought for defending these opening bids. The simplest is still to play takeout doubles. Of course, that does present a problem when you have a hand such as the following:

♠ A J 9 5   ♥ A 6   ♦ K Q J   ♣ A K 6 4

When RHO opens 4♠, what do you want to do to it? You feel like standing on your chair and doubling loudly enough that people in the next town will know the contract is going down.

Ah, but if you make a takeout double, what do you think partner is going to do? Right, he is going to take it out, with the result that your side, rather than the opponents, will likely go minus.

So what else can you do? We said there were two approaches. The other is to double 4♠ on most good hands, whether you are either short in opener's suit or strong and balanced, while still treating a double of other four-level openings as takeout. You will recall that we mentioned earlier the idea that four tricks are easier to take than ten or eleven. That concept really comes into play when you playing this 'Card-showing Double' of 4♠ opening bids. Rather than forcing partner to bid at the five-level, your double simply shows a good hand, and allows partner to make a decision on whether or not to defend.

As responder, you assume that the doubler has enough high cards to beat 4♠ on his own. You do not therefore bid out of fright, just because you have a bad hand. Partner *expects* you to have a bad hand. Indeed, exactly the opposite applies here: you may only take the double out if you think you can make the contract you are bidding. Thus:

♠ J 4   ♥ K 4   ♦ J 5 4   ♣ A J 8 6 4 3

LHO	Partner	RHO	You
4♠	dbl	pass	?

You can safely bid 5♣, and partner will know you have a decent hand because you have removed his double. In fact, if he has a suitable hand, he will raise to slam. If, instead, you held something like

♠ J 4   ♥ 8 4 2   ♦ J 5 4   ♣ J 8 6 4 3

LHO	Partner	RHO	You
4♠	dbl	pass	?

On this hand, you would pass the double of 4♠. You do not expect to make a five-level contract, so you pass and hope that your partner has enough defensive tricks to beat 4♠ doubled. We did say that bidding over four-level openings was a little hit-and-miss. You can now see why. You will no doubt concede your share of -790s and -990s no matter what method you select.

If your doubles just show cards, then sometimes you are going to need some way to force partner to bid his best suit. What if you have this hand:

♠ — ♥ K Q 8 7 ♦ Q 10 9 6 5 ♣ A J 9 7

LHO	Partner	RHO	You
		4♠	4NT

If double just shows a good hand, you cannot really afford to double on this. You certainly don't have much hope of beating 4♠ with this hand unless partner has a fair amount of defense. However, you can use a 4NT bid over 4♠ to show a three-suited takeout; partner simply bids his best unbid suit over this. Had the opening bid been 4♥, 4NT would still be Unusual for the minors since a double would be takeout, asking partner to bid his best suit.

Higher-level openings

You will not encounter opening bids at the five-level (or higher!) very often, but when you do, the principles are similar to those we described for competing over 4♠.

LHO	Partner	RHO	You
pass	pass	5♣	?

You will rarely have the perfect hand for a takeout double here, where you are comfortable forcing partner to bid his his best suit at the five-level. Instead, as over a 4♠ opening, double just shows a good hand (three tricks are easier to take than eleven). If partner bids over your double, he expects to make what he bids.

Summary

✓ Overcalls of 4♣, 4♦ and 4♥ openings show good suits. Doubles are for takeout.

✓ Doubles of opening bids of 4♠ or higher simply show a very good hand. Partner is not allowed to bid out of fright; he must only bid if he expects to make his five-level contract.

✓ An overcall of 4NT over a 4♠ opening is a three-suited takeout — partner is now expected to bid his best suit.

BIDDING OVER OTHER PREEMPTS

NOW TRY THESE...

What is your next bid on each of the following hands?

1
- ♠ K Q J 9 7 4
- ♥ A 3
- ♦ K 10 8
- ♣ 7 4

LHO	Partner	RHO	You
		4♥	?

2
- ♠ A 9 7 3
- ♥ 6
- ♦ A Q 3
- ♣ K J 8 6 5

LHO	Partner	RHO	You
		4♥	?

3
- ♠ 4
- ♥ 2
- ♦ A K J 8 7 5
- ♣ K Q J 10 7

LHO	Partner	RHO	You
		4♥	?

4
- ♠ 5
- ♥ A J 8 7
- ♦ Q J 10 7
- ♣ A Q 9 6

LHO	Partner	RHO	You
		4♥	?

5
- ♠ K Q J 10 5 2
- ♥ A J 8 7 4
- ♦ 7
- ♣ 6

LHO	Partner	RHO	You
		4♣	?

6
- ♠ 2
- ♥ A J 8 7
- ♦ Q J 10 7
- ♣ A Q 9 6

LHO	Partner	RHO	You
		4♣	?

7
- ♠ 10 8 7 5
- ♥ 9 8 7
- ♦ Q 9 8 3 2
- ♣ 6

LHO	Partner	RHO	You
4♥	dbl	pass	?

8
- ♠ 2
- ♥ 8 7
- ♦ Q J 10 7 5 4 2
- ♣ A 9 6

LHO	Partner	RHO	You
4♠	dbl	pass	?

ANSWERS

1   4♠   Don't worry that you don't have a huge hand. Partner will have some high cards (you hope!). You have a good spade suit so, if anyone is going to bid it, it will have to be you. If you pass, then you may find that partner has a decent balanced hand on which he has no sensible bid.

2   dbl   You have the short hearts so it is up to you to bid. If you play that this double shows a really good hand, you have to pass now and hope partner has enough to bid.

3   4NT   A good two-suited hand. Perfect!

4   pass   You would like to make a penalty double but your double here would be for takeout, and you know that your partner will bid spades. He's going to be very disappointed with your dummy! In this kind of situation you have to pass quietly, and hope partner has enough to come back in — preferably with a double.

5   4♠   This is typical of the kind of problem RHO was trying to create when he opened 4♣. What's the right contract going to be — 4♠, 4♥, 6♠, 6♥, even 7♠ or 7♥? You don't know, and there's no sensible way to show both suits any more. All you can do is bid your longer suit, and hope for the best. If they bid more clubs, you can bid 5♥ (you're not planning on defending anything below 6♣), and then partner may be able to take a bid and show you any support he has.

6   pass   Again, double would be for takeout, so you must hope partner can double in the passout seat, when you will happily pass. If he bids 4♠ instead, you can only hope he has really good spades, and that your bits and pieces will fill in his hand.

7   4♠   Yes, we know your best suit is diamonds, but partner will usually have spades when he doubles 4♥, and ten tricks are easier than eleven.

8   5♦   No need to get more excited than this. You're telling partner you have a good suit and some stuff outside it by bidding 5♦ and not just passing his double, and if he has a really good hand with diamonds, he'll bid a slam.

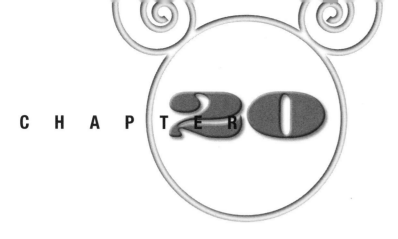

BALANCING — GENERAL PRINCIPLES

 There is scarcely one player in a hundred who does not overbid. Players grip the bid between their teeth, and nothing will persuade them to relinquish it. *Florence Irwin,* **Auction Highlights,** *1913.*

Balancing auctions occur when the opponents try to end the auction at a low level. When you are in the balancing seat you must decide whether to allow them to do so. The most common situation occurs when your LHO opens the bidding and two passes follow. Bidding in the balancing seat is not so different from bidding when the opening bid is on your right, although the strength requirements for balancing bids are generally lower. There are few hands on which you would take action in second seat that would pass in the balancing seat. Indeed, as we shall soon see, you will often bid in the balancing seat on hands that you would have passed automatically if partner still had a chance to bid. Let's investigate why.

Why is bidding in the balancing seat different?

LHO	Partner	RHO	You
	(direct seat)		(balancing seat)
1♥	pass	pass	?

When the bidding comes around to you in this way, you are in the 'balancing' seat (or 'passout' seat — passing now will end the auction) as opposed to partner, who was in the 'direct' seat.

When considering whether to balance, you are not only bidding your own hand, but also protecting partner. So, why does partner need protecting? Consider what he might do with this hand after a 1♥ opening:

♠ 7 4   ♥ A K 3   ♦ K Q 5 2   ♣ Q 9 6 2

LHO	Partner	RHO	You
1♥	?		

If you think back to our earlier discussions you will realize that, although he has a nice hand, there is little partner can do except pass. He is not strong enough to bid 1NT, he does not have a five-card suit to overcall, and he has the wrong shape (length in the opener's suit and shortness in the other major) to make a takeout double.

Let's say your hand in the balancing seat is something like:

♠ J 8 3 2   ♥ 6   ♦ A 8 7 4   ♣ K J 7 5

LHO	Partner	RHO	You
1♥	pass	pass	?

If the bidding were opened 1♥ on your right, you would pass because you are not strong enough to make a takeout double. However, if the auction starts with 1♥ on your left and two passes follow, the requirements for a takeout double are much lower. Looking at the two hands above together, it is clear that you do not want to defend 1♥. Chances are that the opponents can make 7-8 tricks in hearts while you can probably make nine tricks in either minor.

One of you obviously has to bid something. Having decided that partner cannot reasonably bid in the direct seat, it follows that it must be up to you to take some action when LHO's opening bid is passed around to you.

How much less do you need?

You can be much more aggressive in the balancing seat. A good guide is to add a king (or 3 HCP) to the value of your hand temporarily and then make the same bid that you would have made if the opening bid had been on your right. You may think it sounds incredibly dangerous to bid a hand that you don't actually hold, but there is logic to this principle.

Say you have the 9-HCP hand given above. LHO's 1♥ opening showed 12-19 HCP and RHO cannot have more than 5 HCP, having passed his partner's opening bid. Thus, the opponents have a maximum of 24 HCP, and perhaps as few as 13. Even if both opponents have maximum hands, partner will have 7 HCP. He could have as many as 18 (and certainly up to 15 HCP in a hand that had no suitable bid over 1♥). The chances are that the points are split about evenly between your side and the opponents. If that is the case, then you do not want to defend 1♥, as you will surely be able to make a partscore of your own.

Even if the opponents have the balance of points, it is still right for you to bid. If they do have the majority of the cards, the chances are that they will bid again. Then at least you have pushed them higher and they will have to work that much harder to make their contract. You may even manage to defeat them now.

How do you respond when partner balances?

Every silver lining has a cloud! As partner has mentally added 3 HCP to his hand, you must deduct a similar amount from yours. When deciding how high to bid facing a balancing bid, take a king off your actual point count and then bid what you would have bid had partner been in direct seat. Notrump bidding offers a straightforward illustration of how this works:

LHO	Partner	RHO	You
1♥	dbl	pass	?

You will remember this table from Chapter 7:

1NT =	*8-10 points*
2NT =	*11-12 points*
3NT =	*13+ points*

LHO	Partner	RHO	You
		1♥	pass
pass	dbl	pass	?

BALANCING — GENERAL PRINCIPLES

This is the corresponding table for bidding notrump over a balancing double — exactly three points more in each case:

1NT =	*11-13 points*
2NT =	*14-15 points*
3NT =	*not possible — you would have overcalled 1NT in the first place!*

When partner doubles in second seat, you know he will have 11+ HCP (plus distribution) and thus you can bid game with 13+ HCP. When he doubles in the balancing seat, he may only have something like the 9-HCP hand we saw above. If you were not strong enough to overcall 1NT immediately, then it is not possible for you to have enough to bid 3NT now.

Do the same rules apply to balancing overcalls?

Yes, you still need at least a five-card suit for an overcall, but you can make the bid with less high-card strength than would be required in second seat. For example:

♠ A J 8 6 4   ♥ 9 6   ♦ J 8 6 5   ♣ 10 5

You would not overcall 1♠ in direct seat because, expecting you to have more high cards than this, partner will frequently bid too much. However, if LHO's 1♣, 1♦ or 1♥ opening is followed by two passes, you can now safely bid 1♠. Partner knows you are balancing and will proceed with caution. In direct seat you must have a good suit if you are going to overcall with less than opening bid values. In balancing seat, the suit quality matters far less.

♠ J 7 5   ♥ 5 4   ♦ K Q 10 8 6 5   ♣ Q 4

Non-vulnerable, you might have made a weak jump overcall of 3♦ if your RHO had opened 1♥ or 1♠. You would certainly not overcall 2♦, which would show a better hand than this — but remember, *you cannot make a preemptive bid in the balancing seat*. A major reason for making a weak jump overcall after your RHO has opened is to make life difficult for the opponents. Clearly, there is no need to do this when you are in the balancing seat. If you have such a bad hand that you are worried the opponents can make game, you can just pass and let them play at the one-level. If LHO's opening bid is followed by two passes you can safely come in with 2♦ on this hand. Partner knows you are balancing and will proceed cautiously.

In the balancing seat, jump overcalls are intermediate, showing something like a minimum opening bid with a good six-card suit. Your hand could be

♠ K 7 5   ♥ 5 4   ♦ K Q 10 8 6 5   ♣ A 4

If LHO opens 1♥ and that is passed around to you, you can jump to 3♦ on a hand such as this. If partner has something like 10-14 HCP and stopper(s) in opener's suit, he will bid 3NT.

What do you need to bid notrump in balancing seat?

Once again, you can mentally borrow a few points from partner's hand. You can agree to a specific range for a balancing 1NT with your regular partner — something like 12-15 points (borrowing 3 points from partner) would be considered standard. Indeed, if you are a passed hand, you can safely bid 1NT with as little as 10-12 points. Remember, partner knows you have passed and thus you cannot have more than that.

You will usually have a stopper in the opener's suit to bid 1NT, but in the balancing seat, making this bid does not guarantee one. For example:

♠ 8 6　♥ J 10 5　♦ A Q 7 5　♣ K Q 8 4

LHO	*Partner*	*RHO*	*You*
1♥	pass	pass	?

You cannot pass. Partner might also be sitting there with a balanced 12-count. You could even be cold for game your way, and defeating 1♥ by a couple of tricks will be poor compensation. You cannot overcall 2♣ or 2♦ with only a four-card suit, and you cannot double with only two small spades. You have a balanced hand in the 12-15 HCP range, so bid 1NT.

As 1NT now shows 12-15 HCP, you must double first and then rebid notrump with the next range — 16-18. With 19-21 HCP and a balanced hand, you can bid 2NT directly. Notice that 2NT is natural in the balancing seat, not the Unusual Notrump convention.

✓ When an opening bid of one of a suit is followed by two passes, the player in the balancing seat can mentally add a king (3 HCP) to his actual point count and then overcall, double or bid 1NT if it is appropriate.

✓ A 1NT bid in balancing seat shows 12-15 HCP and does not guarantee a stopper in opener's suit. With 16-18 HCP and a balanced hand, double first then rebid in notrump. If you are a passed hand, you can balance with 1NT on 10-12 points.

✓ A jump to 2NT in balancing seat is not Unusual. It shows a balanced hand in the 19-21 HCP range.

✓ When partner has made a balancing bid, deduct a king (3 HCP) from your actual point count and respond as you would have done if he had made the same bid in the direct seat.

BALANCING — GENERAL PRINCIPLES

NOW TRY THESE...

What is your next bid on each of these hands?

1
- ♠ J 5 3
- ♥ A 9
- ♦ A 9 7 6
- ♣ K 10 8 4

LHO	Partner	RHO	You
1♦	pass	pass	?

2
- ♠ J 4 2
- ♥ Q 7 5 4 3
- ♦ 7
- ♣ A 9 7 5

LHO	Partner	RHO	You
1♦	pass	pass	?

3
- ♠ 10 9 6 3
- ♥ K Q 7 5
- ♦ 7 6
- ♣ A J 7

LHO	Partner	RHO	You
1♦	pass	pass	?

4
- ♠ K 10 8
- ♥ A 8
- ♦ A J 7 5
- ♣ K Q 7 3

LHO	Partner	RHO	You
1♦	pass	pass	?

5
- ♠ J 3
- ♥ K J 8 3
- ♦ Q 9 8
- ♣ A 7 4 3

LHO	Partner	RHO	You
		1♥	pass
pass	dbl	pass	?

6
- ♠ J 3
- ♥ 7 6
- ♦ A 8 6 2
- ♣ K J 9 7 3

LHO	Partner	RHO	You
		1♥	pass
pass	dbl	pass	?

7
- ♠ Q 8 6 3 2
- ♥ A 4 2
- ♦ 3
- ♣ K J 7 5

LHO	Partner	RHO	You
		1♥	pass
pass	dbl	pass	?

8
- ♠ K 8 3
- ♥ Q 10 7 5 3
- ♦ Q 8 6 3
- ♣ 5

LHO	Partner	RHO	You
		1♥	pass
pass	dbl	pass	?

9
- ♠ K J 5
- ♥ A 8 4
- ♦ J 9 8 2
- ♣ J 8 5

LHO	Partner	RHO	You
		1♥	pass
pass	1♠	pass	?

10
- ♠ 8
- ♥ A J 8 4
- ♦ K Q 8 5 3
- ♣ Q 10 5

LHO	Partner	RHO	You
		1♥	pass
pass	1♠	pass	?

ANSWERS

1 1NT If the 1♦ opening were on your right and you had the ♠K instead of one of the small spades, you would overcall 1NT and consider that a minimum. In balancing seat, bid 1NT with this hand — again about a minimum.

2 1♥ You would not overcall 1♥ if the 1♦ opening were on your right but in the balancing seat it is clear. Pretend one of your small clubs is the king and now you would have the values for a normal second-seat 1♥ overcall, although perhaps not the suit quality.

3 dbl Mentally give yourself the ♠K and you can see that you would have a normal takeout double of a 1♦ opening on your right.

4 dbl Why not 1NT?, you might think. Remember that in balancing seat, you can bid 1NT with 12 HCP, so you clearly cannot make the same bid with 17. Double first, then bid notrump over whatever partner bids.

5 1NT You have a good hand, but pretend the ♦A is the jack and it doesn't look quite as strong now. As partner has already bid those three points for you, 1NT is plenty. Remember that partner is expected to overbid in balancing seat, so you must underbid in order to compensate.

6 2♣ If partner had doubled in second seat, you would have jumped to 3♣, but opposite a balancing double you need a very good hand to take such action. Take away a king and you'll realize that this one is not close.

7 2♠ This hand is worth a jump, but only to 2♠. Opposite a second-seat double you would jump to 3♠, but you realize by now that you have to underbid by a king (or 3 HCP) on the actual auction.

8 2♦ If partner had made a second-seat takeout double, you might have considered bidding 1NT. After the balancing double you have a much weaker hand than partner is expecting and 1NT would be a significant overbid (it shows 11-14 HCP and you have only seven).

9 2♠ With 10 HCP and a nice fit for partner's suit, you would have been more enthusiastic opposite a second-seat overcall, but 2♠ is plenty (and perhaps even too much) facing a balancing bid.

10 1NT You have a nice hand, but it is not even certain that your side has half of the points. With no fit, you should be very wary.

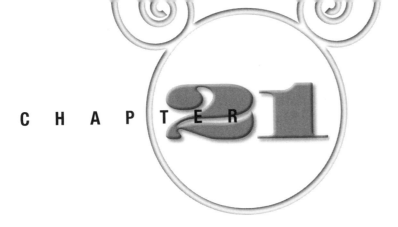

OTHER BALANCING AUCTIONS

 The rules were made to cover 99 cases out of 100, and they do. Occasionally the hundredth case arrives, but it takes an expert to recognize it. And anyone else who tries it will come to grief and drag his partner with him.
Florence Irwin, **Auction Highlights,** *1913.*

There is a balancing decision to be made whenever the opponents try to play at a low level and a pass from you will end the auction, thus allowing them to do so. In some auctions, bidding is extremely safe. In others it is not. Let's try to work out which is which.

How do you know when partner has some points?

LHO	Partner	RHO	You
1♥	pass	pass	?

In the previous chapter, we worked out that the opponents had a maximum of 24 HCP when an opening bid of one of a suit was passed around to you.

However, it is very likely that they have fewer than that. The major reason for this is that your RHO is known to hold a very weak hand — a maximum of 5 HCP since, with six, he would have responded. In theory, opener could hold anywhere between 12-19 HCP, but something near the lower end of this range is statistically more likely.

Most of the time, the points will be about evenly split. Indeed, the non-opening side is the more likely to have the majority. Now compare that auction with this one:

LHO	Partner	RHO	You
1NT	pass	pass	?

Say opener's 1NT shows 15-17. What do you know about RHO's hand?

He probably will not have a five-card major or a six-card minor. However, all you know about his strength is that he has less than 8 HCP (as with that hand he would invite game). His range is very wide indeed, and there is no guarantee at all that your side has the balance of the HCP. Indeed, the odds favor the opposite to be the case.

Things are no different if the 1NT shows 12-14 HCP. In that case, RHO could have as many as 10 HCP (i.e. not quite enough to invite game). Again, your side probably does not have the majority of the points.

This auction is clearer yet:

LHO	Partner	RHO	You
1♥	pass	2♣	pass
2♥	pass	pass	?

The opponents have stopped at a low level, therefore it is safe to come in because partner will have some points, right? Wrong... Opener is somewhere in the 12-15 HCP range. RHO had enough for a two-level response but not quite enough to bid 2NT once his partner showed a minimum, so he has approximately 9-10 HCP. What are the chances that your side has half of the points? Right — they are zero.

Just because the opponents stop at a low level does not necessarily mean that the points are evenly distributed.

Does it make any difference if the opponents have found a fit?

Yes — if they have a fit, it is much more likely that you do too. Indeed, if they have as much as a nine-card fit, then you are guaranteed to have at least one eight-card fit, and perhaps better. To see why is easy enough. Say the opponents hold nine hearts. That leaves your side with just four hearts, and thus twenty-two non-hearts. If we divide those twenty-two non-hearts between the remaining three suits, at least one of them has to have eight cards in it. Similarly, if the opponents have a ten-card fit, you must have at least one nine-card fit or two eight-card fits, and so on.

The best balancing situations occur when the opponents have found a fit and try to stop at a low level. Consider this auction:

LHO	Partner	RHO	You
		1♥	pass
2♥	pass	pass	?

Not only is it likely that you have a fit, but you also know that the opponents have only half (or just over half) of the high-card points. Both opponents have limited their hands — LHO by his simple raise, and RHO by his failure to look for game.

There are two possible reasons that partner has not bid. One is that he does not have enough values. The second and far more likely reason, particularly if you are fairly short in the opponents' suit, is that he had the wrong kind of hand either to overcall 1NT or to make a takeout double.

If you have the right shape, feel free to overcall or make a takeout double on virtually any hand. If you hold 10 HCP, then partner will have approximately 8-11. If you have 8, then he will have 10-13. If you have only 4, that leaves partner with 14-17. Your side's combined assets will always add up to about the same number, no matter how few of them you can actually see.

In the auction above, it was safe for you to bid because the opponents had a known fit. Surely this auction is the same, isn't it?

LHO	Partner	RHO	You
		1♥	pass
1♠	pass	2♣	pass
2♥	pass	pass	?

Again, the opponents have stopped in 2♥. So you also have a fit, right? No — absolutely not. How many hearts do you think each of the opponents has?

Opener has five, but probably not six as he might then have rebid 2♥ rather than 2♣. Responder has only two hearts as, with a fairly weak hand and three-card support for his partner's known five-card major, he would have raised immediately. Thus, the opponents have only seven hearts. Quite probably, they do not have an eight-card fit anywhere, and if they do not, neither do you. **_Coming into a non-fit auction is very dangerous._** The most likely result of doing so is to convert a small plus score into a small minus. Sometimes though, the opponents have enough high-card strength to make 2♥ despite the lack of a fit. If that is the case, they may well double you, and then getting into the bidding will have converted a small minus into a large one.

Can you balance safely over a preempt?

LHO	Pass	RHO	You
2♥	pass	pass	?

Is there a reason to suppose that partner has a reasonable hand here? Have the opponents found a fit? The answer to both questions is no, which means that this is not a safe balancing position. To see why, consider what kind of hand RHO might have.

He may be quite weak but, in that case, he almost certainly has short hearts. With three-card heart support, most players would make a defensive raise to 3♥ to increase the level of the preempt. If RHO has short hearts, then he has length in your potential trump suits. He could easily have something like:

$$ \spadesuit\ KQ\,10\,7 \quad \heartsuit\ — \quad \diamondsuit\ Q\,10\,8\,6\,5 \quad \clubsuit\ AK\,10\,8 $$

Not only might you have no eight-card fit but suits are likely to break poorly. This is a dangerous position in which to bid unless you have full values in your own hand. It goes without saying that the same is even more true of an auction like:

LHO	Partner	RHO	You
3♥	pass	pass	?

Do not bid in balancing seat unless you are very close to a hand on which you would have bid in the direct seat. You'll still run into your share of trouble, but it won't happen as often.

Summary

✓ Partner is guaranteed to have some points only when the opponents are both limited. If an opening bid of one of a suit has been followed by two passes, or if opener's suit has been raised to the two-level and opener has passed, then the points rate to be split about evenly.

✓ If the opponents have found a fit, then your side almost always has a fit somewhere. Having a known fit makes bidding much safer.

✓ If the opponents have not found a fit, be extremely wary of balancing, especially if one of their hands could be quite strong. This particularly applies to balancing over preempts.

OTHER BALANCING AUCTIONS

NOW TRY THESE...

What is your next bid on each of these hands?

1
- ♠ K 9 7 4
- ♥ 3
- ♦ K 9 8 2
- ♣ K 8 7 4

LHO	Partner	RHO	You
		1♥	pass
2♥	pass	pass	?

2
- ♠ Q 9 7 5 3
- ♥ 8 6
- ♦ Q 8 7
- ♣ K 6 5

LHO	Partner	RHO	You
		1♥	pass
2♥	pass	pass	?

3
- ♠ 4
- ♥ J 5 2
- ♦ K J 8 7
- ♣ K 10 7 4 3

LHO	Partner	RHO	You
1♥	pass	1NT	pass
2♥	pass	pass	?

4
- ♠ J 4
- ♥ K J 6 4
- ♦ K J 8 7
- ♣ K 10 4

LHO	Partner	RHO	You
		1♥	pass
2♥	pass	pass	?

5
- ♠ Q 8 6 2
- ♥ A J 8 7
- ♦ A J 10
- ♣ Q 6

LHO	Partner	RHO	You
1♥	pass	2♥	pass
pass	dbl	pass	?

6
- ♠ Q 8 6 2
- ♥ A J 8 7
- ♦ A J 10
- ♣ Q 6

LHO	Partner	RHO	You
1♥	pass	2♥	pass
pass	2♠	pass	?

7
- ♠ J 10 2
- ♥ K 10 8 6 3
- ♦ A 7 3
- ♣ Q 8

LHO	Partner	RHO	You
1♥	pass	2♥	pass
pass	dbl	pass	?

8
- ♠ J 10 2
- ♥ K 10 8 6 3
- ♦ A 7 3
- ♣ Q 8

LHO	Partner	RHO	You
1♥	pass	2♥	pass
pass	2♠	pass	?

ANSWERS

1   dbl   Don't worry that you don't have a good hand. The fewer HCP you have, the more partner will hold. You have support for whichever suit partner bids, so make a takeout double to ask him to choose one.

2   2♠   You did not have quite enough to overcall 1♠ on the previous round, but it is clear to balance now.

3   pass   The opponents have not found a fit, and partner must have short hearts and long spades, yet he hasn't taken a bid at either of his opportunities. This is a very dangerous situation in which to enter the auction. Remember, the 1NT does not promise a balanced hand. RHO could well have long minors and be waiting eagerly for you to bid.

4   pass   You didn't have the right kind of hand to bid over 1♥ and you still don't over 2♥. You have too much in hearts, and no spades, so where are you going?

5   2♠   Partner has asked you to pick a suit, and with four cards in the unbid major that seems to be the obvious choice. You did not think seriously about passing, did you? If you did, then go back and look at Hand 1 again, on which you doubled in partner's position.

6   pass   Partner has already bid every high card you hold. The fact that you have four-card support for his suit just makes it that much more likely that he will be able to make eight tricks.

7   2♠   Time to ask yourself — do you feel lucky? Yes, you could gamble on a pass, but you are sitting under the long heart hand and 2♥ is still quite likely to make. Partner has made a takeout double, and the normal thing to do is to take it out. Remember, when responding to a takeout double, if your only four-card suit is the one bid by the opponents, bid your cheapest three-card suit.

8   pass   What were you thinking of doing? Partner could not overcall 1♠ first time around, so you can hardly have a game.

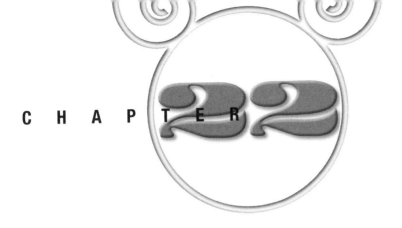

FORCING PASSES

 There is one lesson the average player will never learn, and that is the art of passing on good cards.
Florence Irwin, **Auction Highlights, *1913*.**

There are many situations in which it is useful to use 'pass' as a forcing call — putting partner in a situation where at his turn he is not allowed to pass. In general, a pass should be considered forcing when your side has shown strength and the opposition is clearly sacrificing. In other words, you know it is your hand. In such circumstances, it is inconceivable that you would want to allow the enemy to play undoubled. The decision to be made is whether your side should double and take the penalty or bid on to your own contract.

LHO	Partner	RHO	You
			1♥
1♠	4♥	4♠	?

You have no idea whose hand this is, or who can make what. Partner's 4♥ could have been preemptive, while RHO's 4♠ could be based on a good hand. Pass by you would therefore not be forcing, and partner is allowed to pass out 4♠. He doubles or bids 5♥ at his own risk.

Now look at this auction:

LHO	Partner	RHO	You
3♥	3♠	pass	4♥
pass	4♠	5♥	?

Let's walk through what has happened so far. LHO preempted and, in response to partner's overcall, your 4♥ cuebid showed an invitational raise in spades, asking partner if he was interested in a slam. Partner denied slam interest by signing off in game but now RHO competes to 5♥. Your side has bid willingly to game, making a slam try on the way. The opponents have preempted and then sacrificed once you bid game.

Clearly the hand belongs to you — you raised to 4♠ fully expecting to make it. RHO is obviously sacrificing. He was prepared to defend 3♠ — if he had expected to make 4♥, he surely would have bid it on the previous round. You cannot possibly want to defend 5♥ undoubled. Your side will either double 5♥ or bid on to 5♠.

BY THE WAY

RHO's 'check and raise' tactics on this hand are not recommended. He was probably hoping you wouldn't bid 4♠, but he would have done far better to raise hearts immediately, taking away your cuebid and making life generally more awkward right away.

♠ K Q   ♥ A 6 3   ♦ A J 8 7   ♣ Q 9 7 4

Suppose this is your hand for the auction we are discussing. You have lots of high cards but no clear bid on the previous round. You therefore decided to raise partner's likely six-card suit while making a slam try on the way to game. When RHO backs into the auction at the five-level, it is clear from your hand that you should suggest defending. Double 5♥. Always take your sure plus score.

♠ K J 7 6 5   ♥ 8   ♦ K 10 8 7 5   ♣ A 4

But what if this is what you are looking at? Partner really hit the jackpot with his spade overcall, and your hand is packed with offensive values. You were worth a slam try in case partner had a particularly suitable overcall. When RHO saves in 5♥, it looks to you as if he has done the right thing. There is no way you are going to defend — you may not have a single spade trick on defense against a heart contract. Bid 5♠.

Those two hands are at the opposite ends of the scale in terms of your 4♥ bid. The first one is packed with defensive values but has fairly poor offensive strength. The second example is all offense. In each case, it was clear that you had a view to express over 5♥.

♠ K J 7   ♥ 8 5 3   ♦ K J 8 7 4   ♣ A 4

Now imagine that your hand lies somewhere between those two examples.

You have neither far more defense than your 4♥ bid suggested, nor more offense. In short, you have about what partner would expect. Should you therefore suggest defending 5♥ doubled or should you bid on to 5♠?

Of course, you will have worked out that the answer to that question is 'neither'. You should pass, leaving the decision to your partner, whose hand may be eminently more suited to one action or the other. As we established earlier, there is no chance that your side would want to pass out 5♥ and thus your pass is forcing.

In this common situation for a forcing pass your call says to partner, "I have no particular preference between defending and bidding one more. Would you please choose?"

There is one final point that is worth noting in this situation. Let's say that your hand is stronger and even more offensively oriented than the second one above.

♠ Q J 7 6 5   ♥ —   ♦ Q J 8 7 5   ♣ A 4 3

If RHO had passed 4♠, you were going to make one more slam try. Now RHO's 5♥ bid has interfered with that. Of course, you have no intention of defending 5♥ doubled. However, you should make a forcing pass, and when partner doubles (which you expect), you then pull his double to 5♠. Thus:

LHO	Partner	RHO	You
3♥	3♠	pass	4♥
pass	4♠	5♥	pass
pass	dbl	pass	5♠

This slow route to 5♠ is the strongest slam try you can make. It suggests that you were going to bid on over 4♠. Compare that with the second hand above, where you bid 5♠ immediately. On that occasion, you did not want to invite a slam. You just did not want to defend 5♥.

Does a forcing pass mean anything special at the slam level?

LHO	Partner	RHO	You
	2♣	3♣	3♥
5♣	6♣	7♣	pass

Here's an auction that got out of hand very fast! Partner opened 2♣ and you bid 3♥, showing a decent hand. Partner then cuebid the opponents' suit at the six-level, showing an 'invitational' raise to 6♥ — he is interested in the grand slam. By the time RHO bids 7♣, it is clear that your side owns the hand and that the enemy are sacrificing.

There can be no question of allowing the opponents to play 7♣ undoubled. However, you can convey a vital and very specific piece of information here by making a **forcing pass** that invites partner to bid a grand slam. **You guarantee first-round control of the opponents' suit.**

Perhaps partner is looking at a hand such as:

♠ A K Q J 8 7   ♥ A J 10 7 4   ♦ A   ♣ 5

If your forcing pass of 7♣ said only that you weren't sure what to do, then partner would also now be in a similar position. He would not know if you held:

♠	9 5 4		♠	9 5
♥	K Q 8 6 3 2	*or*	♥	K Q 8 6 3 2
♦	J 7 6 5		♦	K Q 6 5
♣	—		♣	7

You can hardly commit to bidding 7♥ on either of these hands. On the first, you do not know that the minor suits are completely solid. Partner might have bid 6♣ in order to allow you to cuebid a diamond control. On the second hand, you cannot bid the grand slam as you do not know if the opponents are going to be able to cash a club trick.

A forcing pass that invites a grand slam tells partner not to worry about a fast loser in the opponents' suit. If you do not have first-round control of the opponents' suit, you have only one choice: double the opponents.

Can a pass be forcing at a low level?

We could have discussed this situation back in Chapter 13, but chose not to for the sake of keeping life relatively simple; however, it's appropriate here. When you double a 1NT opening for penalties, and they run, it potentially sets up a forcing pass situation:

LHO	Partner	RHO	You
1NT	dbl	2♦	dbl
pass	pass	2♥	pass
pass	?		

What's going on here? The opponents ran to diamonds, and when that got doubled tried hearts instead. Your double of 2♦ showed a good hand, but you weren't so sure about defending 2♥. You are leaving the decision to your partner, and your pass is forcing. You won't be unhappy if he doubles 2♥ — if that were the case, you'd just have bid something over it yourself.

A good general rule is this: once you have doubled the opponents for penalties, they should not be allowed to play undoubled if they run to another suit.

This rule allows you to pass 2♥, simply denying enough trumps to double 2♥. If your partner has trumps, he will double. If he does not, then he will bid. Either way, you will defend 2♥ doubled when that is right for your side, and you will bid on when it is not.

Forcing pass situations can also occur at a low level if the opponents bid once your side is in a game-forcing auction. For example, you cannot defend an undoubled contract if one of you has opened 2♣, or if you have forced to game by using Fourth-Suit Forcing.

Summary

✓ A pass should be considered forcing if the opponents bid after your side has bid voluntarily to game, having shown strength in doing so.

✓ A forcing pass makes partner choose between doubling and bidding on. If you have a particularly defensive hand (or a poor offensive hand) for your previous bidding, you should double, suggesting defending. If your hand is strongly oriented towards offense, you should bid in front of partner. Passing says your hand is somewhere in between, so he should make the decision.

✓ If you pass in a forcing pass situation, and subsequently pull partner's double, you are making a slam try.

✓ At the slam level, a forcing pass that invites partner to bid to the seven-level guarantees first-round control of the opponents' suit — the ace or a void. Without first-round control, double.

✓ Forcing pass situations can also occur at a low level. Passes become forcing if you have already doubled the opponents for penalties and they have run to another suit.

✓ Pass is forcing if the opponents intervene when you are in a game-forcing auction.

FORCING PASSES

NOW TRY THESE...

What is your next bid on each of the following hands?

1
- ♠ J 10 9 4 2
- ♥ 7 3
- ♦ K Q J
- ♣ 10 8 7

LHO	Partner	RHO	You
	2♣	2♥	2♠
3♥	3♠	4♥	?

2
- ♠ K J 9 7 5 3
- ♥ 8 6
- ♦ 8
- ♣ Q J 6 5

LHO	Partner	RHO	You
	2♣	2♥	2♠
3♥	3♠	4♥	?

3
- ♠ K J 9 7 4
- ♥ 8 2
- ♦ J 8 7
- ♣ A 10 7

LHO	Partner	RHO	You
	2♣	2♥	2♠
3♥	3♠	4♥	?

4
- ♠ K Q J 9 7 4
- ♥ —
- ♦ J 8 7 3 2
- ♣ Q 10

LHO	Partner	RHO	You
	2♣	2♥	2♠
3♥	3♠	4♥	?

5
- ♠ A Q 7 5 2
- ♥ K Q 6
- ♦ 3 2
- ♣ K 6 2

LHO	Partner	RHO	You
			1♠
pass	2NT[1]	3♦	?

1. Game-forcing, agrees spades

6
- ♠ A J 7 4
- ♥ Q 8 5 2
- ♦ 6 3
- ♣ K Q 6

LHO	Partner	RHO	You
	1♥	pass	2NT[1]
3♦	4♥[2]	5♦	?

1. Game-forcing, agrees hearts
2. Minimum hand

ANSWERS

1 dbl Your hand is terrible offensively — a poor suit and no distribution. Your outside honors are also defensive assets. Don't worry that you do not have trump tricks — partner knows the opponents have nine or ten hearts between them.

2 4♠ This time, your values are all offensive. Your lack of controls and the doubleton heart (the worst holding you could have on this auction) make your hand unsuitable for a slam try of your own, though.

3 pass You have about what partner would expect, both offensively and defensively. You have no opinion to express, so leave the decision to partner.

4 pass You have no intention of defending 4♥ doubled, but it is also just about possible that you will have three losers in 5♠. RHO's 4♥ bid enables you to make a slam try without venturing beyond game. Make a forcing pass and then pull partner's expected double to 4♠.

5 pass You have no extra offense or extra defense. Pass and let partner decide whether to double 3♦ or bid on in spades.

6 dbl You have good defensive values and minimum offense, having already shown four-card heart support with your Jacoby 2NT bid. Partner can elect to bid on anyway, but warn him that your hand is defensive in nature.

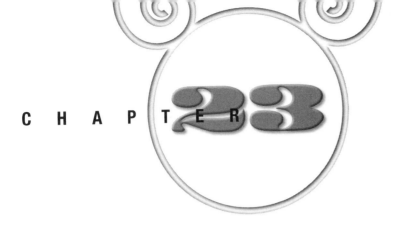

LOCATING STOPPERS
FOR NOTRUMP

 The first great test of a notrump bid is whether the hand holds two unprotected suits. One suit you may safely trust to your partner, but it would be rather optimistic to expect him to take care of two.
Florence Irwin, Auction Highlights, 1913.

It is usually a good idea to have a stopper in all suits when you play a notrump contract. If, for example, you play in 3NT holding Q-x opposite two small in a suit, your only chance is that the opponents do not lead that suit, or underlead the A-K. In order to avoid this, it is sometimes necessary to bid 'stoppers' rather than suits when you are trying to decide whether to play a hand in notrump. It is quite common to know you have the values for game, but to be uncertain about the stopper situation in one suit; for example

♠ A K ♥ 6 4 ♦ K J 5 4 ♣ K Q 10 7 3

LHO	Partner	RHO	You
			1♣
pass	3♣	pass	?

What now? If you knew partner had hearts covered, you'd probably take a shot at 3NT, but you don't. There's nothing worse than going down in 3NT when you're cold for 6♣, so you need some way to find out more about partner's hand — in particular, what the heart situation is.

How can you ask partner for a stopper?

As usual, there isn't a simple answer to that question. There are a number of ways to do it, and the one you use depends on the exact auction that has preceded your enquiry. As a general rule, when there is only one suit in which you can possibly need a stopper for notrump (whether an opponent has bid the suit or not) then bidding it asks for a stopper. When there are two or even three suits, it is normal to bid one in which you hold a stopper. On the example hand, you would bid 3♦, giving partner a chance to bid 3♥ if he can. If he does bid 3♥, you will try 3NT; if he doesn't, you will probably end up in 5♣.

Once you have already agreed on a trump suit, bidding another suit is never advertising that you have lots of that suit. There would be no point ever in bidding diamonds in our last example just to show you have diamonds; no one cares. And partner cannot have a four-card major or he would never have bid 3♣ in the first place. That is how you know that these bids are asking for stoppers en route to 3NT.

A simple example of an auction in which you can ask for a stopper occurs when you have bid three suits between you. Now, if either of you bids the fourth suit, that asks for a stopper (if you had one, you'd just bid notrump yourself!).

♠ Q 4   ♥ J 5   ♦ A K J 7 5   ♣ K Q J 7

LHO	Partner	RHO	You
			1♦
pass	1♠	pass	2♣
pass	3♣	pass	3♥

The bid of 3♥ does not show any interest in playing the hand in a heart contract. It essentially asks partner to describe his hand further. Both 3NT and 5♣ are possible contracts but the former will clearly be hopeless if the defenders can take five heart tricks off the top. One of the ways in which partner can respond is to bid notrump if he can stop the fourth suit.

In this book, we are dealing only with auctions in which the opponents have opened the bidding. In many such auctions, a bid of the opener's suit can be used to ask for a notrump stopper. For example:

♠ A 7   ♥ 8 6   ♦ A Q 7   ♣ A J 9 7 6 4

LHO	Partner	RHO	You
		1♥	2♣
pass	3♣	pass	?

Eleven tricks in clubs looks a long way off. Remember, partner could have raised clubs via a 2♥ cuebid, but he chose to make a limited, weakish simple raise. Even so, you are willing to take a shot at 3NT if partner has a heart stopper. Bid 3♥ to ask for a stopper. Without one, partner will bid 4♣, which you can pass.

Remember that we seldom wish to play a hand in five of a minor, unless we have a singleton or void. It is much harder to take eleven tricks and the score is not nearly as remunerative as 3NT. Five of a minor is for children and opponents!

Similarly:

♠ 8 6   ♥ A J   ♦ K Q 10 7 6 5   ♣ Q 10 6

LHO	Partner	RHO	You
		1♠	2♦
pass	2♠	pass	?

BY THE WAY

A cuebid of the opponent's suit to ask for a notrump stopper is often called a Western Cuebid.

Your hand is weaker this time, but partner has promised a limit raise or better. If you held a spade stopper yourself, you could suggest a notrump contract by bidding 2NT or 3NT. With no stopper in opener's suit but an otherwise suitable hand, you can ask partner for a stopper with a 3♠ cuebid.

When do you show a stopper instead of asking?

Sometimes there is more than one suit in which you need to check for stoppers.

♠ Q J 5   ♥ K   ♦ J 3   ♣ A Q 10 8 6 4 3

LHO	Partner	RHO	You
1♦	1♥	1♠	2♣
pass	3♣	pass	?

Here you have a good hand and you want to investigate a notrump game before climbing all the way to the five-level. You are likely to have at least nine tricks in a notrump contract, provided the defenders cannot cash five before you can gain the lead. You are not worried about spades, as you can stop them running that suit, but what about diamonds?

When there are two suits about which you are unsure, you show the suit in which you have a stopper. On this hand, you would bid 3♠. Effectively, this says to partner, "I have spades stopped, can you stop diamonds?" Similarly, a 3♦ bid would show a diamond stopper and ask partner whether he could stop spades. That seems fairly straightforward when one of you is looking at a clear stopper in the key suit.

How can we locate divided stoppers?

♠ Q 5 2   ♥ A Q J 7 5   ♦ 4 2   ♣ K J 5

LHO	Partner	RHO	You
		1♦	1♥
1♠	2♣	2♠	3♣
pass	3♦	pass	?

Partner has a diamond stopper, but not a spade stopper — with both he would probably have just bid 3NT himself. So, is ♠Qxx a good enough stopper? If partner has only one or two small spades, then the opponents are likely to be able to cash the first five tricks in the suit. If he has as much as ♠Jx though, then that, combined with your holding, will ensure that the defenders cannot cash five quick spade tricks.

What do you think a 3♠ bid would say about your hand?

If you had nothing in spades, you would already know that 3NT was not an option, since your partner has already denied a spade stopper. If you have a full stopper yourself, you would bid 3NT. Therefore, bidding 3♠ should show half a stopper — something like Qxx, Jxx, Qx or Jx.

If partner also has a half stopper, he will bid 3NT. If he does not, he will know that 3NT is not a possible contract. Of course, you may still end up in 3NT with a spade stopper of Qx facing Jx, but that cannot be helped. Besides, sometimes the opponents believe you and duck the first round of the suit in order to keep communications between them open!

In the auction above, we used a combination of stopper-showing bids (3♦) and stopper-asking bids (3♠). This is also possible even when the opponents have not bid any of the suits involved. That's exactly what happens in this auction:

LHO	Pass	RHO	You
		1NT	3♣
pass	3♦	pass	3♥
pass	3♠	pass	3NT

Let's see what happened here. You started by showing a good hand with a decent suit. You could not bid 2♣ because you play Landy, and that would have shown both majors, and thus the jump to 3♣ shows a decent hand with a strong club suit. In such auctions, 3NT is by far the most likely game, and thus it is important to be able to locate stoppers. Partner's 3♦ showed values and/or length in diamonds, although it is not really a suggestion that you play the hand in that suit. You have already shown a good club suit, so if a minor-suit game is an option there is no need to look for a diamond fit.

When you bid 3♥, that simply showed a heart stopper. It would be unusual to overcall 3♣ with a four-card major, so there is no chance that partner will suddenly raise hearts. For the same reasons expressed earlier, partner's 3♠ bid implies a half-stopper in that suit and asks for a little help there — if he had a full spade stopper, he would simply bid 3NT. Likewise, if you had both hearts and spades stopped, you would have bid 3NT over his 3♦ bid. If he had nothing in spades, he would press on in clubs, so once again 3♠ shows you that he has half a stopper, and asks for the other half from you.

With a hand such as

♠ J 3 2 ♥ K Q 4 ♦ 2 ♣ A Q J 10 9 3

you can now bid a confident 3NT.

Summary

✓ When there is only one suit that you can be worried about, bidding that suit asks for a stopper.

✓ When there is more than one suit in question, bid the lowest one in which you hold a stopper.

✓ In an auction where you are showing stoppers, when only one suit has not been confirmed stopped and partner has already denied a full stopper by implication, bidding that suit shows a half-stopper and asks for the other half.

LOCATING STOPPERS FOR NOTRUMP

NOW TRY THESE...

What is your next bid on each of these hands?

1
- ♠ J 9 7
- ♥ A K 8 7 3
- ♦ A 10
- ♣ Q 8 7

LHO	Partner	RHO	You
1♠	2♣	2♦	2♥
pass	3♣	pass	?

2
- ♠ 7 5 3
- ♥ K 8 6
- ♦ 8
- ♣ A K J 6 5 3

LHO	Partner	RHO	You
		1♥	2♣
pass	2♥	pass	3♣
pass	3♥	pass	?

3
- ♠ J 9 7
- ♥ A K 8 7 3
- ♦ A 10
- ♣ Q 8 7

LHO	Partner	RHO	You
1♠	2♣	2♦	2♥
pass	3♣	pass	3♦
pass	3♠	pass	?

4
- ♠ Q 10 7
- ♥ K Q 4 3
- ♦ J 7 3
- ♣ A 10 7

LHO	Partner	RHO	You
1♦	2♣	pass	2♦
pass	3♦	pass	?

ANSWERS

1 **3♦**   You can reasonably expect that partner's clubs will be ♣AKxxxx, in which case you will have nine top tricks provided he can stop the spade suit. Show your diamond stopper.

2 **3NT**   Partner's first heart cuebid simply showed an invitational raise to 3♣. With a minimum for a two-level overcall, you correctly signed off. His second heart bid is a Western Cuebid, asking you for a heart stopper. With ♥Kxx, you are happy to show one by bidding 3NT.

3 **3NT**   Partner knows you do not have a spade stopper — if you did, you would have already bid 3NT. His 3♠ bid therefore shows half a stopper, probably Qx or Qxx. Your ♠J97 should therefore be good enough to prevent the defenders cashing five spade tricks.

4 **3♥**   Partner has asked for a diamond stopper. ♦Jxx is not a strong enough holding to bid 3NT, but you also do not want to bypass game in notrump in case partner has a half stopper. By bidding 3♥, you allow partner the chance to bid 3NT, which he will now do with a half stopper (since he knows that you already know he does not have a full stopper). Anyone for gin rummy?

THE LAW
OF TOTAL TRICKS

 The maxim 'It is a good idea to let the other fellow make a dollar once in a while' is as useful in bridge as it is in a horse trade.
Florence Irwin,* Auction Highlights, *1913.

Are you a Law-abiding bidder? That question has nothing to do with whether you remember your system, but with a completely different kind of Law — one that has been the focus of much attention in recent years. It is a concept called the 'Law of Total Tricks', and it is an idea that can be of enormous help in making bidding decisions in competitive auctions. Frenchman Jean René Vernes first wrote about the Law in 1969, and Joe Amsbury was a vocal supporter of the concept when he was the Editor of IPBM in England. But it was America's Larry Cohen who pushed the Law to the forefront of modern bidding theory with his 1992 best-seller, *To Bid or Not to Bid*. Since Cohen's book was published, it has been rare to read or hear a discussion about a competitive bidding problem without someone referring to the Law.

What is the Law and how does it work?

The basic statement of the Law is this:

> *The total number of tricks available on any deal is equal to the total number of trumps held by the two sides.*

For the purposes of this definition, the 'total number of tricks' means the combined total of the tricks that could be made by the two sides if they each played in their best (longest) fit. For example, if your side can make eight tricks in clubs, and they can make nine tricks if they play in hearts, there are eight plus nine or seventeen total tricks on the hand. The 'total number of trumps' means the combined total number of cards in each side's best trump fit. For example, if your best fit is ten cards in diamonds and the opponents' is nine cards in spades, then the Law says there are nineteen tricks available on the hand. This trick total, however, can be divided between the two sides in many different ways — maybe you can make eleven tricks and the enemy only eight, or vice versa, but the *total* number of tricks is fixed at nineteen.

This example hand illustrates how the Law works:

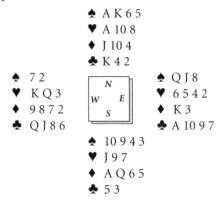

                    ♠ A K 6 5
                    ♥ A 10 8
                    ♦ J 10 4
                    ♣ K 4 2

    ♠ 7 2   ♠ Q J 8
    ♥ K Q 3   ♥ 6 5 4 2
    ♦ 9 8 7 2   ♦ K 3
    ♣ Q J 8 6   ♣ A 10 9 7

                    ♠ 10 9 4 3
                    ♥ J 9 7
                    ♦ A Q 6 5
                    ♣ 5 3

You are South. Your side's best fit is in spades, where you have eight trumps, while your opponents have an eight-card club fit, so there is a total of sixteen trumps on the hand. The Law says that therefore there should be a total of sixteen tricks on the hand. Let's see if there are.

Playing in a spade contract, you rate to lose one spade, one heart and two clubs. Meanwhile, if your opponents play in clubs, they will lose two spades, two hearts and two diamonds. You can make nine tricks and they can make seven, a total of sixteen.

Perhaps you are thinking that we set this hand up just to make the example work. After all, the black suits break evenly, both heart honors are onside for you, and both minor-suit kings lie under the ace. Actually, none of this matters; the Law doesn't care about such things. You don't believe it? Well, then, let's change things around. Say we switch the East and West hands:

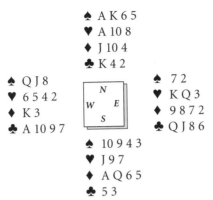

```
              ♠ A K 6 5
              ♥ A 10 8
              ♦ J 10 4
              ♣ K 4 2
♠ Q J 8                    ♠ 7 2
♥ 6 5 4 2        N         ♥ K Q 3
♦ K 3         W     E      ♦ 9 8 7 2
♣ A 10 9 7       S         ♣ Q J 8 6
              ♠ 10 9 4 3
              ♥ J 9 7
              ♦ A Q 6 5
              ♣ 5 3
```

Now both the hearts are offside, and both the minor-suit kings are winners. How does that change things? North-South must still lose one spade, and now you have two heart losers and one diamond, although there is only one club loser this time. So the number of tricks for your side has fallen from nine to eight. What about your opponents' prospects in their club contract though? Well, they must still lose two spades, and they have a club loser now too; but with the red suits moved around they lose only one trick in each of those suits. Their trick total has risen from seven to eight. So the total number of tricks is still equal to sixteen, which is the same as the total number of trumps.

Try swapping North's ♣K for one of South's low clubs. Now you can make only seven tricks but, lo and behold, East-West's total has risen to nine — the magic number is still sixteen. Try switching other key cards and you will see that the total of sixteen tricks remains constant. One side may gain a trick, but if so, the other will lose a trick, and the total number of tricks that can be made never changes.

What is your Law level?

We have seen how the Law works. Another concept that arises from this curious linking of trumps and tricks is the concept of the correct 'Law level', which we have actually encountered in earlier chapters without explaining it in great detail. Look at this hand, on which we'll assume that the opponents are vulnerable and you are not:

♠ 10 9 7 6 4   ♥ 8 3   ♦ K 9 3   ♣ 9 7 2

LHO	Partner	RHO	You
1♣	1♠	dbl	?

How many spades should you bid? To give you a clue, here is a simple rule that derives from the Law:

You are safe to contract for a number of tricks equal to the combined number of trumps held by your side.

We first mentioned this principle back in Chapter 2 when we were talking about how high to raise partner's overcall. What it means is that, in a competitive auction, if your side has eight trumps, then it is safe to bid to the two-level, an eight-trick contract. With nine trumps you have the protection of the Law at the three-level, and with ten trumps the four-level should be safe. Now, we should hasten to add that the Law doesn't promise that you will make what you bid. However, it does promise that if you go down, you will show a profit compared to defending whatever the opponents can make. So, why does this rule work?

Assume your side has ten spades. How many trumps will the opponents have? Since they have only three spades, twenty-three of their twenty-six cards are in the other three suits. Even if those cards are split as evenly as possible between the other suits, they will still have an eight-card fit. Thus, if you have ten trumps, the opponents have at least eight of something, and where there are at least eighteen trumps the Law says there will be at least eighteen tricks.

If you bid to the four-level and go one down (making nine tricks), then the Law tells you that the opponents will be able to make at least nine tricks. Your ten trumps thus ensure that even if you cannot make 4♠, you will not be too badly hurt, since if the opponents have eight hearts, say, there is a total of eighteen trumps on the hand and they should be able to make 3♥. If they have nine hearts between them, then since there will be nineteen total tricks, they should be able to make game if you cannot make 4♠. As a result, since you know that your side has at least ten trumps, you can safely bid a preemptive 4♠ with the hand above. Remember too that all good hands with spade support would start by making a cuebid raise, so partner will know what you have and not get too excited.

What can the opponents do over 4♠? If there are eighteen total tricks, they may be able to double 4♠ for +300 or even +500 against their game — still a profit for you. In the worst case, you will go down one when they could only make 3♥ — still not bad. On a good day, they will bid on to the five-level to find that they have only ten tricks.

By getting to your correct Law level quickly, you use up the opponents' space and prevent them from investigating the hand properly. They will get these high-level decisions wrong much more often if you refuse to give them a chance to describe their hands and bid 4♠.

We must, however, sound a note of warning here. Of course, vulnerability and high cards do have some relevance too. You don't want to get to the four-level vulnerable with no high cards just because your side has ten trumps — going for 1100 into their game is not winning bridge even if they are vulnerable!

How does knowing the Law help?

Armed with your new knowledge of the mechanics of the Law, you may still be wondering, 'How does it help me?' Let's look at a common bidding problem and see how you can use the Law to make the right decision in a very common type of competitive auction. With both sides vulnerable, your hand is:

♠ A 9 7 6   ♥ K 5 3   ♦ A K 10 7 2   ♣ 6

LHO	Partner	RHO	You
			1♦
1♥	dbl	2♥	2♠
3♥	pass	pass	?

Partner's negative double showed four spades. Do you bid one more and push on to 3♠ or do you let the opponents play the hand in 3♥? Once you are familiar with the Law you will find that it is a very useful tool to help you make decisions in these everyday situations. This is a perfect time for the Law to help you with those nasty guesses.

How many trumps are there? The points seem to be fairly evenly divided, since no one is very interested in making a move towards game. Clearly your side has exactly eight spades (partner would have bid 1♠ instead of making a negative double if he had five). If partner had a singleton heart, then he would probably have competed to 3♠ himself, so he is likely to have two hearts, leaving eight for the opponents. That means that there are sixteen total trumps, and thus we expect sixteen tricks to be the total number available.

As you become more familiar with the Law you will know automatically what to do in these common situations, but for now let's use a chart to see what happens with both sides vulnerable when there are sixteen trumps. In every case, there are sixteen total tricks, so if you can make ten tricks in spades, they will only be able to come to six tricks in hearts, and so on. If you do the arithmetic, this is the chart you arrive at:

You play in 3♠		They play in 3♥		
Declarer's Tricks	Your Score	Declarer's Tricks	Your Score	Total Tricks
10	+170	6	+300	16
9	+140	7	+200	16
8	-100	8	+100	16
7	-200	9	-140	16

BY THE WAY

The Law works best on fairly balanced hands — on distributional hands, it tends to give results that are not as accurate. It also works best when you and partner have at least 16 HCP between you. You will find that it helps to deduct half a trick from the total if you have a flat hand, or if you have honors in the opponents' suit. Use the Law as a rule of thumb, not an absolute. If you read Larry Cohen's book, you will find that much of it is devoted to situations where the Law does not work quite so neatly!

THE LAW OF TOTAL TRICKS

As you can see, when the opponents play in 3♥ you always get a better score no matter how the sixteen tricks are divided. This means that you should pass and let the opponents play 3♥. Bidding on to 3♠ cannot be a winning decision. (Of course, if you think your side has a majority of the high cards you can also double 3♥, in which case on this hand you'll do even better.)

If the points are split evenly, then the most likely outcome of the hand is that both sides will be able to make eight tricks. Bidding 3♠ will then turn a plus score into a minus — and how often have we all done that! The lesson from this table is that it will usually be wrong to bid 'three-over-three' when there are only sixteen total tricks.

Summary

✓ The Law states that the total number of tricks on a hand will equal the total number of trumps available with each side playing in its longest fit.

✓ It is usually safe to bid to a contract where the number of tricks you have to take is equal to the total number of trumps held by your side — this is your Law level.

✓ You can use the Law to help you make 'pass or bid one more' decisions in competitive auctions, if you can estimate the number of trumps held by each side.

✓ The Law is a rule of thumb, not an absolute. It is a useful tool which can assist you in making competitive decisions, but it does not always work perfectly.

THE LAW OF TOTAL TRICKS

NOW TRY THESE...

What is your next bid on each of the following hands? (Assume equal vulnerability.)

1
- ♠ J 9 7
- ♥ J 8 7 3
- ♦ 10
- ♣ Q 8 7 3 2

LHO	Partner	RHO	You
1♦	1♠	dbl	?

2
- ♠ J 9 7
- ♥ J 8 7 3
- ♦ 10
- ♣ Q 8 7 3 2

LHO	Partner	RHO	You
1♦	2♠	dbl	?

3
- ♠ J 9 7
- ♥ J 8 7 3
- ♦ 10
- ♣ Q 8 7 3 2

LHO	Partner	RHO	You
1♦	2♥	dbl	?

4
- ♠ J 9 7
- ♥ J 8 7 3
- ♦ 10
- ♣ Q 8 7 3 2

LHO	Partner	RHO	You
1♣	3♠	dbl	?

5
- ♠ A J 8 6 4
- ♥ 8 5 3
- ♦ K Q 9
- ♣ A 3

LHO	Partner	RHO	You
		1♣	1♠
dbl	2♠	3♥	?

6
- ♠ A 10 9 7 5 3
- ♥ 8 6
- ♦ K J 8
- ♣ 5 3

LHO	Partner	RHO	You
		1♥	1♠
2♥	2♠	3♥	?

7
- ♠ A 10 9 7 5
- ♥ 8
- ♦ K Q 8 4
- ♣ A 5 3

LHO	Partner	RHO	You
		1♥	1♠
2♥	2♠	3♥	?

8
- ♠ A 10 9 5
- ♥ 8
- ♦ K Q 8 4
- ♣ A 5 3 2

LHO	Partner	RHO	You
		1♥	dbl
3♥	4♠	pass	pass
5♥	pass	pass	?

ANSWERS

1 2♠ You have three-card support for partner's five-card suit, so you can safely compete to the two-level. Take the two-level away and make them bid higher if they want to come back in.

2 3♠ You have three-card support for partner's six-card suit, so you can safely compete to the three-level.

3 4♥ You have four-card support for partner's six-card suit, so you can safely compete to the four-level. We know this one looks scary, but think it through: you have ten trumps, and they surely can't have more than ten. Therefore the Law says that if you are going down more than two tricks in 4♥, they can make a slam — so make it hard for them to bid it.

4 4♠ You have three-card support for partner's seven-card suit, so you can safely compete to the four-level. Again, the Law will probably protect you. It's harder for the opponents to double you without good trumps, and they won't be sure how many of their high cards in clubs and hearts will make tricks on defense.

5 pass You probably have eight spades, and you have no reason to assume that the opponents have more than eight hearts. Do not bid three-over-three when there are only sixteen total trumps. If partner has either a fourth spade or a singleton heart, he will probably compete to 3♠, but it is not your decision to make.

6 3♠ You know your side has at least nine spades, so you can safely compete to the three-level.

7 3♠ Again, you are only guaranteed to have eight trumps, but this time the opponents are likely to have nine hearts (always assuming they are disciples of the Law). That makes seventeen total tricks, so bidding on is likely to be right. (Partner might have four hearts, of course, in which case you may have done the wrong thing, but there is no way to tell).

8 dbl This is a classic competitive bidding decision. Partner's pass is forcing (see Chapter 22), so you must bid 5♠ or double 5♥; you cannot pass. Your side has nine, or just possibly ten spades. They likely have nine hearts, but may have ten. So there are between 18 and 20 tricks available on the hand. Suppose there are 18; that means if you can make 5♠, or eleven tricks, you can beat them four in 5♥ doubled for a good profit. Now suppose there are 20 tricks available (which is stretching things a bit); even if you can make eleven tricks, they are still down two. That's a small loss against your game, and better than going down in 5♠ when you could have taken a plus in 5♥ doubled.

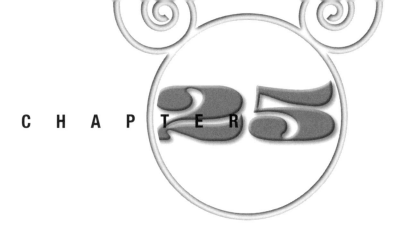

HAND EVALUATION

 Any innovation which tends to increase the advantage of skill and to decrease the advantage of luck should be welcomed by bridge lovers. *Florence Irwin,* **Auction Highlights,** *1913*.

The value of your hand is not fixed in stone; it changes constantly throughout the auction. Sometimes your hand gets better, and sometimes worse. Individual cards may take on enormous value or be rendered completely worthless. When you first pick up a hand, you count your high-card points; that gives you a rough starting point for valuation. However, your estimate of the value of your hand is not a photograph, but is more like a movie in which things are constantly changing. When your hand is unbalanced, you also note your potential extra distributional values, although you cannot count anything for long or short suits until you know that you have found a trump fit. So your estimate of distributional values will also change as the auction progresses. To see what we mean, look at this hand.

♠ K J 8 5 4 3 ♥ Q 7 ♦ K Q 4 2 ♣ K

It starts out as a better than average hand — it has 14 HCP and a six-card spade suit. As dealer, you would have no qualms about opening the bidding.

Now evaluate the hand after the auction starts like this:

LHO	Partner	RHO	You
1♠	pass	2♥	pass
4♦			

LHO opens 1♠ and then makes a splinter jump to 4♦, agreeing hearts. How do you rate your hand? Frankly, you can tear most of it up and throw it away. Quite possibly, the opponents will roll up thirteen tricks in hearts once they get to playing the hand. Your ♥Q is clearly worthless, as are your diamond honors. If the ♣A is on your left, your king is dead and, if declarer needs a spade finesse, that is also working. Wow! That hand sure went downhill fast.

Now consider the same hand after the following start to the auction:

LHO	Partner	RHO	You
	1♦	pass	1♠
pass	2♥	pass	?

What a huge hand you have all of a sudden. Partner has shown at least 5-4 in diamonds and hearts, and has reversed, showing extra values. You could have an excellent play for a grand slam opposite as little as

♠ — ♥ A K J 2 ♦ A J 10 9 5 ♣ A 5 4 3

In the first auction, the ♥Q was worth nothing. In the second, it fills a hole in partner's second suit. When LHO had the ♣A, your king was worth little or nothing, but opposite partner's ace you have both a trick and a ruffing value in the suit.

At each stage of the auction you should be asking yourself, 'How do I feel about my hand now?', because you will find that the answer will change!

Why is point count not totally reliable?

The 4-3-2-1 method of counting high-card points is very widely used because it is a very simple way to value honor cards and it is quite effective. However, it does tend to undervalue aces and overvalue jacks. Aces are always good cards to hold, although even they do not always pull their full weight. At the start of a hand, we assign a standard point-count value to minor honors (holdings such as Qx or Jxx). However, if the opponents bid the suit those honors are frequently worth nothing. On the other hand, when they are located in partner's suits they can be worth far more than one or two points. Sometimes, it will be impossible to tell during the bidding how valuable a lesser honor may be, although you can often hazard a guess.

Say you hold ♠AQ10. This starts out as six points with an additional plus value for the ten. If LHO opens the bidding with 1♠, though, you should immediately look upon both the queen and the ten as questionable

BY THE WAY

Some experts add ½ point for each ace. Others deduct a point for an aceless hand, and add a point if they hold all four aces.

assets. They may not be, of course, as LHO will not always have a suit headed by the king-jack, but you can only really count on one spade trick, either on offense or defense. Now say that it is RHO who opens 1♠. Your holding has suddenly become almost as good as ♠AK10 and, if RHO holds both the king and the jack, you effectively hold ♠AKQ. Even if LHO has a holding such as ♠Jx, he may well lead the jack if you become declarer, setting up three stoppers in the suit for you. If partner is the one who bids spades, you can also upgrade your hand. Almost no matter what his holding is, your secondary honors are likely to be of use. To see why, give him a suit as weak as ♠J432 — you are still guaranteed three spade tricks.

Short-suit honor combinations are always of dubious value, and should only be looked upon favorably if partner clearly has length and values in the suit. For example, QJ doubleton is a very useful holding opposite AKxxx but is worth nothing facing three low cards or AK doubleton. This holding also fails to pull its full weight facing Kx and is 50-50 to take a trick opposite Ax.

Which is the better of these two hands?

♠ K Q 9 6 5   ♥ 8 3   ♦ A J 8 7 4   ♣ 3

♠ Q 9 6 5 3   ♥ K 8   ♦ J 8 7 4 3   ♣ A

Although both hands contain 10 HCP and both have the same 5-5 shape, the first hand is considerably better. When your honors are in your long suits, they are more likely to pull their weight in terms of helping to establish tricks from the long cards in the suit. The combination of honors in spades and diamonds in the first hand also means that each of these honors is likely to be worth more. It is easy to see why this second point is true. Suppose these are your major suit holdings (when partner has only small cards in the suits):

♠   A K   ♥   4 3

You have two sure major-suit tricks (barring an adverse ruff).

♠   A 4   ♥   K 3

Switch the king into the heart suit, and you have only one and a half tricks — one in spades, and one or none in hearts depending on which defender holds the ♥A. Yet both these holdings would add up to seven HCP!

How do you know when you have a good bad hand?

Believe it or not, some clouds do have silver linings. If you don't believe us, try answering this apparently silly question — which of the following hands would you rather hold?

♠ —   ♥ Q J 10 7 4   ♦ Q J 10 7   ♣ K Q 10 9

♠ 10 5   ♥ K 7 4   ♦ 9 7 5 4 2   ♣ 10 7 2

You might think the answer is obvious, but first impressions can be deceiving. In fact, an alert reader may well have answered, 'I don't know without hearing the auction!' If you did, go to the top of the class! OK, let's say that this is the auction:

LHO	Partner	RHO	You
1♣	4♠	dbl	?

You are obviously not going to bid with either hand, but which would you rather put down as dummy? Let's think about what is likely to happen.

When you hold the second, obviously bad, hand, you have only one trick for partner but your spade holding suggests that RHO's double is based on high cards rather than a plethora of trumps. Even though partner will almost invariably fail to make 4♠ doubled, the opponents are virtually certain to be able to make a game and quite possibly a slam. The reason is that besides having no help for partner in a spade contract, you also have little that will hinder the enemy when it comes to making whatever contract they choose to bid.

However, if you are looking at the 0-5-4-4 11-count, it is obvious that RHO has trump tricks for his double. Whether partner has a seven- or eight-card suit, the chances are that RHO has the rest of the spades. You might or might not have a trick for partner, and the chances of 4♠ doubled making are the same as they were when you held the balanced three-count — practically zero. This time though, it really will be a disaster; you have great defense against all three other suits, so it is also guaranteed that the opponents cannot make anything.

Besides illustrating that you sometimes cannot tell at the outset when a hand is bad, here's an extreme example that shows how your view of a hand can change dramatically as the auction proceeds. We're going to take another look at that 'bad' hand.

♠ 10 5　♥ K 7 4　♦ 9 7 5 4 2　♣ 10 7 2

LHO	Partner	RHO	You
	2♣	pass	2♦
pass	2♥	pass	3♣[1]
pass	3♦	pass	?

1.　0-3 HCP.

Partner has opened with a strong, artificial 2♣, and over your 2♦ response he has forced to game, showing a heart suit. When you then gave a second negative with 3♣, he bid his second suit. What do you think of your hand now?

Your hand has become enormous, and if we had to guess at a final contract it would be 6♦, although even a grand slam is possible. Of course, game may be the limit, but it is unlikely. Partner's hand is likely to be at worst something like:

♠ A 5　♥ A Q J 10 5　♦ A K Q 8 3　♣ 5

As three-counts go, this one turned out to be a pretty good one after all!

How do you know
when you have a bad good hand?

♠ A K Q J 10   ♥ Q 4   ♦ K Q   ♣ Q 4 3 2

You just dealt yourself this, and probably feel pretty pleased about it. You have 19 HCP and a solid five-card spade suit. Great hand, right?

Well, possibly. Yes, you have good spades and lots of high cards, but there are a number of negative factors too. The diamond holding is not really worth 5 HCP, and you certainly cannot also add another point for the doubleton diamond. The 9 HCP outside the spade suit could be much more usefully distributed — something like a red ace and the ♣KQ would really improve the hand compared to the scattered stuff you actually hold.

Let's follow the auction along for a bit and see how things develop:

LHO	Partner	RHO	You
			1♠
2♥	3♠	4♥	?

Partner's 3♠ bid is a preemptive raise, promising four-card trump support (remember the Law!). Now we see another disadvantage of your hand. Solid suits are all very well, but they also can be a liability since you will not be able to cross to partner's hand in the trump suit. Also, you don't really need the ♠J and maybe not the ♠Q either, so those are points that are not contributing anything.

What about your heart holding? You have already counted 2 HCP for the queen, and you might think that the doubleton is worth something as a ruffing value too. But is it? Yours is the long trump hand, and taking ruffs in it doesn't get you any extra tricks! One thing is for sure — your doubleton has no ruffing value. As for the queen, at least it has a pretty colored picture on it.

So, should you bid 4♠? Perhaps, but do not do so with any great expectation of making the contract. Partner's hand is likely to be something like

♠ 9 7 5 3   ♥ 8 6   ♦ A 7 4 3   ♣ 10 7 3

Opposite this, you cannot even make 3♠, let alone four. Defending 4♥ will probably produce a plus score, but it will take a seasoned, disciplined hand evaluator not to bid 4♠. Is that you?

Summary

✓ Downgrade dubious honor combinations such as Q-J, K-J or K-Q doubleton.

✓ Constantly re-evaluate your hand in the light of the bidding; you may turn out to have a good bad hand, or your promising collection may become a bad good hand.

✓ Downgrade unsupported queens and jacks in suits bid by the opponents but upgrade them if partner bids the suit.

✓ Downgrade honor combinations in suits bid on your left, but upgrade them if RHO or partner bids the suit.

HAND EVALUATION

NOW TRY THESE...

In each case, evaluate your hand in offensive terms based on the auction so far, using the descriptions 'Excellent', 'Good', 'Average', 'Poor' and 'Terrible'. Then guess where you think you would want to play the hand if you had to make the final bid in the auction now.

1
- ♠ 10 7 4
- ♥ —
- ♦ K 10 8 7
- ♣ A J 8 7 3 2

LHO	Partner	RHO	You
1♥	1♠	2♥	?

2
- ♠ 10 7 4
- ♥ —
- ♦ K 10 8 7
- ♣ A J 8 7 3 2

LHO	Partner	RHO	You
1♥	2♦	2♥	?

3
- ♠ 10 7 4
- ♥ —
- ♦ K 10 8 7
- ♣ A J 8 7 3 2

LHO	Partner	RHO	You
1♠	2♦	3♠	?

4
- ♠ 10 7 4
- ♥ —
- ♦ K 10 8 7
- ♣ A J 8 7 3 2

LHO	Partner	RHO	You
1♥	1NT	pass	?

5
- ♠ 10 7 4
- ♥ —
- ♦ K 10 8 7
- ♣ A J 8 7 3 2

LHO	Partner	RHO	You
1♦	1♠	1NT	?

6
- ♠ A 7 3
- ♥ 8 7 2
- ♦ A Q 8 6 2
- ♣ K 4

LHO	Partner	RHO	You
	1♠	pass	2♦
3♣	pass	pass	?

7
- ♠ A 7 3
- ♥ 8 7 2
- ♦ A Q 8 6 2
- ♣ K 4

LHO	Partner	RHO	You
			1♦
pass	1♠	2♥	2♠
4♥	5♦	pass	?

8
- ♠ A 7
- ♥ A K 8 7 2
- ♦ 10 6 2
- ♣ K 8 4

LHO	Partner	RHO	You
			1♥
pass	2♦	3♠	pass
pass	4♣	pass	?

ANSWERS

1 Average to Good — 2♠ or 3♠. RHO has raised only to 2♥, and so probably has only three-card support. That means that partner will have three or four hearts, and a trump lead will restrict him to only one or two ruffs. As he probably has nine major-suit cards, some of your minor-suit values are likely to be wasted. If you had a fourth spade, your hand would be significantly better.

2 Good — 5♦. Again, partner rates to have four hearts. He will also have six diamonds, and probably two or three spades. Unfortunately, this means that setting up the clubs is unlikely and a trump lead will probably leave him with a heart to lose.

3 Excellent — 6♦. Partner has at most one spade. That leaves him with six diamonds, probably four hearts, and at least two clubs. All he needs for at least a small slam is the ♦A, the ♠A and the ♣K — not unreasonable for a two-level overcall, although he probably has a wasted heart honor.

4 Average — 5♣. You have enough points for game but it's unclear that you will be able to make one. Partner will have wasted heart values and is likely to have only a doubleton club. Since the opening bidder on your left may well have the ♦A, the defense may be able to lock partner out of dummy in a notrump contract.

5 Poor — let them play it. LHO did not open 1♥ and RHO did not make a negative double. Partner cannot have six hearts but he must have five. RHO must also have four, which means that his hearts are poor and/or his spades very good. Your minor-suit values will be mostly wasted on offense. Pass and let them get into trouble.

6 Average to Poor — 3NT or 4♠. Without LHO's overcall you would have happily bid 4♠. Now, with the ♣K almost certainly wasted and the diamond finesse likely to be wrong if partner does not have the king, you may not be able to make any game, although you obviously have enough points to bid one.

7 Excellent — 6♦ or 7♦. Partner has at most one heart and quite possibly none. With a maximum of 9 HCP in the two suits he has bid, he must surely have the ♣A to justify his bid at the five-level facing a known minimum opening bid.

8 Fantastic — 6♦ or 7♦. You had nothing to say over 3♠ with your minimum opener, but have things ever changed! Your major-suit honors guarantee that there are no losers there (partner cannot have more than three cards in the majors), and meanwhile you have a diamond fit and another gold nugget in the ♣K. When this hand came up on OKbridge, partner held

   ♠ 6 2   ♥ 4   ♦ A K Q J 9   ♣ Q J 10 9 5

   Only three of 52 pairs reached an excellent minor-suit slam!

More Bridge Titles from Master Point Press

Around the World in 80 Hands by Zia Mahmood with David Burn
256pp., PB   Can $22.95   US $16.95

A Study in Silver *A second collection of bridge stories* by David Silver
128pp., PB   Can $12.95   US$ 9.95

Bridge the Silver Way by David Silver and Tim Bourke
192pp., PB   Can $19.95   US $14.95

Bridge, Zia... and me by Michael Rosenberg
(foreword by Zia Mahmood)
192pp., PB   Can $19.95   US $15.95

Classic Kantar *A collection of bridge humor* by Eddie Kantar
192pp., PB   Can $19.95   US $14.95

Competitive Bidding in the 21st Century by Marshall Miles
254pp.,PB   Can. $22.95   US. $16.95

Countdown to Winning Bridge by Tim Bourke and Marc Smith
92pp., PB   Can $19.95   US $14.95

Easier Done Than Said *Brilliancy at the Bridge Table*
by Prakash K. Paranjape
128pp., PB   Can $15.95   US $12.95

For Love or Money *The Life of a Bridge Journalist*
by Mark Horton and Brian Senior
189pp., PB   Can $22.95   US $16.95

I Shot my Bridge Partner by Matthew Granovetter
384pp., PB   Can $19.95   US $14.95

Murder at the Bridge Table by Matthew Granovetter
320pp., PB   Can $19.95   US $14.95

Partnership Bidding *A Workbook* by Mary Paul
96pp., PB   Can $9.95   US $7.95

Playing with the Bridge Legends by Barnet Shenkin
(forewords by Zia and Michael Rosenberg)
240pp., PB   Can $24.95   US $17.95

Saints and Sinners *The St. Titus Bridge Challenge*
by David Bird & Tim Bourke
192pp., PB   Can $19.95   US $14.95

Tales out of School *'Bridge 101' and other stories* by David Silver
(foreword by Dorothy Hayden Truscott)
128pp., PB   Can $ 12.95   US $9.95

The Bridge Player's Bedside Book edited by Tony Forrester
256pp., HC   Can $27.95   US $19.95

The Complete Book of BOLS Bridge Tips edited by Sally Brock
176pp., PB (photographs)   Can $24.95   US$17.95

There Must Be A Way... *52 challenging bridge hands*
by Andrew Diosy (foreword by Eddie Kantar)
96pp., PB $9.95 US & Can.

You Have to See This... *52 more challenging bridge problems*
by Andrew Diosy and Linda Lee
96pp., PB   Can $12.95   US $9.95

World Class — *Conversations with the Bridge Masters* by Marc Smith
288pp., PB (photographs)   Can $24.95   US $17.95